Praise for Matthew Jukes' *Wine*:

'He has distilled a career's knowledge into a most approachable and friendly little book' *Sunday Herald*

'*Wine* . . . is a must for anyone who wants to know how to buy a good bottle just by looking at the label' *Red*

'If you have ever felt intimidated by the wine waiter, or been not quite sure what wine to serve at a dinner party, then this is the book for you . . . An essential book for all wine lovers' *The Good Book Guide*

'An entertaining and lively account of wine and its infinite variety' *Wine*

'[Matthew Jukes is] the new doyen of the wine world' *Marie Claire*

'Here, for the first time, is a book written by a dashing young dynamo in the wine trade . . . In essence, he is the palate of the people' *Harpers & Queen*

WINE

by Matthew Jukes

EVERYTHING YOU EVER WANTED TO KNOW ABOUT WINE BUT WERE AFRAID TO ASK

HEADLINE

First published in 1999 by
HEADLINE BOOK
PUBLISHING

First published in paperback
in 2000 by HEADLINE BOOK
PUBLISHING

10 9 8 7 6 5 4 3 2 1

ISBN 0 7472 6329 9

Design by
Town Group Creative

Photographs by
Ian Garlick

Printed and bound in Great Britain by
Butler and Tanner Ltd, Frome and
London

HEADLINE BOOK PUBLISHING
A division of Hodder Headline
338 Euston Road
London NW1 3BH

www.headline.co.uk
www.hodderheadline.com

ACKNOWLEDGEMENTS

My wife Nathalie who tirelessly proof-read the entire book, harvesting commas, training sentence lengths and fermenting phrases. I would never have finished it without you. Mum and Dad, for keeping a small but perfectly chosen cellar and for my first introduction to wine. Simon, Debbie, the Shaws and the Thomas clan over here and over the pond, for sweating and worrying on my behalf. Paul, Norman and Andrew, for holding the fort. Loyal tasting (drinking) chums Philip, Marmion, Roger, Hilary, J.H., Tom, Rupert, Mark, Palmer '61, Susan, Tish, Hore, Hamish, Jason, Dion, Mike Huntley, Neil (heroic lunches) and Johnny. Pete, Tim and David (Pétrus), Dobs (½s of Sauternes). A bottle of 1947 Cheval Blanc, to prove that expensive wine is really worth it. All of the members of the English wine trade, wine-makers, agents, PRs and vineyard workers abroad, who, over the years, have parted freely and enthusiastically with their time and wine, to keep my thirst for this amazing nectar going. Willi's and Juveniles and all of their offspring for introducing me to the Rhône. The team at Bibendum Restaurant, Graham, Fee, Michelle, François, Dicky and Pierre. Inspiration from two people who have sadly gone on to the big vineyard (or tasting room) in the sky, James Rogers and Adam Bancroft. Lastly Doug, Heather and the team at Headline, Nuala for her keen eye and Robert from P F & D for lubricating my enthusiasm.

CONTENTS

WHY WINE?

aperitif

I started working in the wine trade over a decade ago, after being a little too obsessed with the subject during my teens. Why? Blame Roald Dahl's short story, *Taste*. If you haven't read it, track it down; you too might be bitten by the bug, if you have not already become captivated by the subject. I was also fortunate enough to have been exposed to wine at an early age, often watered-down, European style. After an abortive attempt at becoming a physicist (apparently being one of the few people in the world who, ignoring my lectures, concentrated on trying to prove how boomerangs fly – has anyone done it yet?), I used my sound knowledge of my favourite subjects and found that by blending them together skilfully, wine was the only avenue left open to me. After all, where else do you use physics, biology, chemistry, botany, history, geography, French and bit of mathematics in the course of your working day?

So, first of all, to Leith's School of Food and Wine for a short course. There I met Robert Joseph, a lecturer, who kindly put me in touch with a wine shop in Barnes, south-west London. This was an Aladdin's cave of wines: never had I seen such a range of diverse labels and famous estates in the same place. At the time, James Rogers was the wine consultant for the Barnes Wine Shop. It was his job to track down and taste the amazing wines we sold. He had a talent: he was undoubtedly the finest blind-taster I have ever met. His ability to identify a wine, assess whether it was worth selling in the shop, and at what price, was unbelievable. This was definitely the job for me.

The end of the eighties was an unbelievable time to get into wine. Famous estates such as Cloudy Bay and Ata Rangi from New Zealand, Yarra Yering and Cape Mentelle from Australia, Ridge and Beringer from California, Marques de Murietta and Vega Sicilia from Spain, Pieropan and Ornellaia from Italy and of course Domaine de Trévallon and Lafon Meursaults from France were relative newcomers to our shores. I tasted like a man possessed, notching up and noting down thousands of wines in the process. Wine journalism was also starting to influence people's choices in the shops. Every broadsheet newspaper had a wine column. People would drive across London just to buy one or two bottles of a recommended wine. I found this absolutely fascinating and was caught up in wine fever.

The nineties have seen an enormous expansion in the variety of wines shipped around the world. Wine production has exploded beyond all expectation. The choice on wine merchants' shelves and restaurant wine lists is bigger than ever.

Consequently, the most popular questions I am asked when I give wine tastings, radio phone-ins, lectures or even when I'm just talking with friends, are not technical or necessarily that specific, but more like: 'What is the best wine to have with roast chicken?', 'Why do you have to decant red wines?', 'What is the best, all-purpose wine glass to use?' and 'How cold should I serve a Chablis?' The problem is that wine choice has far outrun wine knowledge. These questions and many others are all answered by a basic level of wine learning, and this book can give you a solid grounding in all aspects of wine with which to arm yourself for the twenty-first century.

But why should you spend time and money on wine? As an alcoholic beverage, wine has everything going for it. It is foody, social, respectable, fashionable and lately acknowledged to be positively good for you. Wine wisdom is regarded as an enviable acquired skill like the knowledge of theatre or opera, except that it is more complicated, more impressive – and far sexier. Wine is a living thing; it actually changes all the time, so in effect no one can ever be a true expert as the goalposts are always moving. Practice can, however, improve your familiarity; and practice, in wine terms, is tasting and drinking, and unlike other hobbies there is no downside. It is, quite simply, great fun.

The British, as non-wine producers (OK, there are some notable exceptions), are generally viewed as unbiased commentators - the world's top wine-buffs. We can therefore cast an unblinkered eye across the global selection of fine and not-so-fine wines, delivering our honest verdicts, much to the chagrin of wine-makers the world over. But only in Great Britain could this subject have been so closeted in the upper classes. Abroad, wine is a crucial part of life on all levels, from the social rituals enjoyed with family or friends around the table to a serious export product for some countries. But wine drinking in Great Britain is at last expanding at a huge rate of knots. Wine is now the most popular take-home drink, even eclipsing beer. Every week there is another article expounding the positive health implications of moderate wine drinking. The partnership of wine and food can be fundamental to enjoying a meal. There is already a movement towards the need to enjoy leisure time more fully and a return to sitting over a meal and talking. The explosion of food programmes on television and the seismic expansion of the amount of new restaurants opening only serves to show that there has to be a knock-on effect in wine and the need for wine education.

So why this wine book? I hope that it will demystify the pomp and ceremony surrounding the subject of wine, and throw open the doors of the intriguing but unnecessarily secret world of wine knowledge. Therefore, I hope that you read this book cover to cover. It can be used as a reference book but it works better as a wine course. It should serve as a complete introduction to wine so that when you have finished, you should feel inspired to confront the wine world head on. This book should also talk to you in your language, not the language of a wine snob.

I have split the book into various chapters focusing on different aspects of wine. I don't deal with the wine regions of the world until half-way through and this is entirely on purpose. In order to understand wine fully, it is important to start at the beginning, and at the very root of the subject (no pun intended) are the grapes themselves; followed swiftly by how to make wine and how to taste wine, how to choose, serve, store and match it to food. I have written a huge glossary section at the back of the book (see page 215) that should cover any terms that might be a little alien to you. This section is once again divided into segments covering terms found in vine-growing, wine-making, tasting and even some French tasting terms.

The most important points to remember while reading this book are that wine is fun, and does not need to be expensive to be enjoyable. I also want to stress that when it comes to the taste of wine, you alone are always right. If you don't like a wine, don't buy it again, or at least wait until your palate decides the time is right to have another taste. Don't let anyone bully you into believing that you don't have 'good' taste, because your own nose and mouth are your parameters, so how would anyone else know what tastes you enjoy? I cannot tell you what you should like, only why I like something and why it tastes the way it does. You have your tastes and I have mine: it is just a matter of identifying what you like and why you like it. I hope this book will help you do that.

Bring on the grape varieties . . .

CHAPTER 1

GRAPE VARIETIES

the players

Understanding the concept of grape varieties is one of the keys to solving some of the mysteries behind the taste of wine. Each grape variety has a distinct character and set of smells and tastes. Some are more memorable than others. Some varieties work better when they are combined – a sort of team effort. The loners prefer to be left to do their thing in peace. If a wine is made from only one grape variety then it is called a *single varietal* or just plain *varietal*. If it is made from more than one grape variety, then it is a *blend*. Blends tend to have many flavours, all racing around the mouth at the same time. If you get to know the particular taste characteristics of each grape, you will have cracked it.

This chapter holds the key to demystifying almost all of the wines in the world. Combined with a little knowledge of climate, general wine-making practices and local traditions, it is possible to guess at a wine's taste by its grape variety or varieties.

Before we start, it is important to explain some of the vocabulary needed to progress. When referring to wine, the term variety means type, so the grape variety is the grape type. (If I was writing about apples, the varieties could include Cox, Golden Delicious, Russet and Bramley.) Some grape varieties may be familiar to you. You may not have realised that these names actually refer to the grapes that a wine is made from. Chardonnay, for example, is often thought of as a style of wine, not an actual grape type. Of course, not all Chardonnays taste exactly the same. Imagine the difference in two bottles of wine both made from the Chardonnay grape, one from France and the other from Chile. They will have a certain degree of similarity – after all, they come from the same plants – but they will not taste the same as they were grown and made into wine thousands of miles apart, by different people in different climates using different methods.

There are over 5,000 grape varieties in the world. But don't despair, as the majority of wines available on the shelves in wine shops and supermarkets use a fraction of these. The following list is divided into red and white grapes, each list containing two sections. The first section details my top ten grape varieties. These are some of the most commonly available varieties and the finest of them are often known as 'noble varieties'. I have moved a couple of the lesser-known grapes into this category as I feel that they are interesting and worthy of note. The second section contains the more obscure, eclectic varieties. Weird and wonderful they may be, but you are unlikely to come across these grapes every day. A few other grape varieties not highlighted here pop up in subsequent chapters – these will be accompanied by a short explanation putting each one into context.

IMPORTANT RED VARIETIES

CABERNET SAUVIGNON

Possibly the most famous red grape in the world, Cabernet Sauvignon has every right to be proud of itself. It is a classy beast with breeding and universally appealing character traits. Cabernet Sauvignon is the metaphorical chairman of the board of the multinational Wine Corporation. This grape forms the main part of one of the world's most celebrated styles of wine: it is the backbone of most red Bordeaux, otherwise known as clarets. Its ability to contribute to the ageing potential of wines has meant that is it a favourite for planting in thousands of vineyards all around the world.

CAB-ER-NAY SO-VEEN-YON

Cabernet Sauvignon tends to perform best when blended. In red Bordeaux it is joined by two or three other grape varieties to form the resulting wine. As this style has a proven track record, wine-makers all over the world follow the recipe, so a wine using Cabernet Sauvignon, Cabernet Franc and Merlot is known as a 'Bordeaux blend'.

On its own, Cabernet Sauvignon has distinctive cassis (blackcurrant) flavours. It responds very well to time spent maturing in oak barrels and is therefore often accompanied by a woody flavour. A grape's skin contains its colour and elements of its flavour, and Cabernet Sauvignon grapes have thick skins, so wines using these grapes tend to be deeply coloured and have a tannic taste when young. Tannin is a grape variety's lifeline: generally, the more tannin, the longer the wine will last; therefore Cabernet Sauvignon brings longevity to a blend. The hallmarks of this grape, along with the blackcurrant flavour, are a cigar-box or cedarwood note and sometimes even a dark chocolate texture and flavour. A New World Cabernet Sauvignon can often be recognised by a mint leaf smell.

There are many famous wines made predominantly from this grape, which do not write Cabernet Sauvignon on the label. All 'Left Bank' clarets (see page 113) such as Château Latour, Château Montrose, Château Lafite-Rothschild, Château Mouton-Rothschild, Château Haut-Brion, Château Palmer, Château Léoville-Barton, Château Ducru-Beaucaillou, Château Cos d'Estournel and many, many others contain a huge whack of this noble variety. In California, Cabernet Sauvignon is the lifeblood of society as almost every estate grows this grape. It accounts for the amazing Opus One made by Robert Mondavi, Beringer's Chabot Vineyard, Joseph Phelps Insignia, Harlan Estate, Ridge Monte Bello, Stag's Leap Cask 23, Shafer Hillside Select, Dominus and many others. These wines command astronomical prices and collector's allocations are down to single bottles only. Elsewhere, the super-priced 'Super-Tuscans' (see page 179) – Italy's most expensive wines like Sassicaia, Sammarco, Ornellaia and Solaia – have broken the local classification rules and broken the bank by producing mind-blowing wines from the non-native Cabernet Sauvignon. Prices went through the roof. The wine's classifications went through the floor, all the way down to Vino da Tavola (table wine)! It just shows how jealous the local authorities were of brave Italian wine-makers who put the great Bordeaux grape to the test and won. It goes without saying that Australia, New Zealand, Chile, Spain and many other countries also make fabulous Cabernet Sauvignons. Most of these wines actually declare the grape variety on the label, so thankfully you don't have to try and guess what it is.

All over the world, Cabernet Sauvignon holds a firm grip on wine drinkers' palates and a majority share of most wine lovers' cellar space. When it comes to recognising the flavour of this grape, just think – *aristocratic*.

MERLOT

This grape variety is Cabernet Sauvignon's best buddy: it rarely performs spectacularly on its own. It is the arty, designer-style grape that flatters many blends but cannot really stand alone unless the habitat is exactly suited to its individual requirements. Because it is a juicier style of red grape, it generally needs the structure of Cabernet Sauvignon to bolster its fruity framework. Merlot is in its element on the 'Right Bank' of Bordeaux (see page 121) where it is often the dominant grape in the blend. With an immediately appealing character, it is supple, smooth and velvety. The New World, particularly California, has gone Merlot-crazy of late. Hyper-expensive small production Merlot-based wines are all the rage. Australia and New Zealand plant Merlot and are making some very ripe Bordeaux taste-alikes. The massive expansion of wine-making in Chile has resulted in a host of inexpensive Merlots finding their way into the shops. If you like these plump, juicy, almost sweet flavours, then steer clear of Merlot's other side: that of the thin, watery, unripe red wine that can be made to drink soon after it is bottled and is found in the cheaper wines of northern Italy, eastern Europe and the south of France. Merlot's hallmarks are usually blackberry and plums on the nose, often with a touch of oak; texture and velvety richness in the mouth; and again, like its big brother Cabernet Sauvignon, it can taste a little minty.

MER-LOW

Famous wines made from this grape include most Bordeaux from Pomerol and Saint Emilion, such as Château Pétrus, Château Trotanoy, Château Le Pin and Château L'Angélus. There is also an expensive Tuscan blockbuster called Masseto and a handful of Californian Merlots like Matanzas Creek, Newton and Ravenswood Pickberry. Once again, other wines make a point of having Merlot written on the label if it is the dominant variety. It is also worth noting that most New World Cabernet Sauvignons will have some Merlot lurking somewhere inside, sweet-talking the tannic Cabernet into civility.

CABERNET FRANC

The third most important grape of the 'Three Musketeers' of Bordeaux is Cabernet Franc, the final building block in the making of red Bordeaux. This grape lends a certain aromatic quality to these wines. It generally plays a supporting role (apart from some notable exceptions like Château Cheval Blanc in St-Emilion, where it forms two-thirds of the final blend, with Merlot filling the gap). The tannin element of Cabernet Franc is less obvious than Cabernet Sauvignon. It often has good acidity and a leafy smell, which means it actually smells both green and red! As well as forming part of the formidable Bordeaux triumvirate, Cabernet Franc is very important in the Loire Valley where it produces the good value, muscular, scented reds of Bourgueil, Saint Nicolas de Bourgueil, Chinon and Saumur-Champigny.

Elsewhere in the world, wine-makers have cottoned on to the fact that the Bordelais (people from Bordeaux) have got a good thing going and they will add a little Cabernet Franc to their Cabernet Sauvignons.

Some wineries in California have planted Cabernet Franc extensively, copying the Cheval Blanc pattern, with amazing results. In Australia, Cabernet Franc is a real favourite as it gives another dimension to their Cabernet Sauvignon-dominant wines. New Zealand has also taken Cabernet Franc to its heart as it is easier to ripen than Cabernet Sauvignon and favours the slightly cooler climate. I love the pure blackberry flavour of this variety. It holds its own well in the predominantly white wine growing region of the Loire, where the red wines are usually one hundred per cent Cabernet Franc; so for this reason I favour this grape over Merlot in world importance.

CAB-ER-NAY FRONK

PINOT NOIR

Here we go. Stop me before it all gets a little too romantic. Pinot Noir is known as the 'fickle mistress' of the grape world, mainly because it is a real pain to ripen and has infuriated wine-makers the world over who have fallen head over heels in love with its charms. Pinot Noir's home is firmly based in France, and you may be surprised to learn that it is one of the three main grapes that make champagne. However, it is best known for producing the red wines of Burgundy, and this is where the celestial elegance and brooding power of this beautiful grape are captured. Names like Gevrey-Chambertin, Chambolle-Musigny, Nuits-Saint-Georges, Richebourg, Volnay among many others are wines that owe their fame to the Pinot Noir variety. The nose is often reminiscent of wild strawberries and redcurrants, with a black cherry flavour on the palate. But as these wines age, they take on a slightly farmyardy feel and as the colour fades from dark red to pale brick red, the nose can turn leathery and raspberry-like. Fiendishly unpredictable and as often as not disappointing, Pinot Noir can make outstanding wines with heroic length and baffling complexity when on form; when off form, it can be thin, stewed and unripe! Other French regions that plant Pinot Noir with some

PEE-NO NW-AR

success are the Loire Valley and Alsace. The weather and the producer are important factors in these two northerly regions, as a good growing season and a skilful hand are essential for Pinot Noir to do its thing.

Elsewhere, most wines using this tricky variety will have Pinot Noir written on the label. New Zealand's Martinborough district and parts of Australia as well as Chile, South Africa and even Italy produce some good Pinots. However, the Californians are the only real contenders outside of the famous thirty-five mile stretch of vineyards in France. In California and Oregon's cooler areas, the petulant Pinot has been befriended by a small band of infatuated wine-makers. Calera, Au Bon Climat, Etude and Kistler make celestial Pinot Noirs, but it seems that for the time being the super-rich of America's West Coast are the only people able to afford to drink the tiny allocations on offer.

SYRAH/SHIRAZ

To be honest, in its everyday form this grape variety is a bit of a brute. It is rather clumsy and not especially charming. In order to experience its purity and explosive blackberry and pepper aromas, it is important to head to the top of the Syrah ladder. The northern Rhône Valley in France is the true home of Syrah, although it has been adopted by Australia as its prodigal grape where it is known as Shiraz. In France, no

SIRRAH/SHIRRAZ

restaurant wine list is complete without a mention of the northern Rhône's two most famous wines: Côte-Rôtie and Hermitage, made from this spicy, firm variety. The most famous producer of Côte-Rôtie – the greatest expression of Syrah – is Marcel Guigal. His single vineyards, La Mouline, La Landonne and La Turque have elevated this grape's fame to unimaginable levels, as these three wines are nothing short of perfection. With this estate leading the way, the northern Rhône has had a new lease of life and Syrah is once again firmly in the limelight. Syrah is also one of the main constituents in southern Rhône wines; however, these tend to be complex blends. The Languedoc and Roussillon also employ this fine variety to lend a bit of class to duller, local wines.

It has been easy to ignore Syrah's roots as the name change and phenomenal fame in Australia has diverted wine lovers' attentions from its spiritual home. Shiraz is an institution down under and its unlikely partnership with Cabernet Sauvignon – in France, this would be the unholy blending of Bordeaux with Rhône – works extremely well. The most expensive non-French Syrah is also from Australia, Penfold's Grange, but it is really no surprise that a grape variety that makes Côte-Rôtie – literally, 'Roasted Slope' – enjoys hot climates. The Barossa Valley in South Australia is almost synonymous with big, inky-black Shiraz. (If you have never tried one of these wines, put your seat-belt on because they are BIG.) The latest Australian region to achieve excellent results with Shiraz is Margaret River in Western Australia. These Shiraz wines have more poise, elegance and pepper than the Barossa monsters so if you have not been tempted outside the northern Rhône before, then start in Margaret River and only move on to Barossa when feeling brave.

Outside France and Australia Syrah is planted in most wine-making countries and is having particular success in South Africa and California. The Americans have a fascination with all things Rhône, and the term 'Rhône Ranger' has been invented to describe a hearty bunch of reprobates whose love of the region is such that they are planting many obscure Rhône varieties in land usually reserved for Cabernet Sauvignon and Merlot. Long may the Rhône Rangers ride!

GRENACHE

The other red Rhône grape that makes it into my top ten is the swarthy cousin of Syrah. Where Syrah likes to go hunting alone (the assassin), Grenache likes to have some company (the transit van thug). Grenache forms the bulk of most southern Rhône blends. It can have as many as twelve other mates on board in a Châteauneuf-du-Pape but usually likes Syrah and Mourvèdre in the gang. Sadly, Grenache is a much-abused variety in the south of France bulk market, as it ripens on cue and provides an ocean of wine for house consumption in bars. It plays a similar role in Spain, where Garnacha (the translation) is very widely planted. Garnacha reaches its peak in a partnership with the deft enforcer Tempranillo. This combination makes Spain's most famous wine, Rioja. In all GRE-NASH cases, Grenache is a meaty, earthy variety that only really lets the side down in rosé form when, on account of its unusually high alcohol, it can be thought of as the gangster's moll. The only other style of wine that Grenache makes that is worthy of a search party is the rich, Christmas cake, port-style wines, Banyuls and Maury. These two wines are fortified, like port, but not to the same degree and are found in the far south-west of France, near Perpignan. (Presumably these wines alone account for the ferocity of the rugby players from that corner of France.)

Australia shipped in Grenache at the same time as Shiraz and the two old pals are often blended together in classic style to form a New World ripeness/Old World dependability wine. Shiraz somehow always takes the credit, but Grenache does a lot of the legwork. California has fun with Grenache in its pink and porty forms. But these two styles are not taken very seriously and Grenache still plays a proper supporting role in many grown-up red blends. The Grenache variety is popping up in South America, helping other varieties to boost structure and presence, and has no trouble fitting in as it is no stranger to a hot climate. The only other place where Grenache is successful is Sardinia, presumably keeping a low profile. Here its disguise is known as Cannonau and can be found in pizzerias the world over, countering the spice of a Dragon's Breath Deep Pan or an American Inferno. Unusual, but nevertheless funky.

GAMAY

All Beaujolais is one hundred per cent Gamay, and for that reason you may think that Gamay is the joker in my pack. I think it is a superb variety that makes one of the most underrated red wines of all. But that does not mean that all bottles of Beaujolais are delicious and offer great value for money – far from it. Fine Beaujolais ranges in taste from summer strawberry juice lightness to a wintry,

GA-MAY

robust, black cherry and pepper concoction. Unfortunately, poor Beaujolais, generally the Nouveau fiasco, is little more than a lipstick-pink, banana and bubble-gum scented, headache-inducing alcopop. The innocent Gamay grape is responsible for this vast range of guises. (Of course, that is not quite true, as the praise or guilt lies at the feet of the wine-makers who transform this grape into whichever style suits them best – benchmark quality or fast buck.)

The one reason that we keep drinking good Beaujolais is that it will keep you smiling. You can switch your brain off when drinking these wines as they are packed with simple, fresh, red berry flavours.

The Beaujolais region is wedged into the gap between Burgundy and the northern Rhône and you can taste this in the wines, which have a juicy character with a hint of earthy spice. They require no extended cellaring; in fact they demand to be drunk the second they hit the shelves. They are rarely expensive and complement food marvellously, due to the low tannins and naturally perky acidity. Gamay is also planted in the Loire Valley, and makes similarly thirst-quenching wine in the area of Touraine. This style of wine is a favourite in Paris brasseries and is often served as their equivalent of a house wine. The reason for this – and don't argue with Parisian restaurateurs – is that there are precious few wines from France that offer immediate drinking with year in, year out dependable quality at affordable prices. Make a mental note of some of the village names in Beaujolais, and then find some reliable producers (see the section on this region, page 147). You will thank me, honest.

NEBBIOLO

Like Gamay, this grape variety does not travel very far from its home. And that is the only similarity between Gamay and Nebbiolo – they are light-years apart in every other aspect. Nebbiolo only really exists in Piemonte in the north-west corner of Italy. An immensely tough variety that

NEB-EE-OLO

often needs five years in bottle to be even approachable in the glass, Nebbiolo is a regal sort. It demands respect and gets it. Even the so-called new wave estates in Piemonte still need years to charm this beast into submission. The most famous name that Nebbiolo produces is Barolo, followed by Barbaresco and Gattinara. Because these wines are in fairly short supply and they invariably require extended cellaring to soften the tannins, they tend to be very expensive. A great Nebbiolo can conjure up intense plummy flavours with spicy, gamey overtones, and is a truly memorable variety, if not an everyday requirement for most palates. Its size, structure and tannin might be too demanding on our poor taste buds.

SANGIOVESE

Sangiovese is the second of the Italian grape varieties in this selection of the vinous élite. This time the grape favours a more central Italian vista, as Sangiovese is the main Chianti variety. It also makes the majestic Tuscan wine Brunello di Montalcino. There is no doubt that Sangiovese is a truly sumptuous variety. Extraordinarily charming, this troubadour is warm, ripe and complex in good vintages and troubled, misunderstood, unapologetic but forgivable in bad ones. This grape has bright red fruit flavours on the nose with a whiff of fresh-cut herbs and leather. It always reveals an acidic kick on the finish, and for this reason Chiantis and Brunellos need a little age to be fully appreciated. Sangiovese is another grape that enjoys the company of Cabernet Sauvignon.

SAN-GEEO-VAY-ZEE

When blending these two together, the resulting wine is known as a Super-Tuscan. (Some of the most famous wines in the collector's world are Super-Tuscan.)

The good news is that Chianti is receiving a welcome return to world fame. The pizzeria cloak has been cast off as investment has been pouring into Tuscany. Now, more than ever, it is time to look closely at a region whose wines are synonymous with all things Italian. It is worth spending a few more pounds on these wines – just as you might do on shoes, clothes, cars, motorbikes, prosciutto or olive oil.

ZINFANDEL

I'm not sure that this variety is a fully paid-up member of my top echelon, but it is worthy of a guest pass with the top seeds. Rumoured to have ancient Italian roots, Zinfandel's relations are reluctant to admit parentage so there will always be an enviable air of mystery about this unruly grape. Some of the greatest red wines in the world are made from this almost exclusively Californian variety. Unfortunately, so are some of the worst wines in the world. Over the years Zinfandel has been seen in many unpleasant guises, from

ZIN-FAN-DELL

'blush', a ridiculous name for a semi-sweet bimbo rosé style; to 'jug' wine bought in enormous containers the size of a house; and a sort of port with a kick like a mule. The correct way to enjoy this exciting variety is in straightforward red wine mode. The taste is like a turbo-charged blackberry-meets-a-spice-warehouse. In the hands of top-flight wineries like Ridge, Cline, Nalle, Ravenswood, Elyse and Turley (all in California), the results are breathtakingly invigorating.

OTHER RED VARIETIES

BAGA BAG-UH

The underrated, thick-skinned Portuguese grape variety that accounts for the lion's share of the blend in Bairrada and is also used for Dão. For this reason it is the dubious winner of 'Portugal's best red grape variety'.

BARBERA BA-BEAR-A

Nebbiolo's nice little brother in Piemonte. It is a relatively forward grape, having lower acidity and tannin than Nebbiolo. Despite being a little unfashionable, in the right hands it produces black wine gum juiciness and good structure, and most good Barolo producers grow Barbera in their armoury. Barberas are always much cheaper than Barolos and so are a nice way to be introduced to the wines of Piemonte.

CARIGNAN CARIN-YON

Carignan is a southern French variety that lags behind Syrah and Grenache in terms of style and elegance. It needs the sun as it is a late ripener and is also found further afield in such sunny climes as Spain and South America. Carignan is an awkward fellow that needs support from other varieties to help it along.

CINSAULT   SAN-SO

Cinsault is similar to Carignan, in that it performs best in a blend. This unremarkable variety, whose home is once again the southern Rhône and Languedoc-Roussillon, has one hugely redeeming feature: it is one of the parents of Pinotage, the other being the delectable Pinot Noir. It does make good rosé wines in the right hands.

DOLCETTO   DOLL-CHETTO

Nebbiolo's funny little brother in Piemonte, this grape has low tannin and therefore is the only true glugging red grape from the north-west corner of Italy. With a purple colour and unusual scent, this variety is worth finding as it lends another dimension to the wine aroma spectrum. Liquorice is a welcome scent but you may find a skunky smell as well. You have been warned!

FREISA   FRAY-ZA

Nebbiolo's weird little brother in Piemonte, this grape seemingly cannot make up its mind whether it is a Dolcetto-like glugger or a Nebbiolo-like keeper. Both styles are made; I prefer the young vibrant cherryade version. You will probably only see this grape on holiday or in serious Italian delis.

KADARKA   KUH-DARKER

The Hungarian, Romanian and Bulgarian (where it is called Gamza) grape variety produces spicy, blunt reds with little charm. Think of a wine whose ideal food partner is haunch of yak.

MALBEC MAL-BECK

An unfashionable, old retainer grown in the Loire Valley, Cahors in central France and South America. It is a fairly heavyweight red grape which used to be widely planted in Bordeaux and was used as the tannin/colour provider on account of its thick skin. It can also be known as Cot and Auxerrois.

MAVRUD MAV-RUDD — RHYMES WITH 'HOOD'

Mavrud is a Bulgarian red grape variety with dark, swarthy appeal. It even sounds rustic if you roll your 'r'.

MOURVÈDRE MORE-VED-RA

Mourvèdre is another of the large band of southern French red grapes. But unlike Cinsault and Carignan, this grape has true style. In France, Mourvèdre is an integral part in the finest Châteauneuf-du-Pape blends, loving the company of Syrah, Cinsault and Grenache. Other famous wines that owe their flavours to a greater or lesser degree to this variety are Bandol, Cassis, Palette, Tavel and many other Provençal wines. They may all be a little esoteric, but are worth hunting down. Desperately in need of a suntan, this variety loves the hot weather. It travels extensively abroad to Spain, Australia and California (where it is known as Mataro).

PETIT VERDOT PE-TEE VER-DOUGH

The 'little green one' as it literally translates is sometimes used in small quantities in Bordeaux blends to add acidity to the rich cocktail of Cabernet Sauvignon, Cabernet Franc and Merlot. Keen Bordeauxphiles plant this variety in the hope that an ever more authentic blend will help them to reach perfection. They probably need not bother as a small percentage of Petit Verdot in a blend hardly affects the outcome.

PINOT MEUNIER   PEE-NO MUR-NEE-YAY

Pinot Meunier is the only grape variety that actively needs a PR agent. Virtually unheard of, this poor grape is left in the wings while Chardonnay and Pinot Noir take all the applause. Found in Champagne, it is immediately squashed out of its skin and produces a white wine that is an integral part of many champagne blends. It is even the most widely planted grape in the Champagne region. It brings up-front fruit and crisp acidity to the party and is generally used in non-vintage champagnes, where prolonged cellaring is not a requirement. Pinot Meunier is virtually unheard of outside France, except for some plantings in Australia and some in Germany (where it is known as Schwarzriesling).

PINOTAGE   PEE-NO-TAHGE

A Pinot Noir/Cinsault cross developed in 1925, it produces a rich, rustic wine and is South Africa's most famous red grape. Pinotage is an earthy, spicy, deeply coloured grape with tobacco and plums on the nose, crushed berry fruit on the palate and a hearty finish. It needs food badly.

TANNAT   TAN-AT

Originating in the Basque region of France, this variety did not have to travel too far to find its home in the two wines Madiran and Irouléguy. These two quirky offerings tend to be very dense when young and need a few years for the tannin levels to soften. Strangely, Tannat also is found in Uruguay where it is transformed into a slightly softer, fruitier version of Madiran – in other words, still a bit of a monster.

TOURIGA NACIONAL   TOO-REE-GA NA-SEE-ON-AL

Of the huge number of grape varieties that go into port, Touriga Nacional is the most aristocratic. Immense power, as you would expect, is the main character trait of this grape. Cram-packed with dense black fruit, it is the backbone of the finest and longest-lived vintage ports. Touriga Nacional is lately being used to make red wines with some considerable success. They are, not surprisingly, pretty big spicy creatures.

TEMPRANILLO   TEMP-RA-NEE-YO

This extremely important grape is the main ingredient in Rioja as well as many other Spanish red wines. It is confusingly known as Tinto Fino, Ull de Llebre and Cencibel in different parts of Spain. It also enjoys a favourite holiday location, this time Argentina, where the style is fruit-driven and less oaky than Rioja.

IMPORTANT WHITE VARIETIES

CHARDONNAY

If Cabernet Sauvignon is the king of the grape world, then Chardonnay is most definitely the queen. World domination was on the agenda when Chardonnay took the throne, and she achieved it mercilessly. This remarkably versatile dry variety has reached world fame on the back of a mass-appeal flavour that harmonises nicely with oak barrels and tends to complement food well. SHAR-DUN-AY Chardonnay is planted in every wine-making country and can be found in hundreds of different guises on wine shop shelves. If you are bored of seeing the word Chardonnay on bottles of wine, then try some Chablis, Meursault, Chassagne-Montrachet, Puligny-Montrachet, Pouilly-Fuissé or Mâcon-Clessé – or come to think of it, any white Burgundy; for all of these wines are made exclusively from the Chardonnay variety but do not feel the need to write it on the label (there are a few exceptions, but we will come to those later). It is also one of the three grape varieties used for making champagne (a Blanc de Blancs champagne is one hundred per cent Chardonnay). Chardonnay all over the world aspires to the greatness found in Burgundy's white wines. In California, Chardonnays come tantalisingly close to the complexity and elegance of white Burgundy. However, no one seems to have completely cracked the code. Other countries producing excellent Chardonnays are New Zealand, Australia, Chile and to a lesser extent Spain, South Africa and Italy.

You may think that you have been too reliant on this immensely popular grape and need a change. Some wine drinkers – the so-called ABCs – favour an 'Anything But Chardonnay' policy. They claim that Chardonnay is a boring variety and that we should all look to other white grapes for our titillation. Nevertheless, you will always feel the need to top up your taste buds with white Burgundy: it is an essential part of life. (That might sound a little dramatic, but when you do taste one, remember that it is a Chardonnay you are drinking, and you will know why all the adulation began.)

RIESLING

Here is a grape variety whose name sends a shiver down one's spine. Outside the wine world, Riesling is usually regarded as a cheap, sweet wine with a comedy German name. Blue Nun and Black Tower – look no further. Inside the wine world, Riesling is hailed as the greatest of all white varieties, including Chardonnay. Why? Well, Riesling produces a vast array of styles of wine. Everything from bone-dry aperitifs, through structured and foody, via long-lived,

REES-LING

complex and off-dry, ending up at heart-achingly beautiful sweeties. This variety has superb balance. The grape's acidity and fruit characteristics are stunningly complementary and can lead to a long and happy existence slumbering in the cellar. This variety is the unspoken, modest, spiritual leader of a wine lover's palate. Riesling has spent many years as an outcast in society, but there is always a hardened band of like-minded disciples keeping the fires burning.

Riesling's home is in Germany, yet over the French border in Alsace incredible wines are made. Here, Riesling Clos Sainte-Hune, made from a single vineyard owned by Domaine Trimbach, is the finest expression of dry Riesling available: the perfume is extraordinary and the taste on the palate spectacular. Italy and Austria produce delicious versions of this grape and further afield, particularly in New Zealand and cooler parts of Australia, Riesling is having huge success. The Riesling revolution is whispered about every year and one day it will happen; you only have to look at how many wine-makers are planting this variety and how many New World wine lovers are adding a Riesling to their portfolio, showing signs of support for this underdog. Dry Riesling is an uplifting aperitif. Sweet Riesling is a joy to behold. In between there lies a cornucopia of flavours and styles. Try one. Do your bit for the cause.

SAUVIGNON BLANC

Many wine drinkers regard Sauvignon Blanc as a court jester: a mere trifle not to be taken seriously. This is wrong, categorically wrong. True, these wines are not made to last for ever: the majority of Sauvignon Blancs in the world should be drunk within three years. Granted, there is a lot of mediocre Sancerre and Pouilly-Fumé on the market, and this is the grape that has made these two wines so famous. Sauvignon Blanc

SO-VEEN-YON-BLONK

does not take to oak barrels as well as Chardonnay, it doesn't age as well as Riesling, it can't cope with sweetness as well as Chenin Blanc or Sémillon, and rarely has the texture or oiliness of Gewürztraminer or Viognier. But it has something all of those other grape varieties don't: upfront, brazen, outgoing, happy-go-lucky style. You do not need a degree to appreciate its appeal. You do not need to have memorised the 1855 classification of Bordeaux châteaux to understand every element of its charm.

At home in the Loire Valley in northern France, this grape likes cooler climates.

New Zealand would never have been discovered by the likes of the English wine trade were it not for the gooseberry explosive nose and tropical fruit palate of their Sauvignon Blancs back in the early eighties.

I am always excited to taste great Sauvignons and now the skill of capturing the aromatic nose and zingy palate has crossed the water to cooler parts of Australia, Chile, California and South Africa as well as doing great things in northern Italy, southern

France and of course the Loire. The final vote-winner should be that Sauvignon Blanc is a saviour when it comes to oriental food. No other grape copes with the sweet and sour, spice and heat of all types of Pacific Rim, Asian fusion or even the real-Eastern-thing quite like this thirst-quencher.

SÉMILLON

This workhorse grape variety only really hits full speed in its sweet form. Once again, its birthplace is in France, more specifically Bordeaux. Here, often in conjunction with the underrated Sauvignon Blanc, it makes the most celestial sweet wines. Sémillon is luckily prone to 'noble rot' (see page 215), and this rot is encouraged. Despite the grapes looking unpleasant on the vine, the juice that

SEM-EE-YON

emerges when they are pressed is incredibly high in sugar. Under the right supervision it can result in a heavenly potion, whose well-known names are Sauternes and Barsac. Sadly these wines are few and far between, not to mention fairly pricey. The dry wine, again often made using a proportion of Sauvignon Blanc in the blend, can be sublime. Unfortunately, there is a large quantity of very dull dry white Bordeaux on the market as well. Sémillon blends well with Chardonnay and tries to emulate its more talented partner in the taste department. It can handle oak barrels, not as effortlessly as Chardonnay can, but well enough for it to be trusted on its own with these flavours. It also loves to travel. Flying solo, Sémillon has surprising success in the Hunter Valley and Barossa Valley among other areas in Australia. In New Zealand, several estates pioneering single varietal Sémillon have come up with an interesting alternative to Chardonnay. Relying on its CV as a fine producer of sweeties, it comes as no surprise that when asked to perform the pudding wine thing, it steps up to the mark and leaves every other grape in its wake.

CHENIN BLANC

Chenin Blanc is like the friend that favours music, clothes, food – come to think of it, everything – when it is out of fashion. Never quite getting the timing right, Chenin

Blanc is a dear old thing that tries hard and only really gets invited out when the company can put up with its eccentric behaviour. Found in the Loire, along with geeky Sauvignon Blanc and awkward, uncommercial Cabernet Franc, Chenin Blanc is another grape variety with an almost inhuman ability to outlive everyone in the room. Like Riesling, it has an uncanny balance of acidity and fruit when youthful. Acidity being the

SHUH-NAN-BLONK

vinous equivalent of a healthy supply of multivitamins, Chenin loves to always appear to have something in reserve – Loire Chenin Blanc always seems to be a little too young.

The other fascinating aspect of this variety is that it makes the full range of styles of white wine from remarkably efficient sparklers, through lean, zippy aperitifs to medium dry, charcuterie and pâté friendly wines to full-on honey and succulent peach sweeties dripping in unctuous mouth filling richness (using the rot that Sémillon loves).

So despite being a little unusual to say the least, this grape is a talented individual. For this reason it travels well. In South Africa – known as Steen – it flourishes, mainly in dry form. In Australia and New Zealand, Chenin copes admirably with oak barrels and thanks to the warmer climate can develop some considerable structure.

GEWÜRZTRAMINER

Gewürztraminer has the most distinctive smell of any single grape variety. Pungent lychee, spice and rose petals on the nose are accompanied, more often than not, by an oily texture on the palate and a long ripe finish. This grape has the unusual

GUH-VURZ-TRAM-INNER

knack of always smelling sweet and then sometimes surprising you, just when you least expect it, by tasting bone dry. Altogether other-worldly and more perfumed than winey, this grape is an acquired taste. Born in Germany but more at home in Alsace, France, it can produce extremely concentrated, flavoursome wines that range from light, fresh and dry to unctuous, decadent and sweet.

Curiously, the nose always gives the variety away, but not until the taste is it possible to tell whether the wine is dry, medium or sweet.

A popular way of making Gewürztraminer is to pick the grapes a little later than others grapes destined for dry wines. These wines are called *vendange tardive* (literally, *harvested later*). This complements the grape variety well and these wines are never cloyingly sweet, just ripe and smooth. Gewürztraminer is always a treat for your palate, as it exercises the taste buds you never knew you had.

Unlike the other well-travelled white grapes in this section, Gewürztraminer doesn't quite make the grade abroad. Seemingly a little jet-lagged or just homesick, it lacks the power and concentration of the Alsatian back home. Australia, New Zealand, Chile and North America all have a go at this grape and all make interesting, if not captivating wines. In Europe, northern Italy loses the *Gewürz* (German for *spice*) and plain Traminer produces the equivalent of a diluted Gewürztraminer nose with a crisp, dry finish. Spain and eastern Europe do their bit in growing this variety, but to little effect. It seems that Gewürztraminer loves its homeland and just can't stand to travel. Sulky and spoilt? No, just happy and content at home.

MUSCAT

The Muscat grape has a huge number of relations. Whether they are directly related varieties, sub-varieties and clones or just happen to sound vaguely similar, I am grouping them all together in this sprawling clan.

The range of tastes that emanate from this family tree are also extraordinarily diverse. From the lightest, fizzy soda-siphon grape juice, like fairy dust dancing on your tongue, all the way to the deepest, darkest, headiest liqueur like a rugby player's liniment, it just about covers the full complement of flavours.

The common factor in all of these wines is that Muscat is the only grape variety that actually tastes of grapes. For all of the other varieties in this chapter it is possible to come up with many different descriptive words to try to convey their taste, but with Muscat it is a struggle to find a more useful word than . . . grapey!

The main Muscat – the head of the family – is Muscat Blanc à Petits Grains (no wonder that just plain Muscat will do). This grape is responsible for the dry wines of Alsace (Muscat d'Alsace – another synonym) and the sweet wines from southern France, Muscat de Beaumes-de-Venise and Muscat de Frontignan. The Italian translation for this Muscat is Moscato Bianco. This

> MUS-CAT

version makes the frothy Asti wines in Piemonte and some fabulous sweet wines in Trentino. Although fairly widely planted in Italy, there is always another strain looking over its shoulder. In South Africa it is known as Muskadel and in California as the Muscat Canelli or White Muscat. The inferior Muscat of Alexandria is starting to crowd out the Muscat à Petits Grains and is responsible for Muscat de Rivesaltes, a fortified wine that hits the spot in a clumsy sort of way; and also Moscato di Pantelleria from Sicily, an orange-peel-crossed-with-syrup style of wine. More commonly used as a table grape, Muscat of Alexandria only really finds it comfortable in hot climates. It is made in Portugal into the tolerable clodhopper of a sweet wine, Moscatel de Setúbal. It is also found in the fortified Australian monsters known as Liqueur Muscats and some South African wines under the comical synonym Hanepoot – literally, *honeypot*. The other Muscat worth noting is the Muscat Ottonel, a cooler climate buddy who is trying to shove Muscat à Petits Grains out of Alsace. (So not much of a friend after all.) At least this Muscat is happy in Romania, Austria and Hungary.

The family of Muscat is not a happy one, more dysfunctional than functional; they are continually treading on each other's toes with no one version reigning supreme as climate compatibility plays a large role in which version is planted where.

PINOT BLANC/PINOT BIANCO

Not the most demanding of grape varieties, it is very easy to condemn Pinot Blanc to the B-list; but I welcome it into our happy band of overachievers. Another grape whose fame is almost exclusively European,

> PEE-NO BLONK/PEE-NO BE-ANCO

Pinot Blanc is found in Alsace; Burgundy (in minuscule quantities – here is one of the exceptions mentioned in the Chardonnay section); northern Italy (swap Blanc for Bianco); Germany (as Weissburgunder – pretty literally misplaced) and to a lesser degree in Austria, Chile and California.

So, what is Pinot Blanc's appeal? Almost all the Pinot Blancs made world-wide are unoaked, dry and relatively inexpensive. Find an estate with a good reputation and the chances are that their Pinot Blanc will be on form.

Very few Pinot Blancs will make you rush out into the street screaming with joy. They are not boring; they just seem to like to set the scene for other wines. They are the compères of the wine world: amusing, likeable, dry, multi-skilled crowd-pleasers which won't put anyone off before the real show begins – the best variety to start off an evening's wining and dining.

TOKAY-PINOT GRIS/PINOT GRIS/ PINOT GRIGIO/TOKAY D'ALSACE

So called because it has a greyish skin, Tokay-Pinot Gris is another grape variety that loves it in Alsace. Its flavour is somewhere between Pinot Blanc and Gewürztraminer - admittedly, there is a world of flavours in that gap! The distinctive nose of this grape is one of spice and honey. It does not have the rose petal perfumed element that Gewürztraminer has and also tends to be drier, like Pinot Blanc. There are some notable exceptions to this, as late, judicious picking can lead to extremely sweet wines; but on the whole, it is a savoury taste collision between a fruit bowl and a spice rack. The Alsatian version of this grape is not that commonly available; however, the Italian style – Pinot Grigio – is. But what a different can of beans this wine is. The richest, most exuberant Pinot Grigio is still a virtual lightweight next to the oleaginous Alsatian. Pinot Grigios from Trentino, Alto Adige and Friuli are spicy on the nose and then spritzy, almost buzzing with electricity, on the palate. This freshness comes from the Italians' eagerness to harvest

TOCK-EYE PEE-NO GREE
PEE-NO GRIDGE-EEO
TOCK-EYE DAL-SASS

a little early and capture all of the mouth-watering acidity that this grape has to offer. This grape definitely has a split personality.

In Germany, Pinot Gris is called Ruländer and it enjoys a fair degree of success in the relatively warm Baden region. Here it puts on some of the weight in which it revels in Alsace, and for that reason is appreciated as an enjoyable, food-friendly wine. Never quite reaching the aromatic zip of Pinot Grigio, or the weight and spice of Tokay d'Alsace, this grape also manifests itself in Austria and eastern Europe – don't bother.

VIOGNIER

Divine, sensual, provocative temptress, or fashion victim's folly? Your guess is as good as mine. With its haunting perfume of peach kernels and apricot blossom followed by an ample body with plenty of charm and a lingering aftertaste, Viognier seems hard to resist. But resist it you must: there are too many new Viogniers out there hitching a ride on the bandwagon. Viognier is the enchanter who found initial fame in the fiendishly expensive northern Rhône white wines,

VEE-YON-YAY

Condrieu and Château Grillet; and to give credit where it is due, these grapes from the steep slopes around Côte-Rôtie have spawned some magical wines. It was only a matter of time before somebody had the courage to plant Viognier elsewhere. Suddenly there were not one but thousands of estates clamouring for attention, and it is now widely planted in the Languedoc-Roussillon and southern Rhône and abroad in Australia, Uruguay and California. Central Italy has also gone for Viognier in a big way as it blends well. Even Frascati producers are turbo-charging their wine's aromas with the addition of a little Viognier.

It also forms a fine partnership with Chardonnay, where the Viognier, lacking in acidity, finds the ability to age for a little longer than normal. The main thing to remember is – be careful. In Viognier's case, all that glisters is not gold, and beauty could be only label-deep.

OTHER WHITE VARIETIES

ALIGOTÉ ALEE-GOT-AY

Most of the white grapes planted in Burgundy are Chardonnay. The Pinot Blanc appears in minuscule quantities, but the other grape that is seen around is the fresh and fruity Aligoté. It produces a dry, lean style of white wine that is designed to be drunk young. Traditionally this variety was mixed with a dribble of cassis (blackcurrant liqueur) to make a Kir. The dry flavour of the wine balances nicely with the rich blackcurrant taste to produce a delicious aperitif. But as most of France's Aligoté is planted in Burgundy, vineyard plantings have shrunk in favour of the nobler Chardonnay, so Aligoté is often relegated to the worst vineyard sites, such as next to the motorway. Only in the village of Bouzeron is Aligoté upgraded to a relatively serious commodity. Here it has its own appellation, Bourgogne Aligoté-Bouzeron, and yields are closely monitored to ensure high quality. Further north in the Chablis district, it is again viewed with a touch of respect and makes simple and refreshing summery wine. Aligoté is also grown in Chile, California, Romania and Bulgaria, although only one country really champions this often-bitter little warrior – Russia, where it is the second most planted white wine grape (but don't bother trying to find any).

ALBARIÑO/ALVARINHO AL-BA-REEN-YO

I once described this grape variety as having a Viognier nose with a Riesling palate. High praise indeed, for it was a particularly good example of a Galician Albariño. This variety really can have a peachy aroma like Viognier and a flowery, spicy palate like Riesling. I'll also stick my neck out and claim that it is certainly the best indigenous Spanish white grape variety. But sadly, that is not saying very much. In the far north-west corner of Spain, the province of Galicia churns out fine Albariño for wealthy Spanish wine drinkers to enjoy. The Rias Baixas zone in Galicia produces Albariño that has a cult following, and several examples have made their way out of Spain to test the international waters. The reception has been surprisingly warm and no doubt a love affair with Albariño will follow. The Alvarinho spelling refers to the superior grape used for a version of Vinho Verde, from across the border in Portugal.

BACCHUS BACK-US

A (Riesling x Sylvaner) x Müller-Thurgau cross (or is that a criss-cross?) with some redeeming characteristics. It ripens in cold climates and is responsible for some of the wine made in England and, to a greater degree, in Germany. Oh, and it is named after the god of wine. Not to be sniffed at, if you see what I mean.

COLOMBARD COLUMN-BARD

Colombard is one of the grape varieties whose primary job is making the dull, acidic base wine that, once distilled, is transformed into Armagnac and Cognac. It has very high natural acidity and so enjoys work abroad as a blending partner, mainly in Australia and California. But work is hard to come by these days.

FURMINT FUR-MINT

A native of Hungary, this distinctively spicy grape helps to produce the legendary sweet wine Tokaji (not to be confused with the grape variety Tokay, which is pronounced in the same way). Several dry wines have emerged using this variety, proving the grape to be a fairly talented individual.

MACABEO/VIURA MACK-A-BAYO, VEE-YOUR-AH

Macabeo is a dreary grape variety found in the south of France. Known as Viura in Spain, it found success enlivening white Rioja and now represents more than ninety per cent of the white vines planted in the region. Viura is better suited to producing light wines, which might account for the recent change in styles of white Rioja from the old-fashioned, oaky breed to a more fruity, fresh and forward wine. In Penedès, Viura teams up with local grapes Parellada and Xarello to make the Spanish sparkler, Cava.

MANSENG   MAN-SENG – GROW AND PE-TEE

Gros and Petit Manseng are found in south-west France where they produce, among others, the superb wines of Jurançon and Pacherenc du Vic-Bilh. These two wines, particularly Jurançon, have become very fashionable. The complex nose and citrusy, floral palate accompanied by a very crisp finish have made them highly sought-after restaurant wines. Thankfully, prices have stayed down and they are certainly worth looking out for if you are struggling to stay within some sort of affordable budget while eating out in an expensive French restaurant. The Petit Manseng is the finer of the two Manseng grapes. It has an enviable ability to hang on to its vine well into autumn. The grape shrivels and the sugar content is concentrated, thus resulting in a delicious sweet wine. The longer the grape stays on the vine, the sweeter the resulting wine. Some wines are named after the month of harvest, almost as if they have won an endurance award, like Jurançon Symphonie de Novembre, by Domaine Cauhapé.

MARSANNE   MARCE-ANN

Marsanne is a plump, rich, oily white grape that makes Hermitage, Crozes-Hermitage, St-Péray and St-Joseph in the northern Rhône. It can fly solo, but likes to have a co-pilot to achieve perfect balance. The experienced Roussanne (see below) or trendy Viognier (see above) are usually first past the post. In California, Rhône Rangers feel the need to plant Marsanne to complement other French varieties in residence. Marsanne loves the warmer climate and behaves a little flirtatiously, like a slightly giddy Chardonnay.

MELON DE BOURGOGNE   MELON DUH BOR-GONE-YUH

This is the variety responsible for the super-famous and much maligned white wine, Muscadet. Found at the mouth of the Loire River in northern France, this hardy grape manages to achieve a good degree of ripeness every year, rewarding the wine drinker with a fabulously dull wine that somehow still catches the eye. Show me a restaurant without Muscadet on its list! The gulf between fine Muscadet and bad may be less like a gulf and more like an ocean, but there is no better wine with which to enjoy a dozen oysters.

MÜLLER-THURGAU   MOOLLER TUR-GOW

Widely planted in England and New Zealand, this cold-climate grape is most prolific in Germany. Müller-Thurgau is a Riesling x Sylvaner cross and tries to be a pretender to the Riesling throne, but lacks Riesling character in just about every department. It does ripen early, so it is not as prone to disease and downpour as its noble parent. It also produces a huge crop; in some cases, double that of Riesling yields. But these two points do not make up for a loose-knit structure, weird, green smell and short life-span. I am sure that you have guessed what is coming next. Yes, Müller-Thurgau is responsible for Liebfraumilch, Piesporter and various other brand names worth avoiding. If you are a Liebfraumilch lover, please do not be offended. Taste a Riesling from the Mosel region and discover the definition and complexity of the true star of Germany.

MUSCADELLE   MUSK-A-DELL

Confusingly, this grape has nothing to do with the huge Muscat family. Muscadelle is found in Bordeaux playing a supporting role to Sauvignon Blanc and Sémillon. Third best by a long way, the majority of Muscadelle is used for the lesser-known sweet wines of Sauternes' neighbouring areas, Ste-Croix-du-Mont, Loupiac, Cadillac and further afield in Monbazillac. In fact, out-of-fashion Muscadelle is being pulled up as opposed to planted. It does, however, have a following Down Under where it is responsible for a blunderbuss of an Australian liqueur called Tokay – which has nothing to do with Hungarian Tokaji or the grape variety Tokay. The plot thickens – so does this liqueur.

PALOMINO   PAL-UH-MEENO

Palomino deserves a very brief mention in this section, as it is the grape that is grown around Jerez in southern Spain and makes – you guessed it – sherry.

PEDRO XIMÉNEZ   PED-ROE HEE-MEN-ETH

This grape produces the sherry-like wines of Montilla in Andalucía in southern Spain. More interestingly, Pedro Ximénez is used to make a fortified wine that is rich, dark brown, sweet and tastes of chocolate, raisins and goes under the name of PX. It is like a top-secret potion. This wine can keep after having been uncorked for weeks and is not only delicious poured over ice-cream but could actually replace pudding altogether. (It is also an awful lot easier to pronounce than Pedro what-d'you-call-it.)

ROUSSANNE   ROO-SANN

Roussanne is the more delicate, talented half of the northern Rhône white grape double act. It is leaner and more aromatic than its fat friend Marsanne and also holds the distinction of being one of the four grapes allowed into white Châteauneuf-du-Pape, whereas Marsanne is not on the list. A little like an exclusive vinous fitness club, with a tough membership policy.

SCHEUREBE   SHOY-RAY-BUH

A Sylvaner x Riesling cross that thankfully works well in Germany and Austria. When dry, it makes delicious ripe, zesty wines. When sweet, Scheurebe makes succulent, fruit cocktail aromas on the nose with balanced, not cloying, fruit on the palate. They always have a zip of acidity running through them. This grape is also grown with good results in England.

SYLVANER   SIL-VAH-NUR

The most boring of the Alsace wine-growing fraternity, or just misunderstood? Frankly, this widely planted grape rarely gets into second gear and is often left at the lights by Pinot Blanc, which is saying something. A good Sylvaner generally has some texture and good acidity, but its marked lack of classic descriptive adjectives leaves the palate unexcited and the brain soon switches off. If Sylvaner had to be in a mixed case of Alsatian wine it would be the cardboard packaging ensuring the other bottles didn't break.

UGNI BLANC/TREBBIANO   OO-NEE BLONK/ TREB-EE-AH-NO

Ugni Blanc (French) and Trebbiano (Italian) are names for the same white grape. But whatever the name, this little grape tends to produce lower-end, dry, one-dimensional wines. It is possible to find bucketloads of cheap wines made from this grape in your local wine shop, like Vin de Pays des Côtes de Gascogne. Occasionally, these wines exhibit a fresh, lively lemon zest character with a nice, tidy finish. More often than not, the flavour disappears the second it touches the tongue. It is widely planted in France and Italy and makes some good wines – Frascati and Soave are some of the better-known names. Surprisingly, this plain grape also makes a simple base wine for Cognac and Armagnac (as does Colombard).

With one or all of these raw materials at his disposal, it is then down to the wine-maker to perform his wizardry and transform harvested grapes into wine. That is the subject of the next chapter.

CHAPTER 2

HOW WINE IS MADE

farming and alchemy

Well, it's pretty simple really. Go to a vineyard, pick some grapes, crush them, ferment them (sugar turns to alcohol). Bottle the juice and Bob's your uncle, *voilà*, wine. It sounds easy, so why all the fuss? Making wine should be a relatively straightforward process. The truth of the matter is that each one of those stages described above is a little more complicated than you might expect. Since no two vineyards are alike and thousands of grape varieties are available, it is crucial to decide upon both site and variety first. When you are up and running – this could take three or four years - decisions have to be made as to how to make the wine of your dreams.

In this chapter, I will take you through the process of vineyard site selection, viticulture (the farming of grapes) and vinification (the alchemic transformation of grapes into wine).

This chapter alone should slow down your eager corkscrew a touch in your quest to destroy the contents of a bottle before considering where it has come from and what went into creating it.

Most of the world's wine regions are found between 30° and 50° latitude in both the northern and southern hemispheres. This is because outside these two zones, it is either too hot or too cold for vines to grow grapes suitable for wine-making. Within these boundaries there are huge chunks of the earth that could, in theory, be used for vine-growing. But there are other factors that have to exist in order to consider planting a vineyard. The obvious statement of the day is that grapes grow on vines, and vines are plants. Now I have got that off my chest, I will elaborate.

As a vine is a plant, it can be planted anywhere. Imagine popping down to the local garden centre and buying a rose bush. There are many different sites in your garden where you could plant it; you could even give it to a friend for their garden. One thing is certain: roses grow best in certain spots and green-fingered gardeners will do a better job of deciding on that site than a novice would. Like roses, vines are very picky about suitable places to be planted. Also like roses, there are many different types of vine, each with their own specific likes and dislikes. Which soil is best, how much sunlight is needed, what sort of drainage is required and what style of trellising is essential for a good bloom? But enough of that analogy, because vines are far trickier to grow than roses (and the resulting crop is a damn sight more tasty).

The two most important factors affecting the growing of vines are the precise location and its climate. Location means the country, region, sub-region, area and exact plot of land on which the vineyard is situated. The vineyard itself has two main components, an above-ground element and below-ground characteristics.

Above ground, several factors come into play. The aspect or topography of the vineyard refers to the angle of the slope of the vineyard. A vineyard planted on a hillside will absorb more sunlight than a vineyard planted on the flat. Generally, sloping vineyards not only have a better view of the sun but also have better drainage than flat vineyards. However, not all slopes in wine regions are cultivated. In the northern hemisphere, south-facing slopes are chosen as they maximise the length of sunshine hours on the vineyard. Conversely, in the southern hemisphere, north-facing slopes are used. The direction that vineyards face plays an important part in concentrating the sun's rays down on to the vines for the longest period of time possible.

The altitude of the vineyard can also have an effect on the grapes. The higher the altitude, the cooler the temperatures and the longer the growing season for the grapes. High-altitude vineyards are fine in hot climates as they take the edge off the searing heat, but they are not so good in cool climates. For this reason many vineyards in northern Europe tend to have trees on their hilltops, the best portion of the vineyard being the middle of the slope. Valley floors tend not only to lack the full direct power of the sun but also are more prone to flooding and frost. They also tend to be too fertile, giving rise to inferior crops. Many vineyards are planted on the slopes of river valleys (the Rhône, Mosel and Loire are but a few). These spots are ideal, provided the slope is angled in the right direction, as they receive the added benefit of reflected sunlight.

We cannot affect the climate and therefore must try to pick a kindly one before choosing a vineyard site. Depending slightly on the specific chosen grape varieties, as some require more sun than others do, the ideal climate should include a long warm summer, allowing the grapes to ripen slowly and evenly, with a dry, sunny lead-up to picking time in the autumn. The winter can be pretty cold as vines can withstand minus 20°C, though this would be regarded as extreme. Vines, like most fruit-bearing plants, spend the winter months lying dormant waiting for the spring sunshine.

That, of course, is the perfect scenario: it doesn't always slot into place like that (just think of the last time you went abroad skiing when there was no snow, sailing when there was no wind or sunbathing where it bucketed down for a fortnight). Unfortunately, the weather is very much in control of this stage of wine-making; you have to make the most of it (as I'm sure you've said to yourself before, huddled freezing under a beach umbrella).

> Vines are not very keen on some of the dangers that affect us in our own gardens. At particularly vulnerable times such as flowering or ripening, hail, frost and strong winds can damage the crop and even strip it of flowers or grapes.

Uneven flowering due to a particularly cold or rainy snap can result in partially developed grapes that are not suitable for wine. One of the worst problems is rain at harvest time. The vines can, if given the chance, drink their fill in a short space of time and the resulting grapes will be dilute and lacking in classic varietal flavours. Rainy weather also leads to rot on the vines and, unless there is a breeze to dry the vines out, will lead to an imperfect harvest.

Basically, vines need heat – an average throughout the year of about 15°C (60°F); sunshine for photosynthesis (1500 hours over the growing season is perfect); and water – if it is not falling from the sky then, if allowed, irrigated (a vine needs approximately 80 cm of water per year). So above ground we have our shopping list of ideal conditions, rapidly narrowing down the suitable world areas by the minute.

Below ground, the soil's profile takes into account the type and depth of the soil strata. A soil profile indicates the soil's ability to hold or drain water and retain heat. Vines live through their root systems: too wet or too dry and you have problems. In the Old World, where most of the region's vineyard areas were mapped out years ago, it is possible to see where the best sites for vine growing are. In most New World areas where there tend to be fewer rules governing where and what you plant, new vineyard sites are springing up every day – some successful, some not quite so.

Vines like relatively thin topsoil for good drainage and subsoil with some water-retention characteristics. The best soils for heat retention are gravel, loamy soils or sandy soils. Chalk comes next, with clay bringing up the rear. Good heat retention is essential for an even ripening of grapes and can make up for very cool evenings by keeping the vine's toes warm. Many of the great vineyards of the world have particular soil types. The chalk soils of Champagne must have a huge influence on the famous wine itself, not least having spawned the most fabulous cellars in which to age the bottles! It follows that chalky soils promote grapes with high acidity, but also allow good drainage (essential in a rainy northern European climate). The gravelly soils of the Left Bank in Bordeaux have good heat retention, superb drainage and relatively low fertility, thus forcing a vine's roots deep to search for nutrients. Cabernet Sauvignon thrives in this medium. The Bordeaux commune (village) Graves is named after its gravelly soils. The extra-large pebbles in the vineyards of Châteauneuf-du-Pâpe are famous for their heat-retention qualities, capturing the sun's rays during the day and acting as hot-water bottles at night, keeping the vines warm. Slate soils also warm up quickly and retain their heat, helping the great wines of the Mosel-Saar-Ruwer in Germany to ripen fully in a fairly cold climate.

Below ground we now know the characteristics of the soil needed for the vineyard. The next stage is viticulture: the growing and tending of the vines. These days it is not unknown for wineries to employ viticulturists whose sole job is to look after the vineyards. They are in charge until the crop is handed over to the wine-maker at harvest time. These people are expert geologists, biologists, botanists, meteorologists and probably a few other 'ologists' that I am not aware of. Battling against the weather for the whole year is a thankless task and, as great wine is made in the vineyard, everybody expects viticulturists to do a good job. Sadly, rather like goalkeepers in football, they are rarely awarded the top honours for superb wines, as the wine-makers (the centre forwards) generally get the plaudits.

VITICULTURE

The old adage I've just quoted that 'wine is made in the vineyard' is absolutely true. The neatest, tidiest, best-planned and of course, best-sited vineyards often yield the finest fruit. Before planting a vineyard the method of vine training must be decided upon (see glossary, page 213). It is necessary to make the most of your naturally occurring conditions such as aspect, soil and climate. There are many training techniques used in vine growing. The common aim is to maximise the sun's effect on the vine and to try to allow air movement around the vine to prevent any excessive humidity that would lead to rot or mildew. The buzz-words in vine training are 'canopy management'. For years, it was thought that low yields concentrated a vine's efforts into a smaller crop and the quality would inevitably be higher; and to a certain extent this can be true. However, with the advent of enormous research by some key players in the business, principally Dr Richard Smart in Australia, the science of vine training was born. Nowadays the methods of spreading the canopy of leaves out, designing the trellising systems and measuring the distance between each vine and row of vines to match the exact climate are gradually being tested by keen viticulturists the world over.

With the 'training plan' sorted, the next hurdle is planting. It is now time to introduce you to the demon of the wine world: a little bug (or more correctly a louse) whose name is *Phylloxera vastatrix*.

Sounding more like a comedy mate of Asterix and Obelix, this little creature (the devastator) has ravaged the wine world for ages. Hailing from America, it appeared in a starring role in Europe in the late nineteenth century where it proceeded to munch its way through the roots of over six million acres' worth of vineyards in France alone.

At the time this was viewed as one of the greatest agricultural and economic disasters of the century. In hindsight, and after finding a way to control it, Phylloxera was seemingly the single most important cause of a new-found replanting programme that raised the quality and concentrated the minds of wine-makers in Europe. It was, in effect, a huge clear-out that resulted in the best vineyard sites and wines remaining. From this huge upheaval, the French Appellation d'Origine Contrôllée system was born.

How to prevent this louse? Resistant rootstocks were the answer. So in vineyards around the world, resistant American rootstocks have been planted with a vine variety grafted on to them. In effect two vines are joined together, one good below ground, the other good above. Without trying to overcomplicate matters, there are many resistant rootstocks available; again, it is a matter of matching them to soil, climate and the actual vine destined to be joined to them. Curiously, Phylloxera has not yet infected some parts of the world. Particularly sandy soils are not the natural habitat for this bug, and as yet Argentina, Chile and a handful of others have not yet had to graft. Recently, the so-called 'billion-dollar bug' charged through the vineyards of California. The University of Davis in California, specialists in wine courses, recommended a rootstock called AXR_1. However, the Phylloxera bug had a strain called 'biotype B' that enjoyed the taste of this rootstock, and the rest is history. Californians will tell you that the vineyards needed to be replanted and re-trained anyway! Suffice to say that anybody that used this rootstock has succumbed to the louse and has had to replant. Anyone who disregarded Davis's advice has continued to make wine without a hitch.

We now have the vineyard, training system, correct rootstocks and chosen vine variety. There is one last detail to contend with: once the vine variety has been decided upon, there is the little matter of clones. Clones, without wanting to sound too scary and Big Brotherish, are pure versions of varieties taken from the best vineyard sites that have been reproduced over and over again, eliminating any offspring that are inferior. This concentrates the characteristics of the individual clone and ensures (cross fingers) a good result, as long as the chosen vineyard site for the young nursery plant is compatible to that of its original host. The only problem with relying too much on individual clones is that the crop might be fabulous but will lack the complexity of flavour in the end wine. In this case, several different clones of the same grape variety with slightly varying taste characteristics can be planted alongside each other in the same vineyard, giving a far more varied base from which to make the end wine.

The annual life cycle of a vine is much the same as any other fruit-bearing plant. There are crucial periods during its life when finger-crossing, long-range weather forecasts (and even prayer mats I'm sure) are employed to try to calm the nerves of anxious wine-makers. The following section explains the changes that occur in the vineyard over the eight-month period leading up to and including the harvest. (As the harvest in the southern hemisphere takes place six months ahead of that in the northern hemisphere, I have used seasonal periods as opposed to actual months to describe what is going on.)

Late winter: having survived the cold winter, the dormant vine wakes up gradually. This can be seen when the cane ends start to weep sap (presumably for joy).

This shows that the vine is warming up and the roots are starting to absorb water in the soil. At this point, frantic pruning takes place in preparation for the subsequent spurt of growth. Frost alert – early pruned vines are at risk from frost.

Spring: a month or so after the weeping has started and then stopped, the budbreak (or budburst) takes place. Vines planted in warmer soils, or with warmer weather (or even certain grape varieties, like Chardonnay), will break first. These are more prone to frost. During this period the vines are fastened to their various training systems. By late spring, leaves and shoots begin to appear and tiny, green circular clumps are visible on the vine. These little bunches are the flowers that eventually blossom two months after budbreak. Spraying will prevent any unwanted diseases (particularly *coulure* and *millerendage* – see glossary, page 215). At this time of year it is important that the weather stays fair until after the flowers have been pollinated. Once again, frost here would be a killer. Fertilisation occurs and the flower turns into a berry. At this point they are tiny, round, hard and green. This stage is called 'fruit set'. It is now possible to check the success of the fruit set and estimate the maximum size of the potential of the harvest.

Summer: spraying will continue and the weather should be sunny and warm to ripen the grapes. Summer pruning, the cutting off of excess leaves to focus the vine's energy into the grapes, will be used if necessary. The grapes grow in size and become more recognisable as true bunches when *veraison* happens. This is the moment when the skin on the bright green grapes either turns yellow/green (for a white grape) or purple/blue (for a red one). The sugar content in the grapes is now gradually increasing. Pruning excess bunches of grapes at this time will focus all the vine's efforts into a smaller but higher quality harvest. Once again, leaves can be plucked off the vine to create more space for airflow around the bunches, thus avoiding rot.

Autumn: this is the most important period in the wine year, when human intervention plays as big a part as the weather. The harvest takes place as soon as the grapes reach target ripeness. Measurements are taken of the sugar content in the grapes to see when they are at their peak. White grapes are usually picked first. With this head start, they can sometimes whiz through the winery before the arrival of the red grapes. Each wine-maker generally knows the order in which his different grapes will arrive at the cellar door. If the estate has only one grape variety growing in the vineyards (such as Sauvignon Blanc in the case of a Sancerre producer), specific vineyard sites will tend to ripen quicker than others because of their differences in soil, microclimate or aspect. Practice makes perfect in this department. The only spanner in the works is the all-important weather. If there is any sign of rain, the wine-maker/gambler instinct will emerge.

> There are two choices: pick right away to avoid the grapes getting bloated, thus harvesting dilute or even rotten bunches; or hold on as a sunny patch could be around the corner that will dry out the grapes and continue to ripen them even further after their little impromptu drink.

Early winter: the only grapes left on the vine in late autumn/early winter are destined for the production of sweet wine. These grapes start to shrivel as their supplies from the vine are cut off and their water content starts to evaporate. Late-harvested grapes are not particularly pleasant to look at but this concentration in sugar and acid means that they have the ability to produce sweet wine. One stage further than this is when the 'noble rot', *Botrytis cinerea*, attacks the grapes. This occurs naturally in some vineyards thanks to favourable weather conditions, but can also be artificially introduced by the wine-maker. Noble rot further concentrates the sugar and acid within the grape and can produce tiny amounts of unctuous, rich, sweet wine. If the climate is suitable, then Eiswein (literally, ice wine) can be made. Only occurring when the temperature in the vineyard drops below zero, the grapes actually freeze on the vine. They are picked in late December/early January and lightly pressed so that only the intense sugary juice is collected as the water content is still frozen in the press. Needless to say, the vineyards are pretty empty at this time of year.

VINIFICATION

Given the finest quality grapes, there is no doubt that it is possible to make an incredible wine. But it is far easier and less stressful to make a mediocre wine. The greatest wine-makers seek to retain all the goodness and taste of the vineyard in their wines. Attempting to lose none of the natural power and aroma of the grapes at harvest is an art. After all, it is not very easy to add flavour, but it is all too easy to take it away. Great wine-makers have an ability to turn a poor harvest into something special.

As some wine-makers actually control the vineyard management as well as that of the winery, their knowledge is understandably broad. If a vineyard manager is employed, then the relationship between him and the wine-maker should not be underestimated. There is a right hand/left hand aspect to these two positions. In the weeks leading up to the harvest, the wine-maker will work closely with the viticulturist, spending time in the vineyards tasting grapes and checking their sugar and acid levels. The wine-maker is the person who decides exactly which day to start the harvesting. The viticulturist will then instruct the pickers or mechanical harvesters to go into the vineyards and remove the crop as quickly and efficiently as possible. Any delay in harvesting will endanger the grapes, as once picked they are susceptible to oxidation and heat spoilage. For this reason the grapes are taken to the winery straight after picking. Meanwhile, in the winery, the cellar-hands will have cleaned and tested the winery apparatus, ready for the off. Adrenaline will be at an all-time high and sleep will be very low on the agenda.

I have set out below the classic ways in which white, rosé, red, sparkling, sweet and fortified wines are made. This could be done in a very scientific fashion that would not only baffle me, but also bore you. I have therefore decided to explain these techniques with reference to the way they affect the *taste* of the end wine.

Firstly, I will give you a brief explanation of some of the key stages and practices that occur during wine-making. If you can understand these principles, the rest will be a doddle. Remember, the elements of wine-making are universal. Like making a cake, casserole or cocktail, the basic method is the same: only the ingredients differ.

ALCOHOLIC FERMENTATION

This is the chemical process that turns sugar and yeast into alcohol and carbon dioxide: in other words, grape juice into wine. Yeast occurs naturally on a grape's skin as the so-called *bloom*, seen as a dusty coating. If crushed grapes are left in a tank then fermentation will eventually occur. These natural yeasts are called 'wild' yeasts and this method is the time-honoured, old-fashioned way of making wine. However, with the advent of chemical engineering, cultured yeast can be added to the grape juice by the wine-maker. This process is called *inoculation* and these yeasts have proven characteristics that control the fermentation with favourable results. Certain yeast strains work well with specific grape varieties, enhancing the aroma of the final wine or enabling the wine to be pushed to higher alcohol levels.

Fermentation halts when all of the sugar is exhausted or when the level of alcohol reaches a point where it is actually poisonous to the yeast. This is the natural end to fermentation, but fermentation can be stopped in a number of other ways:

racking: the process of draining the wine off its lees (the cloudy sediment at the bottom of a fermentation vessel), thus removing it from its yeasts.

pasteurisation or chilling: this works because yeast cells are unable to function at extremes of temperature, approximately below freezing and above boiling point.

fortification: this is the addition of alcohol to a level that is toxic to the yeast.

filtration: simply filtering out the large yeast cells from the wine.

centrifugation: this spinning process separates the wine in terms of density. The yeast cells are denser and so can be removed by this rather expensive, time-consuming method.

MALOLACTIC FERMENTATION

This 'fermentation' is really a degradation of malic acid into lactic acid. Malic acid is a hard, bitter-tasting acid found in grapes (also in unripe apples, leading to a lot of cheek-sucking and fish impressions!). Lactic acid is much softer. The riper a grape is at harvest, the lower the acid. In cooler climates where the natural acidity in the harvested grapes is fairly high, 'malo' is almost always encouraged.

> Only in hot climates, where acidity is hard to hang on to and where the grapes ripen at a very fast pace, might it be necessary to inhibit the malolactic fermentation.

Conversion of malic acid to lactic acid tempers the raw taste of a wine and softens the flavours out, often adding another dimension to the taste of the wine.

Malo usually occurs naturally straight after the alcoholic fermentation as the enzymes needed to start this stage are again found on the grape skins. Just to make sure, the winery is usually warmed a little to start the malo process. Some grapes are more susceptible to malo than others. Chardonnay is a natural candidate, whereas Riesling and Chenin Blanc often avoid it.

STAINLESS STEEL

At one time it was rare to see stainless steel tanks in Old World wineries. Nowadays proud French wine-makers show you their gleaming tanks, as if to say, 'Check this out, I'm bang up to date.' Don't tell them the rest of the world got rid of glass-lined cement tanks and dirty old barrels years ago. Stainless steel is the perfect material for tanks as it is inert (does not affect the taste of the wine inside); stainless (easy to clean); long-lasting (much better than a barrel in that respect); and perfect for temperature control (cold water is pumped around pipes surrounding the tank which chills it, allowing the wine to retain all of its aromatic qualities and freshness). Stainless steel is so popular that any wineries with more than a few stainless steel tanks are called 'tank farms'!

OAK

Oak barrels have been used for wine-making since the times of Herodotus. In the past they were almost exclusively used for storage and transportation, but these days oak barrels are used for two purposes in the winery: fermentation and maturation. Whereas stainless steel imparts no taste to a wine during fermentation or maturation, oak barrels do. When wine is either fermented or matured (or both) in oak, its flavour is greatly altered. This is the primary use for barrels – to enhance the flavour of a wine by adding another dimension of taste, namely that of oakiness and other associated nuances.

Before talking about the different types of oak barrels available it is important to explain the pros and cons of oak. The one massive pro is that if handled correctly, the flavour should be augmented considerably. Now for the cons: barrels are very expensive; they are also labour-intensive (they need cleaning, repairing, manhandling, they can leak and are awkwardly shaped); they are porous which means that the wine inside will gradually evaporate and need to be topped up occasionally which costs money and, of course, allows oxidation of the wine which enables it to be drunk younger – accelerated ageing, if you like. Finally, they have a shelf life. New barrels have tons of flavour, one-year-old barrels a lot of flavour; two-year-old barrels have some flavour, three-year-old barrels a little flavour; four-year-old barrels need chucking away! But only as far as distillers, who will use them in turn.

The bigger an oak barrel, the less surface area to volume of wine ratio. The smaller the barrel, the more wood touches the wine. The classic dimension of an oak barrel is the Bordeaux *barrique*. These barrels hold 225 litres of wine (which equates to about 25 cases of 12 bottles).

The other piece of important barrel trivia is that during the barrel-assembling process, the staves are heated in order to bend them into a curved shape. This can be done over a fire. If so, the finished barrel will have a slightly charred inside. Wine-makers can order barrels with various levels of 'toast' from low to high. The charring of the barrel can complement the flavours of the wine and this accounts for the 'toasty nose' of many bottles of oaked wine.

There are two main sources of oak barrels in the world of wine, France and America. French oak barrels are largely considered to be superior to American oak barrels in that they impart subtler, more complex oaky flavours to the wine. They also tend to have more tannin content. Tannin is the natural preservative of wine, so this means that wines using French oak tend to need ageing a little longer than those using American oak. These qualities are also reflected in the price of French oak barrels. A single French oak barrel can cost £500. This cost in turn has an impact on the final cost of the wine. Oaked wines tend to be that bit pricier than their stainless steel cousins. The broader, sweeter, dry-roasted flavours that American oak gives to a wine are considered less elegant and more 'in your face' (or should I say, up your nose). So it is obviously not as simple as just using French oak if you are loaded, American oak if you are a bit strapped for cash and stainless steel for your wine if you are broke.

French and American oak bring different taste profiles to the wine. Where would we be without the soft vanilla flavour that has become the accepted hallmark of Rioja? This stunning taste is picked up by the red wine spending a considerable amount of its life slumbering inside American oak barrels. The peak of Chardonnay excellence found in the Burgundy cellars of France would never consider using American oak as a taste enhancer, because the bold flavour would overshadow the tight-knit, compact young fruit, pulverising the final wine. Roxburgh Chardonnay, the flagship white wine made by the Australian outfit Rosemount, has recently tempered its huge, mouth-filling flavours by moving from American oak to French oak. This change has not meant any loss in the wine's overall appeal, just enabled it to enjoy a little more longevity. The massive boom in South American wines could not have had such a huge impact on the world market were it not for their immediate drinkability. Many of the juicy red wines were oaked, but had French oak been used, the wines would be more expensive and require a few years cellaring before drinking, thus blowing any chance of a fast sale. So there is an argument to support all cases. And all barrels!

Very few white grape varieties can handle the strong flavour of oak. Occasionally Sauvignon Blanc has a go and Sémillon can handle it on a good day. There are unsuspecting varieties that get forced, kicking and screaming, into a barrel by brave wine-makers, but the one grape with the muscle to cope is Chardonnay. 'Oak-Aged' or 'Barrel-Fermented' can be seen on the labels of many a bottle of Chardonnay.

Most red grape varieties, however, can handle a dunking in an oak barrel. The richer the wine, the longer the time spent in the barrel or the newer the barrels used. Either way, barrels should be used to complement the wine, not overpower it. A popular analogy is the use of salt and pepper on a plate of food. Just the right amount brings the flavour to a peak; too much can ruin it.

FINING

This wine-making process clarifies and stabilises a wine. Minute particles held in suspension in the wine can, in time, cause haziness or greater problems, such as bacterial spoilage. Fining is a speedy way of clarifying a wine, thus preventing faulty bottles. Clarification would naturally happen if a wine was left to stand for several months; however, most wines are ready to bottle shortly after the end of vinification and fining quickly stabilises the finished product.

A clarifying agent is added to the wine which sticks to the invisible, unwanted particles and falls to the bottom of the tank or barrel, forming a sediment. The fining agents themselves are an unlikely bunch. Egg whites, isinglass (fish bladders), milk, bentonite (clay), charcoal and a few others can be used to clarify wine. It is important to stress that none of these substances are left in the wine that is bottled; they form the sediment at the bottom of the barrel or tank, and once the wine has been racked off (see page 222) it is clean and clear.

COLD STABILISATION

This is another preventative measure to avoid the formation of crystals in the bottom of a bottle of wine. The wine is chilled to a very low temperature to encourage crystals to form and fall to the bottom of the tank. The wine is then racked off and bottled. These crystals are tartrate deposits that are completely harmless but can cause a fair degree of panic for an unprepared drinker as they look like little pieces of glass. Cold stabilisation is practised by almost all commercial wine-makers, thus avoiding any consumer panic. However, many expensive wines are not cold stabilised as the process could remove some of the original, valuable taste elements. Fine wine-makers prefer to print a little disclaimer on the label – *vin non filtré* or some other such note – warning the drinker that should the wine have crystals, pour carefully and enjoy. I would go even further than that and say that I, for one, actively enjoy seeing tartrates at the bottom of a bottle of fine white wine, as it is an extra hallmark of quality.

LEES CONTACT

Lees are the dregs or sediment that settle at the bottom of a barrel or fermentation tank, made up of dead yeast cells, grape skin fragments, grape seeds and tartrates. Usually the lees are discarded as soon as fermentation is finished by one of the techniques discussed above. However, some wines are deliberately left on their lees in order to extract more flavour from these heavy particles. This is called 'lees contact', and lees contact is incredibly trendy. It not only encourages malolactic fermentation, but also adds complexity to the finished wine. Lees stirring affects the taste of wine particularly if it is in oak barrels. These wines will have much subtler, softer, more integrated oak flavours than those that are left undisturbed. Most Chardonnay producers (Burgundians particularly) are very keen on lees stirring, as it give their wines depth and texture. The lees are stirred with a big oar, so in France this process is called *bâtonnage* (i.e. done with a baton!). Another famous wine that is traditionally made on its lees is Muscadet. Muscadet is rarely made in oak barrels but the lees contact does make a big difference to its taste. Watch out for *sur lie* (on the lees) on labels of Muscadet.

The difference that lees contact makes to red wines is less obvious as they are generally more structured than white wines. However, lees contact also helps to start malolactic fermentation in reds.

MAKING DRY WHITE WINE

The first few stages of white wine-making are performed at speed, the main aim being to retain all of the flavour and freshness of the harvested grapes. Any delay can result in air and heat causing unwanted oxidation in the bunches, so after the grapes have been picked they are taken quickly to the winery. A quick check through the bunches will be carried out either in the vineyard or winery to remove any rotten or unripe grapes. Then, depending on the style of wine, one of two techniques will be used. For lighter wines, the grapes will be lightly crushed and destemmed, then pumped into a press. (The stems are removed as they contain bitter flavours.) For heavier or aromatic styles, the grapes will be crushed and destemmed and then left to 'macerate' – soak in contact with their skins – in a temperature-controlled stainless steel tank for twelve to thirty-six hours. Cold maceration extracts more flavour compounds from the skins into the juice, a practice sexily entitled 'skin contact'. (Apart from the slightly tired 'this one's ready to lay down', 'a good firm body' and 'exciting in the mouth and longer than you'd expect', you rarely get the opportunity for bawdy talk in a winery, so make the most of this one.)

At all times, the wine-maker will ensure that the temperature of the white grapes, juice and wine is cool which is crucial in order to retain freshness and aroma in the wine. For this reason if the climate is particularly hot, the grapes will be picked at night when it is cooler. The harvest can be refrigerated on its way to the winery if necessary. The grapes can also be refrigerated at the winery before crushing, in large, walk-in cold rooms. Maceration will be temperature-controlled and the next stage, the pressing, will also be fairly quick in order to get the juice into a tank to settle at a cool temperature again. It may seem over-particular but, of all the recent skills learned over the last few decades in the winery, temperature control is the most important.

The grapes are pressed gently and the juice, known as *must*, is collected. The reason for a gentle pressing is that the juice that naturally falls out of the grapes first is of the highest quality. Even before the press is started juice will have been released from the grapes as a result of the crushing process (this is known as 'free-run' juice).

The first pressing will be the best juice. Rarely will the second or third pressings be used in the best wines, as the harder the press squeezes the grapes, the more bitter the flavours in the must.

The must is pumped into a stainless steel tank for settling (*débourbage* in French). At the very least a basic settling of the must is carried out, usually at a cool temperature. In some cases two separate settling stages are required to brighten the must further, in order to make it cleaner. The must can now be manipulated before fermentation. Loads of tricks can be used like filtration, fining, centrifugation and cold stabilisation, all of which clean up the must and remove any solid particles and unwanted impurities. At this stage sulphur dioxide is usually added to kill any bacteria and prevent oxidation.

The juice is now pumped into a fermentation vessel. This could be a tank or a barrel, depending on the grape variety and style of wine. The wine-maker can now add cultured yeasts or just let the naturally occurring yeasts in the cellar start the fermentation. A cool cellar or temperature-controlled stainless steel tanks will ensure that the fermentation takes place in a relatively cool atmosphere, between 10°C and 17°C. This will enable the wine to have good aromatic qualities and crispness on the palate. Any warmer than that and the wine might lack zippy freshness but gain complexity. Very few white wines are fermented at any warmer than 25°C. In cool climates, where the grapes have failed to reach optimum ripeness, a process called 'chaptalisation', where allowed, is practised. This is the addition of sugar or concentrated grape juice to the must, before or during fermentation, to raise its total sugar content. This can increase the final alcoholic strength of the wine by one or two degrees. In hot regions, the harvested grapes can have a lot of sugar but too little acidity. To correct the overall balance of the wine, tartaric or citric acid can be added.

Malolactic fermentation follows alcoholic fermentation either naturally or, once again, is started off through inoculation by the wine-maker. Some producers will not allow their wines to go through malo as they wish to retain the extra acidity in their wine. This only happens in wines where high acidity is required for the style or where the fruit was especially ripe in the first place with low acidity at harvest.

We now have wine! There are a few last details to take care of before it is bottled and labelled. The final few decisions are purely 'recipe' procedures, and they will be wine style or grape variety specific.

After malo, tank-fermented wine can be transferred into barrels for a period of maturation. These wines pick up an oaky taste in barrel, and often 'oak-aged' or words to that effect will be used on the wine label to denote this style of wine. Oak-aged wines are a little different to barrel-fermented wines, which usually ferment *and* age in oak barrels, thus resulting in a more pronounced oaky flavour. It's also time to get out the *bâton* for a little *bâtonnage* if this will enhance the style of the wine. Depending on the type and age of the oak barrels, the wine could hibernate here for anything from a few months to several years.

Finally, after fermentation and maturation, when the must is well and truly converted into wine, the racking, fining, stabilising and filtering options can be used if desired prior to blending, bottling, labelling and at last (hurrah!) drinking.

MAKING RED WINE

Red wine making is always regarded as being a little trickier than white wine making as there is one small but desperately important difference between the two techniques: the skins. Red wine can only be made from red grapes as the skins contain the red colour pigments. Take a peek inside a grape and you'll see that the pulp is clear, regardless of the colour of the skin. So in theory, you can make a white wine from red grapes if you crush the grapes quickly and get rid of the skins. The best example of this is champagne, which is usually made from two-thirds red grapes.

As with white wine, the first step is to crush and destem the bunches in a cleverly entitled crusher/destemmer (*égrappoir* in French, which always sounds better). The stems contain very harsh tannin flavours and they tend to unbalance the wine and rarely soften even with age. It is sometimes advisable to put a small percentage of stems into the fermentation if the vintage is too hot and juicy or a little feeble, as this will give the wine a touch more grip.

There is not the same urgency when making red wine as there is making white: the process is often deliberately slow. This is because during the first few stages the grape juice has to macerate with the skins in order to extract colour, flavour and other qualities, which takes time.

In fact, in some wineries, a 'pre-fermentation maceration' takes place at cold temperatures just to try to get all of the potential goodness out of the skins. (The reason that this maceration is done at cold temperatures is that if the temperature were allowed to rise, the natural yeasts on the grape skins would kick off fermentation.)

Every red wine maker wants rich, dark, juicy red wines. However, not every vintage produces these hallmarks. In wet years, when the crop is dilute, some technological wizardry can be employed (scientific breakthrough time). In some estates wine-makers can remove water from swollen grapes via some very expensive machinery which extracts water using reverse osmosis or evaporation under a vacuum -- baffling stuff! However, if this can concentrate the sugars in a wine that until now would have ended up pretty weedy and watery, then it can only be a good thing.

Once the crushed grapes have been pumped into a tank or vat (or large open-topped oak barrel called a *cuve* – now very old-fashioned) the fermentation will start either naturally or induced with cultured yeasts and a warm winery. Late autumn is one of the best times to visit a winery as the cellar is usually warm (a rare event) and the smell is heavenly. Fermentation can take anything from a few days to a month. The temperature is allowed to rise to much hotter levels than in white wine making, to around 30°C (but no more than 35°C otherwise the yeasts could die and the fermentation become 'stuck'). The warmer the temperature, the more flavour is extracted from the skins and the deeper the colour of the wine. During fermentation a mass of grape skins and pips (and stems if some are included) form a cap (*chapeau* in French) which rises to the top of the tank due to the carbon dioxide released from the fermentation. This accumulation of skins will sit on top of the must (juice) at the top of the tank, reducing the amount of colour extraction unless it is either pushed down into the must (a process called *pigéage* in French), or the must is pumped or sprayed over the cap. 'Pumping over' (or *remontage*) is a widely practised technique. Chaptalisation can be employed at this time if the grapes lack sufficient sugar to reach an acceptable level of alcohol. At all times the temperature police keep an eye on the thermometers, making sure that temperatures stay within a safe range. If they rise too high, cold water will be pumped over or around the cooling jackets on the tanks. As you can imagine, some wineries these days have control panels similar to a space shuttle.

After fermentation has finished the skins can be left in contact with the wine for a further period, extracting yet more flavour and richness. Lighter reds will be separated from the skins immediately.

The total time that a wine spends in contact with its skins is called *cuvaison*. The wine that runs out of the tank of its own accord, leaving its skins behind, is called free-run juice. Left behind is the sodden cap *(pomace)* which once pressed releases 'press wine' which, as you would expect, is much darker, heavier and more tannic.

These two liquids are kept apart as the press wine is vastly inferior to the free-run wine and will only be added in small quantities if the harvest was poor and the wine needs beefing-up.

Over the next few months all the different batches of wine will be tasted over and over again by the wine-makers. They will know which tanks or barrels come from which grape varieties and also from which vineyards. As all vineyards differ not just in aspect and the like but often in vine age and reliability, the wine-maker will watch and taste making a mental note of all the lots. Usually the best vineyard sites produce the best wine, so experience and local knowledge counts for a lot in the art of blending. The finest tanks or barrels will be selected as the premium label and the rest will be sold as lesser labels or even in bulk. If the estate makes blended wines (red or white) then test blends will be made up. Once the perfect blend has been assembled, the separate lots will be blended (*assemblage* in French) in bulk in a large tank and from now on will be earmarked as the Château label, second label, Prestige Cuvée or whatever (these terms are explained on page 93). Lesser blends will spend their time following a different regime to the top wine, as they tend to require a separate 'oak programme'. Some wine-makers, usually of single varietal wines, leave the final assemblage until just prior to bottling. (Dealing with one grape variety means that the only two variables are the quality level and either oak or stainless steel handling, but it is still pretty difficult.)

The wine is now pumped into clean tanks or barrels for malolactic fermentation – the softening of the acidity. Following this, after a short wash and brush-up, simple, forward-drinking wines can be bottled. More complex wines will be put into oak barrels for a period of maturation. Fine reds will spend a considerable amount of time in oak barrels picking up the flavours and mellowing out. Decisions will be made as to what percentage of the wine will go into new barrels and what into one-year-old, two-year-old or older barrels. This choice will be based partly on the strength of the harvest – good years can handle more pungent new oak - and partly on the style of the wine – heavier grapes need more oak than light ones. Local tradition will play a role as well.

During oak ageing the wine will be racked several times to clarify the wine. The lees will be left behind in the barrel. Fining will also take place in the cellar, to clean up the wine prior to bottling. Many wine-makers will use a filtration system to further remove any solids from the wine, as it provides them with the safety of a perfectly clean and stable wine.

Filtration is rarely used for top reds as it can strip out too much flavour and leave the wine a little hollow. It is widely believed that judicious racking and fining will make red wine stable and clean enough without removing any of the character of the wine.

The freshly bottled wine will now be rushed out of the winery on to the shelves for sale, into merchants' cellars for ageing or will be kept back by the winery for ageing. Bottle ageing as opposed to oak ageing is crucial for many fine wines, both red and white. Occasionally wineries take the noble, if costly, decision to hold bottles back, delaying their release in the hope that the wine will benefit from this period of rest and development. If not then we, the consumers, are expected to do that on behalf of the wine. Hence the need for wine cellars.

CARBONIC MACERATION

Before we move on to rosés, sparkling wines and sweeties, there is one other method of red wine making that is important: *macération carbonique* or, in English, carbonic maceration. This process makes very forward, juicy, low acidity, low tannin but highly coloured wines, ideal for immediate consumption. Think of the fruitiest, most forward style of wine – Beaujolais. This wine and many others besides employ this practice, which involves whole berry fermentation in sealed tanks. Carbon dioxide forces uncrushed grapes to ferment quickly under pressure inside their own skins. Some producers use a 'semi-carbonic' process in which only some of the grapes are crushed beforehand. All very chemistry-orientated and awfully difficult to explain in detail, but it works and thank goodness we can drink some red wines young and fruity.

MAKING ROSÉ WINE

Making rosé wines is dead easy. OK, I suppose there are a few twists, but the basic principle is straightforward. The crucial word is *skins*. As red wines get their colour from the skins, then rosés must do also. But just not quite as much colour and therefore not quite as much skin contact. Several rosé-making methods are detailed below.

bled rosés (*saignée* in French) are made from the free-run juice that bleeds from just-crushed red grapes. This is very high quality, aromatic juice that makes the finest, palest and most succulent of rosés. As a result of bleeding the remaining red grapes will have a greater proportion of skin to juice and will go on to make a red wine of improved concentration and structure.

limited maceration rosé is the easiest style to understand. This is red wine making stopping short of making red wine. Set your stopwatch and remove the skins when the colour suits – eight to twelve hours usually works. Then, ignoring the colour, just proceed as normal for a white wine.

blending red and white wine is a terrible suggestion that has, in the past, given rise to some hideous wines. They are generally and understandably out of balance as they are neither red nor white but some Frankenstein blend. The only proper wine that is made with this method is the thoroughly delicious rosé champagne.

MAKING SPARKLING WINE

Remember that carbon dioxide is a by-product of fermentation: sugar + yeast = alcohol + CO_2. Normally this gas is allowed to escape from the wine into the atmosphere. If this gas is prevented from leaving, either by putting a lid on a tank or a cork in a bottle, then it will dissolve into the wine. The resulting wine, when uncorked, will release the

CO_2 in the form of bubbles. Eureka: fizzy wine. Dom Pérignon and his keen wine-making monk pals discovered that some of the bottles of wine in his cellar were fizzy when opened (some bottles even exploded). In this case, the fermentation had not completely finished when he had bottled the wines, so some carbon dioxide was dissolved in the bottles. This was the precursor to modern day sparkling wine production. Today sparkling wines are made from one of the following methods.

champagne method: *(méthode champenoise, méthode traditionnelle, méthode classique)* due to European Union law no one outside Champagne is allowed to use the term *méthode champenoise*, although you are allowed to use the other terms. This is the finest way to make sparkling wine and many estates, not just in Champagne, use this labour-intensive, costly method to produce their wines. The main difference between this style of wine-making and the others is that the second fermentation is carried out in the bottle in which the wine is sold. I will fully explain this method later in the Champagne section (see page 149).

transfer method: a touch down-market, this style copies the champagne method until the crucial last moment. The second fermentation takes place in bottle, but not the bottle in which the wine is sold, as the wine is transferred under pressure into a tank for filtration and re-bottling.

tank method: *(cuve close, charmat)* the entire process takes place in a large temperature-controlled tank (including the second fermentation). This process is used for bulk sparkling wines, but does not always result in low quality. Asti is the most famous wine made in this style, and while it is not everybody's cup of tea, there is no doubt that it can be absolutely delicious.

pompe à bicyclette: though literally this means 'bicycle pump', here it describes the technique of pumping carbon dioxide gas into a wine in a similar way to making fizzy soft drinks. Cheap and effective, but not a good way to make long-lived or elegant wines.

MAKING SWEET AND FORTIFIED WINE

The normal way to make sweet wines is to aim to harvest fully ripe fruit, in most cases leaving the grapes on the vine as long as possible and picking them late. The riper the fruit on the vine, the more concentrated the sugar in the grapes and therefore the higher potential of sweetness *(residual sugar)* and alcohol. Some grape varieties are more suited to making sweet wines than others. The top three performers are Sémillon, Riesling and Chenin Blanc, although many other varieties do the job well. The trick is to pick late, as with luck the grapes may be affected by 'noble rot' *(Botrytis cinerea)*. This rot lives on the skins and dehydrates the grape by sucking out its water. Despite sounding rather dangerous and looking very unattractive, it actually does the job of concentrating the sugar within the grape to levels that would be impossible to achieve naturally. The great wine-makers of Sauternes, Loire, Alsace and Germany all cross their fingers at harvest time, willing their vineyards to attract this rot if the weather conditions are favourable. It is possible to cheat slightly and spray the vines with a potion that introduces botrytis to the vineyard. This trick is used in California, Australia and elsewhere where the weather conditions would not always give rise to this rot naturally.

The wine-making process for sweet wines is the same for that of dry white wine except that the grapes are naturally much higher in sugar before they start. Before the fermentation is totally finished, while there is still unfermented sugar in the must, fermentation is stopped. This can be done by the addition of sulphur, which kills off the yeast. If the sugar levels are naturally very high in the first place, once the level of alcohol reaches sixteen per cent the yeast will be killed anyway, leaving a high-alcohol sweet wine.

There are other ways to make sweet wines, the crudest of which is straightforward chaptalisation – the addition of sugar. But there are some other interesting techniques employed in the making of sweet wines.

If botrytis does not occur, grapes can be left on the vine until they dry and shrivel, like raisins. This, once again, concentrates the sugars in the grape. The French term for this is *passerillé* and wines such as the tangy, tropical, Jurançon Moelleux are made by this method. Drying the grapes after harvest, either on mats or hung up in barns, can also be a way of raisining the grapes and raising the sugar levels for making sweet wines. *Recioto* is the Italian term for wine made in this style, such as the delicious, honeyed Recioto di Soave.

The final way to make sweet wines is by freezing the grapes, either naturally on the vine – Eiswein (the German for 'ice wine') – or in the winery, 'cryogenically'. *Cryoextraction* is a process designed to freeze the water content of the grape then crush out the sugar only.

Wines made from this process can be made any year, unlike the ice wine process that needs particular weather conditions. These wines are excruciatingly sweet and are consequently rarely bottled in any size bigger than a half-bottle.

Fortified wines come in many shapes and sizes, from the light, refreshing Muscat de Rivesaltes to the huge, monstrous, vintage ports. The one common theme is the addition of alcohol, usually grape spirit, to the wine. This addition of spirit immediately stops fermentation. The earlier the spirit is added, the sweeter the resulting wine. Fortified wines generally have an alcohol level of between sixteen and twenty per cent. Curiously, despite the huge range of flavours of fortified wines, they are all made in a very similar method: only the raw materials and the amount of alcohol varies. 'Vin Doux Naturels' such as Muscat de Rivesaltes, Muscat de Beaumes-de-Venise and Banyuls as well as Madeira, Marsala, port and Australian Muscats are all made where alcohol is added to the fermenting grape juice. Sherry is the only fortified wine where the alcohol is added to sweeten the wine after it has already fermented to dryness.

CHAPTER 3

HOW TO TASTE WINE

whet your whistle

The miracle moment arrives when, with the corkscrew in hand, you drag the cork kicking and screaming from its hiding place, never to return again. The poor little bark guardian is cast aside with glee as anticipation reaches a peak. Glasses ready, the first drops of precious liquid are poured from the bottle.

But wait a second! I don't want to spoil the moment, but there is something you should think about. That bottle, no matter where it is from or what it cost, has taken a minimum of a year to create. The wine-maker has sweated blood to make it and get it to you.

The wine has been slave to the weather, human error in the vineyard, human error in the winery, the bottling line, the economic climate and countless other variables (no doubt bad driving being one of them) that might have prevented it from ever making it this far. You have already seen its birth certificate (the label - of which more later) and it has a story to tell. So please, take a little time to get to know and acknowledge it for what it is - more than just a drink. In that split second before taking a sip, realise that in order to ever understand and totally enjoy wine, it is crucial to remember that it is a living, breathing thing, made with love and skill and requiring love and a little bit of skill to enjoy.

Why, though, taste wine? After all, tasting is little more than slow drinking with the brain switched on. But tasting is also the process by which all of a wine's secrets can be unlocked, revealed and enjoyed. Tasting is like reading a book rather than guessing the story from a glance at the cover. With previous knowledge of an author's work and a racy title, coupled with the blurb on the back cover, one can guess at a book's story. The same is true of wine - a reputable château, good vintage and back label can serve the same purpose. But reading the book or tasting the wine is the true test.

Can you taste? Do you have what is required to be a wine taster? The answers are yes and yes. You taste things every day. Wine might not occupy your daily regime, but toothpaste, coffee and toast, followed by lunch, dinner and choccies in front of the telly can all form part of the daily tasting schedule. Within each mouthful you can easily identify between the roast potatoes, broccoli and chicken. Eyes and nose help, but even if you were blindfolded it would still not be too difficult. It is honestly very similar with wine. Everybody has the apparatus in their own head.

Before embarking on your wine tasting, remember that the wine you have in front of you has been tasted many times before to assess its quality, readiness to drink and potential. The wine-maker will have tasted it countless times during the wine-making process, to ensure that it is representative of the style of wine he is trying to make. An agent will have tasted the wine to decide whether or not to buy it to sell on. Then a wine merchant, restaurant or other outlet will have sent a taster to the agent to assess the quality of the wine, perhaps comparing it to other similar wines in order to determine which one fits the slot in their shop, wine list or portfolio. Only then do you get a chance to see for yourself what the end result is.

Wine tasting is an organoleptic assessment, or sensory examination. Sounds painful? Well, it isn't, of course. Tasting just involves using all your senses to analyse a wine's elements. So here comes the skilful bit – tasting. This should also be good fun!

SIGHT

Hold a half-full glass of wine by the stem (this will prevent warming the glass and sticky fingerprints) and tilt the glass over – not too far! Look through the glass on to a pale background, a white tablecloth, plate or piece of paper. It is helpful to be in a room with natural light because artificial light can affect the colour and tone of the wine. Before concentrating on the colour, just check that there is nothing floating in the wine – pieces of cork, flies, dust, sediment and many other unmentionables could have found their way into the wine or the glass. Check that the wine is clear and not hazy (this could be a problem). It should just appear bright. Are there any bubbles? If there are, the wine will probably be a full-blown sparkling wine. But there may be just a few tiny bubbles on the surface of the wine, known as a spritz. These bubbles would indicate that the wine is young and fresh, a good pointer to a zippy, refreshing style of white.

Now assess the colour and its intensity. Try to get beyond just white and red. White wines can be described as colourless, pale yellow, yellow-green, yellow, yellow-gold, gold, and deep gold. (You do not need to stick to these descriptions: many other words could be used.) For reds, try opaque, black-red, deep purple, red-purple, ruby, garnet, brick red, orange-brown. Again, make up your own if it helps you. Colour can tell you a number of important things. For white wines, the paler the colour, the lighter, dryer and, if there are green tinges to the wine, the younger the wine. The deeper the colour, the heavier, richer, older or sweeter the wine. Oak aged whites will be a little deeper in colour than a similar wine made in stainless steel tanks. For red wines, the lighter the intensity of red colour, usually the lighter the weight of the wine. If the colour is bright and has a blue or purple rim, the wine will be younger than that of a wine with a brown or brick red rim. Climate can make a huge difference to a wine's colour. Hot climate wines will be riper and so tend to have stronger, more intense colours.

Remember, colour is only useful when combined with the smell and the taste. As you progress through the discipline of tasting a particular wine, you can build up an identity for it.

Just a quick note about 'legs', the patterns that wine makes down the side of a glass after having been swirled around. Ignore this phenomenon: it is merely a demonstration of the viscosity of the wine. It doesn't tell you anything about where the wine is from, what it is made from or its quality.

HEARING

Not really worthy of a listing as the only time a wine really makes a noise is the glorious moment when the cork is popped; guaranteed to raise a smile and also heralding the arrival of a glass, hopefully heading your way. Other wine noises are of course the pouring of a glass of wine and the fizz on a champagne or sparkling wine.

SMELL

This is the big one. In order to release the maximum amount of smell from the wine, gently swirl the wine around in the glass, again holding the glass by the stem. A little practice will enable you to swirl in mid-air. If this introduces a hitherto undiscovered wine spillage problem, place the glass on a table or flat surface and holding the stem like a pencil, draw tiny circles. This should get the wine swirling slowly around the glass. You will soon graduate to fully-fledged aerial swirling. If you think that this is all a little too pretentious, then take a non-swirled glass and have a sniff. It will not smell as intense as the swirled one, so there is a point to it, beyond that of looking like a pro.

And now for the first sniff. This is your formal introduction to the wine so take a steady, long, gentle inhalation, resisting the temptation to snort the wine as this can be particularly painful. When sniffing, try to bend over the glass rather than tilting the glass to you. Don't be afraid of sticking your nose into the glass as the smell will be strongest close to the wine. This part of tasting is known as the *nose*. The fun part is breaking this whoosh of winey smells into parts and trying to give them names. We are very privileged to have an awesome olfactory system that possesses a busy department that I call 'Smell Memories'. Whenever a smell whizzes up your nose the smell memories get working. You can be stopped dead by a smell and then spend the next five minutes trying to remember where and when you last encountered it. Whether it be a familiar pipe tobacco, an alluring perfume, honeysuckle blossom, old leather car seats, mown grass (particularly cricket pitches), home baking, freshly ground coffee, warm summer rain or a beautifully balanced salad dressing – all engage the brain for a fleeting moment. (Many of my friends have the enviable talent of being able to detect a fish and chip shop, after pub closing time, several streets away!)

The purpose of trying to identify wine smells is to look for links between one wine and another, and try to attach a regional or varietal 'smell memory' to it. Practice makes perfect and although a bit of effort is required to remember these smells, it is remarkable how quickly specific triggers in the brain begin to identify characteristics in the glass, so stick with it. An important rule to remember when tasting is that *you are always right*. Which is brilliant, because if you detect a specific smell on a wine, nobody can tell you that you are wrong. After all, it is your nose that has sensed the aroma and your smell memories that have unearthed the name for the smell. It is then a matter of applying that knowledge to the wine in question and unravelling its story. In blind-tasting, where the objective is to guess the origin of a glass of wine without looking at the label, many triumphs have occurred just by smell recognition alone.

Overall, the wine should smell clean, by which I mean not out of condition. 'Corked' wines occur with alarming regularity and should be weeded out instantly on the nose. The smell will be very pungent and woody coupled with that of five-year-old jogging shoes – it will not be remotely enjoyable. Also, if in doubt, taste the wine to check that this musty, unpleasant flavour is here as well.

Once the wine has been given a clean bill of health, the challenge begins to give names to the smells in the glass. It is like a photo-fit. First, check if there is oak present or not, as your nose is the best judge of this. Then search for fruit flavours. Are there any spicy or earthy overtones, and then any other aromas that come to mind, like honey, nuts or flowers on whites or beetroot, boot polish or cough syrup on reds? Also, decide how much intensity is behind the nose, as this could be a guide to quality and/or climate. This may all sound a little bizarre but you will be surprised what you find.

TASTE

OK, you have waited a long time for this: go ahead and take a medium-sized mouthful. This part of the operation is called the *palate*. Roll the wine around your mouth. A weird expression for this is 'chewing' the wine – it may sound strange, but if you try this it will become clear what the term really means. If you are feeling brave you can attempt to release yet more flavour from the mouthful by drawing in a small stream of air through your lips. This can also sound a little strange but it is all in a good cause. (Make sure that you don't choke! It's worth practising with a glass of water in order to perfect the action.) Then swallow the wine; or if you are intending to taste a range of wines, you can spit them out in order to keep your head clear. Finally, concentrate on the *finish*. As you would expect, this is the flavour after swallowing and the length of time that it lingers on the palate. Repeat if necessary and then by all means progress to straight drinking as soon as you are happy with the information that your brain has amassed. That is all you have to do to taste wine.

But what can the palate tell you about a wine? It will not really reveal any more about the key flavours of the wine, as your nose will have done much of that work already. When the wine is swirling around your mouth, your nose will continue its good deeds collecting flavours and nuances while your palate detects other elements.

Firstly, the **dryness** and **sweetness** of a wine is only revealed on the palate. Some white wines smell sweet but taste dry, like Gewürztraminer. These wines are not therefore sweet, just *ripe*. Again, a New World Chardonnay may have more body and structure than a Chablis but it is no sweeter, just riper, as they both have good levels of acidity and are dry on the finish.

Talking of **acidity**, the palate is also the determining tool in the detection of this vital element of a wine's make-up. Acidity is a crucial component in the balance of all wine, giving it bite and freshness on the finish. If it is difficult to separate the sensation of acidity from the rest of the wine in your head, then just taste a young Sauvignon Blanc. As white wines do not have tannin, the perky, zippy, zingy, refreshing quality that lends a tartness to the taste is the acidity. White wines without balanced acidity are referred to as 'flabby'. Red wines often have discernible tannins, so it is difficult to decide which part of the flavour is tannin and which acidity.

They both give rise to drying in the mouth and consequent cheek-sucking, but the acidity is the refreshing element whereas the tannin is the more bitter part.

With red wines, **tannin** can be a major slice of the overall flavour. This happens when a wine is too young. If the tannins are not in balance with the fruit, oak (if oak-aged) and acidity, this indicates that a wine has yet to reach its peak of drinkability. Tannins do soften with age, although that does not mean to say that if a young red is in perfect balance, it is not drinkable – far from it. If the tannins are hard, the fruit flavours huge and the acidity firm, there is no reason why the wine cannot be enjoyed now (probably with some hefty food). Only wines with prohibitively strong tannins should be sent back to the cellar for rest, recuperation and further hibernation.

Your palate can also detect **body** or **structure** within a wine. The best way to explain this sensation is to use a great American expression: 'mouth feel'. The richness of a wine, its texture and weight on the palate are all easy to spot. Wines can range from thin, via creamy, through smooth and ending up at velvety; not to mention lightweight, medium-weight, heavyweight and blockbuster. This is a guide to the alcohol levels, vinification techniques and grape variety (or varieties) that the wine is made from. Taking the point even further, the body of a wine along with its colour should also point you to a style, climate-type and even a good guess at the country of origin. **Body** and **colour** are generally connected as a result of the degree of sunshine that a vine has been subjected to during the year. So a luscious, golden white wine or a deep, dark red wine will probably be from a hot area or country. Conversely, pale, thin whites and light, weak reds usually come from cooler climates. Sometimes you may get a really tricky wine that has a deep, dark colour but is from a cooler region. If this is the case, either a brilliant wine-maker has had a hand in making it or it was a once-in-a-blue-moon excellent vintage.

Oak on the palate should always complement the fruit flavours in the wine. Over-oaked wines either need more time in the cellar to 'knit together' or else the wine-maker has been a little overzealous with the barrels. Oak flavours usually blend in with the grape flavours to add an extra dimension to the taste. If oak is detected on the nose, look out for the harmony on the palate. Also remember that oaked wines are generally more expensive than un-oaked wines, as this may help with your deduction process when playing the Price Point Game (see glossary, page 229).

Flavour, like the nose on a wine, is very much a personal thing. Once again, you cannot be wrong as your palate tells you what you recognise. Don't worry if everyone else tastes passion fruit and you get kiwi fruit. They are both tropical so you are all in the same ball-park.

The **finish** is an all-important quality marker.

Fine wines tend to hang around on the taste buds for minutes whereas cheaper styles can be gone in seconds. Keep a note of which flavours remain on the palate.

If the fruit is last to go then the wine will probably be at its peak or slipping downhill. If the tannin or acidity (or both) are last to leave, the wine will probably be better off being kept for a few months or even years as it will need to soften further. The units of measurement for finish are short, medium, long and heroic (I threw the last one in). 'How long do you think this one is?' – cue uncontrollable sniggering.

I am a **balance** freak, and as I have already mentioned, balance is fundamental to great wines – and by great wines, I do not mean expensive bottles. The one element that unites all of the world's best wines is that they have in-built impeccable balance. If the concept of balance is slightly baffling, then imagine two see-saws, one for reds and one for whites. The red see-saw has four arms, and on each arm sits a different element in a red wine's make-up: fruit, acidity, oak and tannin. For whites, there are only three arms to the see-saw: fruit, acidity and oak, if present (if not, there will be only two arms). If any of these elements is too heavy, the see-saw will be weighed down on one side. If all elements are present in equal and complementary proportions, the wine will have perfect balance. I do hope that is helpful as it sounds a touch preposterous, but it works for me!

The final part to consider is the **complexity** of the wine. I often refer to simple wines as one-dimensional, others as having many dimensions. One wine could be like hearing a solo instrument playing, another like hearing the whole orchestra. There are occasions, perhaps when sitting over a meal and relaxing, which call for a wine that can awaken the taste buds and challenge the mind. Other times the wine is a simple partner to a quick salad at lunch-time. The complexity of a wine is often another hallmark of quality, and more often than not, has an impact on the price of a wine. But usually genuine, regional wines made by skilled wine-makers have in-built complexity and integrity coming from the soil and local traditions that transcend price.

Tasting when performed at Olympic levels can require Herculean amounts of concentration and it can take for ever to get to the bottom of a single glass. Competitive or what? But social drinking can and should involve tasting – done at high speed for your own benefit or privately in your own personal space.

Pour, observe, sniff, sip, swallow, think, and return to the conversation. It only takes two seconds and can heighten your enjoyment of the glass of wine enormously.

Finally, remember, with wine in mind, practice makes better, never perfect. The most important aspect to tasting wine is the very simple question that many of us fail to ask ourselves: do I like it?

SETTING UP YOUR OWN TASTING

This can be good fun and a novel way to storm through copious bottles of good wine in the name of furthering your own powers of deduction. Here is a short check-list of what you will need.

an invitation: obviously, it always helps to know where and when the tasting is, but it is important to emphasise the start time – it's very difficult to retrace one's steps in a wine tasting if you are late.

a theme: concentrate on a single grape variety, region or vintage. There are so many wines in the world that it is best to narrow it down for the purposes of a tasting.

the order: dry to sweet for whites and light to heavy for reds. Group similar grape varieties along the way.

lighting: natural daylight is best, as artificial light tends to show dull colours.

glasses: ISO glasses are the world standard wine-tasting glasses. They are relatively inexpensive, useful for all styles of wine and widely available from wine shops or glassware manufacturers. If you do not have any of these, then tulip-shaped glasses will do – the shape should prevent wine whizzing out when swirling! Avoid cut, engraved or coloured glass as these all interfere with the colour of the wine. Make sure that the glasses are clean with no detergent smell.

no smoking: this will mess with your taste buds and other people's noses.

no strong perfume: this will also mess with your taste buds and other people's noses.

tasting sheets: a numbered sheet on which to record your thoughts, tasting notes and perhaps marks out of ten for each wine. This will serve as an aide-mémoire at a later date.

spittoons: if necessary.

food: again, if necessary, but crackers or water biscuits are a bare minimum to fend off the undesirable effects, at least for a time. Try to match wine to food.

wine: of course, the most important ingredient. Ensure that each wine is served at the correct temperature (of which more on page 77), and poured in no more than half-glass quantities. After all, there may be some left at the end for avid fans of particular wines. Always keep the receipts for the wine in order to play the 'price point game' (see glossary, page 229).

Remember that when tasting in groups, the 'sheep phenomenon' sometimes takes over. One person may say, 'This tastes like strawberries,' and everyone else will lazily nod and agree. It is always important to give everybody a fair crack at analysing a wine as this will throw up loads of adjectives and nuances that will benefit the entire crowd.

THE WINE TASTER'S LANGUAGE

I am sure that you are aware of the extraordinary language used for describing the taste of wine by wine tasters. While many of the words and phrases used are common and recognisable, there are some bizarre expressions that can appear totally alien when referring to wine. Please turn to my extensive wine taster's glossary (see page 221) for details of some key phrases. (I promise you that these are all genuine!)

In the mean time, here are just a few widely recognised 'nose' hallmarks for a collection of classic red and white grape varieties, some of which I have already touched on. See if you can pick out these and other aromas from your wines.

RED GRAPES

Barbera	Black wine gums and boot polish.
Cabernet Franc	Grass cuttings and black fruit.
Cabernet Sauvignon	Blackcurrants, tobacco, chocolate and mint.
Dolcetto	Black cherry, liquorice and occasionally eggs!
Gamay	Bananas and bubble-gum on cheapies, pepper and blackberries on more expensive bottles.
Merlot	Plums, red wine gums and coffee.

Nebbiolo	Leather and stewed prunes.
Pinot Noir	Strawberry and redcurrants, violets and horses!
Sangiovese	Cranberry, fresh herbs and red cherries.
Syrah/Shiraz	Ground pepper, cigar-smoke and blackberries.
Tempranillo	Strawberry, raspberry and vanilla.
Zinfandel	Black cherry and mixed spices.

WHITE GRAPES

Chardonnay	Honey, butter, nuts and fresh flowers and fresh-baked bread, lime juice, butterscotch and vanilla (if oak-aged).
Chenin Blanc	Beeswax, honey and wet woolly jumpers!
Gewürztraminer	Rose petals, lychees and spice.
Muscat	Grapes!
Pinot Blanc	Very little.
Riesling	Rhubarb, petrol and honey.
Sauvignon Blanc	Asparagus, gooseberries, lemons, elderflower and cut grass.
Sémillon	Honey, orange blossom and lime juice.
Tokay/Pinot Gris	Mixed spices and fruit salad.
Viognier	Peaches, nutmeg and apricots.

WINE FAULTS

How do you know when a wine is genuinely faulty, as opposed to just not very good? There are a few ways to find out. After all, if you are served a faulty wine in a restaurant or you buy a wine in a shop that turns out to be faulty, you are entitled in both instances to a refund or to swap the bottle for another of the same. The one point to remember is that you must speak up. It is always easy in a restaurant to catch someone's eye and rustle up another bottle; however, people are generally lazy about bringing a bottle back to a wine shop and so miss out on the opportunity to claim a refund. Do not feel guilty about complaining as the merchant and restaurant will themselves get reimbursed from the wine-maker or importer in turn. Always record the date that you opened the wine on the label, as the shop will taste the wine to try to determine the fault as well. It is helpful for them to know how long the wine has been exposed to air in order to discount any mild oxidation from its list of possible ailments.

POINTS TO LOOK OUT FOR
(OR SMELL OUT FOR) IN FAULTY WINES

Apart from sediment in red wines and tartrate crystals in whites, there shouldn't be any other visible problems. Both of these two naturally occurring substances, if anything, point to confident wine-making and a lack of filtration before bottling. As filtration can take flavour and body from a wine, these two elements are positively attractive. Anything other than true sediment or tartrates is questionable. If a wine shows a permanent **'haze'** or cloudiness, there could be a bacterial problem with the wine, usually that yeast is still present. This is a genuine fault and the wine should be returned as soon as possible. Wines with haze will not necessarily harm you as such, they are just biologically unstable. But they may be unpalatable and are clearly not what the wine-maker intended, so it is best not to drink them.

Occasionally you may spot **bubbles** in a still wine. Some whites are given a little squirt of carbon dioxide when bottling to give them a lift in order to try to retain the freshness of the style. This is not a problem as this spritz will disappear shortly after pouring a glass of wine. A difficulty arises when a wine is actually and actively fizzy. Still reds and whites can be unintentionally bottled with yeast still active in the wine. This is a huge error, because whereas in champagne this trick is used for the positive development of bubbles, in still wines this gives rise to unwanted fermentation.

The nose on a wine can detect other faults. While a browning in the colour of a wine could be an indication of **oxidation**, the best test is to take a sniff. The smell will be sherry-like. Any **vinegary** or strong **sulphur** smells can also be off-putting and point to bacterial or wine-making cock-ups. Mouldy smells could indicate dirty wooden barrels, bacterial spoilage or just plain unhygienic wine-making. Wine should always smell clean. **'Bottle stink'** is a term used to describe slightly musty wines that need air to freshen up. If you have a wine that is not obviously faulty but just a little stale-smelling, then allow it to breathe or even better, decant it. This could give the musty wine a much-needed kiss of life.

The biggest problem of all must be **corked** wines. Until everyday wines are sealed with screw caps or plastic corks, this problem will continue to plague drinkers. A corked wine is the result of a contaminated cork affecting the taste of the wine (not a few pieces of cork floating in a glass). This problem is irreversible and as many as one in twenty bottles world-wide could be affected, perhaps even more. This fault is not just associated with cheaper wine, although the chance of a corked bottle of fine wine is, thankfully, greatly reduced. Corkiness arises from a problem encountered during the cork production process. Chlorine is used to bleach corks prior to washing and drying. This chlorine reacts with phenol in the cork and is converted, by mould found on the corks, to a chemical compound called trichloroanisole (TCA). It is thought that changing the bleaching process could make a difference, although mould growing on corks can still generate these corked smells, and corks can be contaminated at any time during the production process.

Corked wines have a distinctive mouldy, stale, pungent aroma. They are usually easy to spot as the smell is not remotely winey – more like a strong, musty, woody smell.

If you are eating in a restaurant and are in any doubt, ask a wine waiter to check the wine. If you are at home, do not pour it out but re-cork it and return it to the shop it was bought from. If it is corked it will be replaced; if not, there should be an explanation as to why the wine smelled so peculiar and you will probably be given a replacement to try again.

The palate is not really required to detect faults, merely to confirm them. Corked wine generally tastes pretty awful, as does vinegary wine and so on. I would avoid tasting anything that smells unpleasant anyway.

If you have a problem with a bottle of wine and a second shows the same problem too, it is definitely a sign to move to a different wine. It is rare for two bottles of the same wine to both be corked or oxidised, but if bad wine-making is the reason for your concern, you are unlikely to enjoy the same bottle again.

HOW TO SERVE WINE

There is an amazing amount of pomposity associated with the rituals surrounding wine drinking. Crusty old buffers would blanch at the youth of today drinking Zinfandel with chocolate, chilling down red Crozes-Hermitage or decanting a Meursault. Some of the old practices are necessary in order to get the maximum flavour possible from the wine. Others sadly just perpetuate the myth that wine is a snobby drink, only to be enjoyed by those privileged enough to be in the know. In this chapter I will strip away all of the unnecessary wine etiquette and leave for you the bare dos and don'ts of wine drinking. After all, how difficult is it to drink a glass of wine? In my experience, it is not very tricky at all. Here are a number of logical steps and some useful information to ensure that you enjoy your wine to the full.

CORKSCREWS

There are thousands of corkscrews on the market these days and I am sure they can all extract a cork from a bottle of wine. However, I do favour certain styles over others. Firstly, consider the objective. Corks can vary greatly in length and composition. Old corks can be very crumbly, and new corks very hard, so the corkscrew needs to be sharp and long (5.5 cm minimum). The helix, or the spiral shaft, needs to be straight, so look down the helix from the pointed end to see a

clearly defined inner and outer circle of metal. It also needs to be smooth in order to facilitate the manoeuvre. I am not keen on corkscrews with a central shaft that resemble a DIY wood screw, as these tend to just bore a hole in the cork and end up pulling the centre out of the cork rather than removing the cork from the bottle. The most well-known style of corkscrew must be the 'waiter's friend', favoured by restaurant staff. I must admit to using this style myself, as it does the job well and folds up so as not to cause injury in the pocket. The famous 'screwpull' is the safest and most foolproof of modern corkscrews and the top of the range 'lever arch' model is a must for the devoted connoisseurs. The only model that I am still completely baffled by is the so-called 'butler's friend'. This has two prongs designed to be inserted between the cork and the bottle and by using a pulling/twisting action the cork is allegedly squeezed and extracted unscathed! I am sure that butlers the world over can complete this task, no doubt sneakily pouring out the fine wine for themselves and replacing it with a less fine brew for their employers in the space of a few minutes; I, alas, cannot.

OPENING A BOTTLE OF WINE

While steaming through various wines, you will inevitably come across many different styles of bottles. Some are a doddle to open, others a pain. A bottle of wine should not present too much of a challenge but there is a right and wrong way to go about it. First, take off the capsule (the plastic or metallic case over the top of the bottle). Some people like to cut around the capsule leaving a neat skirt of colour, but I prefer complete removal as I have sliced open my fingers and thumbs countless times on razor-sharp edges. This also makes it easier to see through the neck of the bottle if the wine requires decanting. Next, screw in the corkscrew, vertically, straight and all of the way. Screwing the corkscrew in at an angle or only putting it in half-way is encouraging the cork to break and that is a hassle that you really do not want to contend with. Then lever or pull, depending on the style of your corkscrew. Constant pressure as opposed to a nervous jerk will again prevent the cork breaking and will also stop you elbowing someone into next week. Well done: have a rest and pour yourself a half-glass of wine. This is the ideal amount as you can swirl it around without spillage.

OPENING A BOTTLE OF CHAMPAGNE

Undoubtedly, opening a bottle of champagne is the most testing of procedures. There are several basic points to grasp before showering your friends with a bottle of fizz. Make sure that nobody has shaken up the bottle before you get hold of it. Always have a target glass nearby to pour the first gush into.

Twist the bottle (not the cork) slowly after the capsule and wire have been removed. Remember to keep your hand over the end of the cork in case it attempts to fire out of the bottle and lodge itself in someone's eye. Point the bottle away from everyone and ease the cork out slowly.

The noise of the gas emerging should be a hiss or young maiden's sigh (if you know any), not an ostentatious pop unless you're feeling particularly vulgar. Pour a small taste for you to nose, checking to see that the wine is in good condition. After it has been given the seal of approval, pour half a glass for each drinker, then top up the glasses after the mousse has subsided. This pouring procedure eliminates any chance of glasses overflowing and people getting a sticky-champagne-hand.

GLASSES

It is essential to have some good glasses in order to fully appreciate wine, as it is the medium through which wine is transferred from the bottle to your mouth. There are many different styles of glassware on the market today and it is worth investing in appropriate glasses. The finer the glasses, the less likely they will break when polishing and the better they will look on the table. It is possible to have a different glass shape for every wine imaginable. It is more sensible to have a white wineglass, a red wineglass, a champagne glass and a smaller glass that will accommodate sherry, port, sweet wines and digestifs. Glasses will look nicer if they come from the same set. If you are on a very tight budget then one medium-sized glass will take care of any wine style (champagne excepted). The main point to remember is that all glasses should curve in slightly at the top so that wine does not spill out when swirling it around. The rest of the decisions are purely down to your personal taste. Do try to avoid cut or engraved glass and coloured glass as they distort the hue of the wine. A popular question asked on the subject of glasses is should you change glasses after every wine? You should definitely give your guests the option of using new glasses. But usually, people will rinse their own glass out with water and just carry on. In a restaurant, you would expect new glasses for each wine (see 'glasses' in 'Setting up a Tasting', page 69).

TEMPERATURE

The exact same wine, white or red, poured at fridge, cellar or room temperature will taste completely different. Any wine served straight out of the fridge will be very cold (4°C–7°C). Very few wines really need to be this cold as temperature inhibits the fruit character of a wine, making the acidity taste much stronger. Generally, only sweet wines with huge, ripe flavours can handle these cold extremes. Champagne, traditionally an ice-bucket favourite, rarely needs to sit in ice for the duration as the fresh flavours can disappear so completely that the palate is just left with searing acidity. Light whites need to be a touch warmer, so it is a good idea to take the bottle out of the fridge and leave it on the side for a few minutes before serving. The majority of white wine ought to be served between 8°C–10°C, and finer whites like white Burgundy, and New World Chardonnays and Sémillons can be drunk at anything up to 13°C. Vincent Leflaive, a venerable wine-maker in Burgundy, taught me the best lesson in the effect of temperature on a wine. He kindly gave me a very expensive bottle of Le Montrachet, Burgundy's most famous white wine, to drink later that day with my dinner. He told me to give it to the wine waiter at the restaurant I was visiting that evening and to tell him that M. Leflaive said not to put it in a fridge or ice bucket. Serve it after dinner, warm, instead of, as he put it, 'the British habit of a glass of port'. The wine was sublime, and it was possible to taste the thousands of layers of fruit and complexity that would have been masked by any kind of chilling.

The opposite is often true about red wines. A room temperature red can taste too soupy and lose its definition. A quick dunk in an ice bucket can return a red to its tighter, more balanced state. Do not make the mistake of drinking red wine too warm. There are many reds that actually benefit from being drunk a bit colder than normal. All Beaujolais, many Pinot Noirs, most Cabernet Francs, Valpolicella, young Syrah and New World Grenache are but a few of the styles and grapes that appreciate a cooler environment. Even huge blockbuster styles rarely actually need true warmth to open up, just air.

A popular expression in the world of wine is 'cellar temperature'. Short of measuring the actual temperature of a cellar, it really is a term for a point somewhere between fridge and room temperature that is ideal for wine. If you are lucky enough to have a real cellar under your house then you will not need to refrigerate many white wines. Some reds will require bringing up to the house to acclimatise prior to opening; but a cellar under a house is not only the best place for your clobber but not surprisingly also the best place for your wine.

The general rule is that fruity, young reds can be served cooler than big, rich styles; and dry whites should not be as cold as sweet whites. The more the concentration of a white wine, the warmer it can be.

Be prepared to leave a white out of the ice bucket, and use ice for warm reds. Topsy-turvy, but essential for the total enjoyment of the bottle from start to finish.

DECANTING

Decanting is the process of pouring the wine from one container to another, often with the purpose of leaving any sediment formed in the first container behind. Racking fulfils the same objectives as decanting, when the contents of one barrel are poured into a fresh barrel, leaving the lees behind. As far as serving wine is concerned, decanting loosens up, warms up and opens out red wine, as well as performing the more obvious job of getting rid of sediment. Most red wines that have thrown a sediment require decanting before serving, as the sediment tends to billow in the wine if the bottle is disturbed and this can ruin the taste of the wine. A decanter is usually a glass stoppered vessel into which wine can be poured and served.

There are many different shapes and sizes of decanter available and antique decanters are immensely collectable items. However, I tend to go for a simple, classic decanter that looks plain and does the job of aerating the wine. I am always terrified of breaking expensive glass and so, to date, my decanter is one of the cheapest, but most used gizmos in my kitchen.

In order to decant a bottle of red wine, stand the bottle upright for at least a day, allowing any sediment to settle. Open the bottle of wine carefully, avoid shaking it, and remove the capsule completely. Get a clean decanter (or other container) for the wine. Then pour the wine slowly and evenly into the decanter. Look through the neck of the bottle at a pale background, or more traditionally the flame of a candle, to watch the flow of the wine. Stop pouring the second the sediment, initially sitting at the bottom of the bottle, creeps near to the neck of the bottle. This takes a little practice but, once proficient, there will only be a little wine left in the bottle with the sediment. If there is no sediment and the purpose of decanting is to let the wine breathe, there is no need to be so careful; just whack it in the decanter.

Once in the decanter, the wine starts to breathe. This aeration of both red and bigger white wines immediately improves the taste as well as slightly warming the wine. Pulling the cork on a bottle of wine then letting it sit on the piano in the drawing-room for two-and-a-half hours is not always possible. Besides, decanting does the same job in a matter of seconds. Younger wines need to breathe more than old bottles whereas very old wines can fall to pieces unless drunk quickly as they over-air and become too frail. Decanting is a great way to enjoy wines that ideally, if just opened and poured, would taste better the next day. Barolos, Zinfandels and hefty Syrahs are but a few of these monsters who could, if decanted, get the chance to open and approach their optimum flavours by the time you are ready to drink them. Do not be afraid of swilling the wine around the decanter a little to allow as much surface area as possible to come into contact with the air. If a decanted white gets a little too warm, just pop it into an ice bucket.

A nice trick along the same lines as ordinary decanting is 'double decanting'. This is decanting from a bottle into a decanter, then back into the original bottle. Between decants, wash out the sediment from the wine bottle with water. It is then possible to serve the wine in its original bottle, without the danger of any sediment and also having had a quick aeration. Double decanting enables the drinker to see the wine label unlike the anonymous decanter.

Remember that old red Burgundy is never decanted. It is a sort of tradition, because Pinot Noir rarely throws a big sediment, and old Pinot Noir is a delicate sort that may collapse with too much air.

ORDER OF DRINKING

If you have lined up a diverse array of wines for dinner it is important to get the order right, otherwise you may risk overshadowing a wine with the taste of the one drunk before. The order in which to serve wines is always similar to that of an organised wine tasting: usually, dry before sweet and light before heavy will do the trick. I do not necessarily subscribe to the school of thought that says that whites should be drunk before reds or that old wines should be drunk after young wines. There are many occasions when a light, fruity red is a good precursor to a rich oaky white and also many old bottles of red wine simply cannot follow the power and structure of a young red as the flavour would be too dominant. The best solution to this dilemma is to think through the order of wines for a meal as if you were at a wine tasting and ask yourself, could I taste each wine one after the other without detracting from their flavours? Then look at your menu and guess at the food and wine compatibility and where the natural breaks for courses would be. Sometimes it may be necessary to drink a wine in between dishes (fondly called 'inter-course') if it doesn't work directly with a dish or there is a break in style or grape variety.

Good luck, this is a great challenge. Food and wine matching (dealt with later on) and menu planning is an art. But it is also good fun to try out different combinations and flavours.

WINE APPARATUS

None of the following wine paraphernalia is essential. Some are more useful than others but that does not mean that they would not enhance your wine cellar a little!

Wine storage for expensive wines is often very tricky. Constant temperature, darkness and no vibration can rarely be found in cellarless houses unless you buy a **'Eurocave'** or other large wine storage cabinet. These not only protect the wines but also have separate sections that can be set at different temperatures. They are very expensive, but are a worthy addition to the serious collector and are essential if you are storing fragile, old wines.

Another luxury is a **'Chilla'** or quick-refrigeration machine that will bring down the temperature of a wine in a few minutes. If fridge space is limited, this machine proves invaluable and is also useful for taking the edge off warm reds. There is a domestic version of this restaurant machine available on the market.

Decanting cradles seem to be inexplicably popular with wine lovers. They are very steady decanting machines which pour a bottle slowly using a screw mechanism. Decanting cradles can be used for old wines or wines with heavy sediment like port, but are no substitute for a confident, steady hand. They also take ages and look ridiculous.

Drip-stoppers are little collars that can be placed around the neck of a wine bottle preventing dribbles of wine rolling down the outside of a bottle and marking the furniture. Another crazy invention that does do the job, but why not give the bottle a little wipe with a cloth, if necessary?

Wine thermometers can be used to detect the temperature of a wine in order to serve at the correct temperature. Do not bother. They often record the temperature of the glass and not the wine. Use your palate: it is far more accurate and sensitive to the relationship between taste and temperature than a thermometer will ever be. And people will think you are mad if you seen taking a bottle's temperature.

Foil cutters are a neat gadget for removing the top of a capsule. As I have already mentioned, I prefer to remove the whole capsule, but if you have one of these at least there will be no jagged edges left.

HOW TO STORE WINE

Most wine nowadays is consumed within hours of the actual purchase. Many people do not have the money or space to buy and store wine. But dark passageways lit only by candlelight, ending at a portcullis behind which cases of pre-war clarets sleep, are a rare sight. That does not mean that looking after several bottles or even cases of wine should be undertaken with any less care than the bottles in my imaginary cellar. Storage of wine is a rare art form. Looking after your wine, stacking or racking it in such a way as to maintain its condition and facilitate ease of location, is crucial. A cellar book can be used to record details of your collection and will also be useful when making tasting notes.

When finding a place at home to store your wine, bear in mind the following list of requirements. The storage area should be dark, moderately humid, have no vibration and a constant temperature (7°C–11°C is ideal). Under the stairs is usually the best place unless the boiler is there. The cardinal sins are central heating, bright lights, too little humidity and lots of vibration, so next to a washing machine would rate as the worst place, followed closely by a kitchen. If the room is light, keep the wine in its cardboard or wooden case. Many people mistakenly think that a garage is a good place to store wine, but the temperature range in a garage throughout the year could cause considerable damage. Always lie your bottles down to keep the corks moist. Wine racks are now available at any DIY shop or department store, and they can be custom-built to fit into awkward places, making the most of your storage space.

It is sometimes possible to store wine with your local merchant. Storage charges will be payable, usually a year in advance.

RESTAURANTS

With such a huge choice of wines available these days, it is amazing that so many restaurants have such dreary wine lists. Add to that the exorbitant mark-ups that some restaurants insist on charging and this makes dining out an expensive and often disappointing pastime. It seems that restaurateurs have forgotten that greediness is all too transparent. With the huge selection of wine available in shops and supermarkets and the consumer's price awareness, it is staggering that some restaurateurs manage to retain customers. A wine on a restaurant wine list should never cost more than two-and-a-half times that of the same bottle retail. As a wine buyer myself, I avoid all wines that could result in this sort of price comparison, preferring to sniff out more exclusive bottles.

Wine service in restaurants also tends to range from the enthusiastic and helpful to the rude and dismissive. 'Sommeliers' (French for wine-waiters) are a crucial part of the fabric of a restaurant; in fact they will probably visit the table more times than any other member of staff. It is important that a restaurant does not throw away an opportunity to impress customers with a snooty, ill-mannered sommelier.

Wine provides the fundamental framework on which to hang the whole event, not just the food. From an aperitif with which to enliven the palate and peruse the menu, to deciding upon a nice bottle (or bottles) to complement your choice of food, finishing with a sweet wine or digestif, wine is the link between all aspects of the experience of eating out. Great wine lists show as much balance as great wines. From inexpensive to extravagant, light and fresh to huge and brooding, from Aligoté to Zinfandel, wine lists should try to cover as many flavours and styles as possible, taking care to complement the style of food of the establishment. This does not mean that all wine lists have to have hundreds of bins (choices).

Far from it: I believe that five white, five red, a few fizzy and a few sweet wines can do the job, as long as they are chosen with care and represent good value.

Not all restaurants employ sommeliers, as they tend to be the flashy centre forwards of the restaurant world and command pretty stiff salaries. If a restaurant does, the sommelier should be regarded as the salesman for the wine department. It is in their interest that you enjoy what you order, or indeed what they recommend. They should never push you into a sale that is inappropriate and should try hard to match food to wine and keep the price of the bottles to within your budget.

Nothing is more embarrassing than a sommelier recommending a bottle and you not admitting that you would rather spend half that amount. The sooner you speak up, the better. This will not dent your street cred; rather, it should galvanise the sommelier into trying to sell you another bottle later.

The most misunderstood part of eating out is the ritual surrounding ordering and tasting the wine. It should be a simple process, but sometimes can go horribly wrong. Here is the definitive checklist on what to do and when to do it.

First, decide on a wine and then keep the wine list open in front of you. You can always point at it if the name looks unpronounceable, or the wine waiter looks a little slow. Sometimes restaurants have 'bin numbers' that help the staff locate the wine, so quote that if you are unsure. Remember the name of the wine and its vintage. There are occasions when a restaurant may have many different wines with the same name (for example, Nuits-Saint-Georges), so check that you have the right one. Some wines can be red, white or rosé, like Sancerre, so again be clear on exactly which wine you want. If the list just says 'Sancerre, £17.50', it is important to ascertain whose Sancerre it is (which *domaine* or estate) and from what vintage. It could be a young, fresh vintage from a top producer or a tired old Sancerre from Domaine Peint-Strippeur, and you don't want that. You are perfectly entitled to ask to see as many bottles as you like if the wine list does not show the relevant information.

Then the waiter will arrive with the bottle. Check that it is the same one you ordered before it is opened. If you let the sommelier open the bottle after having lazily checked the wine, only later to find out that it is not the right one, you are still obliged to pay for it. You may decide to ask the wine waiter to decant some wines. Ask this now.

The bottle should then be opened carefully at the table. The person who ordered the wine will then be asked if they would like to taste it. Always say yes. The wine waiter will then pour a quarter glassful and let you do your routine. See 'How to Taste Wine' (page 61) for the full version; but usually in a restaurant, as you have ordered the wine and checked that it is the right bottle, there is no need to go into a full-blown ritual of snorting and slurping. Your dinner guests will be parched by now anyway. All that is needed is a quick sniff to check that the wine is not corked or out of condition. Once done, give a quick nod to the wine waiter to go ahead and pour. The staff will be impressed, as will your guests. If the wine appears to be corked then ask the waiter to taste it; if there is any other problem, do speak up. If the bottle is a little too warm or a little too cold, tell the sommelier and they can make provisions.

The wine should be poured for any guests, ladies first and the orderer last, even if the orderer is a lady. The same order applies to topping-up.

It is important to note that if a second bottle of the same wine is ordered, get someone to taste it in order to check that it is not corked before topping up the glasses. This way you will avoid mixing a corked or faulty wine with a good glass, having to throw the whole lot down the sink.

If you have enjoyed a sommelier's service, the nicest way to show your appreciation is to allow them to taste a small glass of the wine, particularly if it is an expensive or unusual bottle.

Remember that a wine list, if properly put together, can demonstrate the harmony between the kitchen and the cellar. To the trained eye it can show a degree of collaboration of styles, tastes and flavours. The best restaurants in the world pay as much attention to wine as they do food.

CHAPTER 4

WINE IN SHOPS

exercising your wallet

Buying wine can be bewildering. There are so many different independent wine merchants, let alone the huge choice of supermarkets and off licences. Where do you start? Well, if it were clothes you were after, you might have a favourite designer or at least a good department store in which to hunt around. You would buy your socks from one store, your shoes from another and jeans from the next. It would not be too difficult to work out which shops sold the sort of clothes you liked. While buying, you would choose a few items and try them on in the fitting-room and imagine which of your own clothes might go with these new items.

That seems to work for clothes and probably many other items of shopping, but not usually wine. We don't seem to have any idea which wine shop is best for which style of wine. There are very few wine merchants that have comprehensive coverage of all of the world's wine; that would be nearly impossible as the choice would be infinite. Every wine seller stocks a specific style of wine, whether it is dependent on the customer profile, the palate of the owner or the proximity to the market. Wines for sale in supermarkets invariably try to be as commercial as possible – not downmarket, just commercial as in universally appealing. Supermarket wines will never need laying down as they are all sold for current consumption. Once again, that does not mean that they do not have the ability to age, just that they are all chosen for drinking now. It is also very convenient to buy wine in supermarkets, which is probably the main reason why wine departments have expanded of late. The last point in favour of supermarkets is that their buying power is enormous compared to a small independent shop, so the prices they charge will probably be the cheapest around for the bottles they sell, though they rarely offer discounts.

All in all, this makes supermarkets a force to be reckoned with in the world of wine buying. Points against supermarkets are that the selections rarely contain unusual or eclectic choices, preferring to favour safe bets.

This can make the choice in a supermarket a little boring. Also, the wineries that supermarkets buy from tend to be huge as they have to keep up with the demand from several hundred outlets. This again means that smaller wineries lose out – and most of the finest wineries in the world tend to be on the smaller side. Lastly, supermarkets rarely offer wine tastings, so you don't get the chance to 'try for size'.

They do have grading scales to help you find out the dryness to sweetness of whites and the lightness to heaviness of reds, but that does not always tell the whole story. My advice is to use supermarkets for everyday wines that are designed to be simple quaffers and you will find they do the job and don't cost a packet.

> That leaves the other side of the spectrum: the wine-specific retailers, both chain stores and independent wine merchants. Chain stores provide very good ranges of wines that tend to be a little more exciting than supermarkets.

They occasionally offer discounts for buying in bulk (this can mean deals on as little as two bottles, not just case purchases). And they occasionally hold in-store wine tastings, giving you an opportunity to decide for yourself whether the wine is for you. Independent wine merchants, as the name suggests, rarely have the buying clout of a big chain, so they have to rely on clever buying to woo the customer. They will spend half their time searching high and low for unique wines and exclusive agencies. The personal touch is more important in independent wine merchants, so it is important to let the shop assistant know your precise likes and dislikes. They will be able to find exactly the right wine for your palate. They always offer discounts and will often open any bottles for you to taste if there is the chance of a worthwhile sale. Not wanting to compete directly with the chain stores, independents rarely list any of the same wines found in the multiples, so the selection will not only be different but usually more challenging and exciting. Wine knowledge in independent wine merchants is generally very good, as most of the staff will have tasted the wines and had some say in selecting them. These shops also stock wines that can be laid down and will always have a far larger choice of older wines. Independents tend to stock a selection of more expensive wines, which tend to be out of the average spending range for a supermarket customer.

> So there are horses for courses. I recommend a blend of all three styles of wine buying: that way you can get the best of all worlds. Here is a mixed case of tips to look out for when buying wine:

▌ If you find a good cheap wine, red or white, then buy as much as you can afford. This will not only save time and money in the future but will also save any disappointment when shopping around.

▌ Don't buy port in December as the prices will always be high in preparation for Christmas; buy a few bottles in the summer instead when the prices are low. This technique applies to all seasonal wines.

▌ Southern hemisphere wines usually arrive in the shops in autumn, so watch out for old vintages that will still taste good but will be discounted to make way for the new wines.

▌ The same goes for northern hemisphere wines in the spring.

▌ Look for wine at sale time. Summer sales and New Year sales can be a good way of finding uncommercial oddities that will broaden your wine knowledge.

▌ Always ask for a case discount or find out if any offers are available in the shop. Quite often there are 'seven for six' deals or 'buy one get one free', and if you don't ask, you won't get!

▌ Ask wine merchants about the wines you are buying as they will know how long they need to breathe, if they need decanting, what temperature to serve them and so on.

▌ Make a note of wines that you like, then try to follow your taste buds when buying. Let a merchant know your thoughts on wines that you have bought as they will try to understand your palate and after a time will be able to accurately recommend wines for you to enjoy.

▌ Wine shops usually have glasses that they rent out for parties. As long as you buy your wine there, there will be no charge for the glasses.

▌ Don't buy any wines that are in window displays or near bright shop lights as they will not be in top condition.

▌ Avoid wines that are too ullaged (the ullage is the space between the top of the wine and the bottom of the cork). It is to be expected in very old wines, but in wines less than ten years old there should be no more than a 2 cm gap. If it is greater than that, there may be a leak or the wine could possibly be oxidised.

▌ Invest in a wine saver, whether it is a vacuum pump or a gas system. They are cheap and can prolong the life of an open bottle of wine for a few more days if you have not finished the entire bottle in one sitting.

WINE LABELS

A wine label is its birth certificate. It is the only piece of information that can help you figure out what is inside the bottle. After studying all the writing on a label you should be in no doubt as to what the wine should taste like. Sometimes bottles have back labels with additional background information about the wine. Here is what to look out for.

a geographical reference: this could be a country name, region, specific appellation or even the exact vineyard. Within Europe, all of the wine must come from the region stated. In the United States and Australia there is an eighty-five per cent rule, allowing up to fifteen per cent of the wine to come from another region.

the vintage: in Europe the vintage does not need to be stated for a table wine as they are usually drunk young, so it is generally safe to assume that a non-vintage French Vin de Table is only a year or two old. If a wine does declare a vintage (most do), then the eighty-five per cent rule usually comes into play again.

the quality level: wines made in the European Union must carry a quality level description on the label, like Vin de Table, Vin de Pays, VDQS or Appellation Contrôlée for French wines. Spain, Italy, Germany and other countries have their own classification systems – see pages 92–97. If the wine is made outside Europe, the word 'wine' must appear on the label before it is allowed to enter the EU.

volume of the bottle: this must state the amount of wine in the bottle. 75cl is referred to as a full bottle, 37.5cl a half bottle, 150cl a magnum, et cetera.

the alcoholic strength: usually stated as a percentage of volume; e.g. 13% vol. = thirteen per cent of the wine is ethyl alcohol or ethanol.

name and address of the producer:
straightforward enough.

bottling information: Château bottled, Domaine bottled,
estate bottled. The main French term used is *mise en bouteille* and then notes
where it was put into the bottle. In Italian the word is *imbottigliato* and in Spanish
embotellado.

grape variety information: this is not necessary,
although a lot of wine-makers decide to let the buyers know what grape(s) the
wine is made from. In Europe, if a single varietal is stated on the label, once again
eighty-five per cent is the minimum permitted amount in the blend. This rule
applies to Australia as well. The USA only needs seventy-five percent to use a
single varietal on a wine label; I think that that is a little too little!

other information: some governments require health warnings,
heavy machinery warnings and pregnant mother alerts ('do not drink wine if you
are pregnant,' not 'this wine may lead to pregnancy'!). Wine made in Europe does
not need to list any additives used in the wine-making process. The USA warns that
wine 'contains sulfites' (sic) and Australians have to declare any additives like
sulphur dioxide, which has its own code number, 220. This does take away from
the romance of the product, but as most wine is made using some degree of
sulphur dioxide (or sulfites) I suppose that it is inevitable that this warning will
appear, despite its seemingly ominous tone.

Those are the main, and in most cases, legally binding details that have to be
included on a wine label. But bottles can have a lot more information listed on the
label. Labels have become increasingly more designer-styled in order to stand out
from the crowd on a retail shelf, but beware skin deep beauty. Many of the wines
available in shops today have a back label that will tell you how irresistible the
nectar is within and no doubt regale you with a cute story as to why the wine is
called Koala Ridge. But these back labels can also have useful details about the
wine: perhaps a little map, a breakdown of the grapes if it is a blend, or maybe the
method of vinification is outlined. All of these pieces of information can be put

together to form a mental picture and help you decide whether it is the wine for you. Bottle shapes and glass colour can also make for an attractive and eye-catching twist to the art of selling wine. The Italians (who else) came up with neat designer bottles, which are biceps-achingly heavy or fridge-defyingly awkward. These now seem to be the norm for any expensive, top-of-the-range wine. Art labels are an interesting proposal kicked off by Château Mouton-Rothschild in Bordeaux, who invited top artists to design a different piece of art to put on each vintage of their wine. So far they have notched up Dali, Henry Moore, Picasso, Chagall, Miró and Andy Warhol to name but a few. Not surprisingly with this roll-call, they are the leaders in this style of design. Their wines are not only eminently collectable, but the labels are too. There have been many attempts to copy this attractive style of labelling, but only one other estate has really succeeded and that is Leeuwin Estate in Western Australia, who focus purely on Australian artists.

But ultimately, I am only interested in what is in the bottle and you should be too, as label design plays a non-existent role in the taste of a wine. I can't tell you how many wine salesmen have told me how beautiful a wine label is on a bottle they want me to buy for a restaurant. Don't they realise that most people choose wine from a list? Many classic wines have unusually simple labels that just let the Domaine or winery name alone do the talking.

There are a number of extra titbits that some producers write on a label. There is a full list of these in the glossary (see page 215), but here are some of the most common.

FRENCH WINE LABELS

Blanc de Blancs	Literally, white wine from white grapes. On a bottle of champagne it would mean one hundred per cent Chardonnay.
Blanc de Noirs	Literally, white wine from red grapes. Rare, but sometimes seen on some champagne (meaning made from Pinot Noir and Pinot Meunier).
Brut	Dry.

Château	The castle, although they rarely are castles! Some are no more than a potting-shed.
Clos	A term for a walled vineyard.
Côte	A slope or hillside, followed by which slope or hillside, like Côtes du Rhône (Hills of Rhône).
Crémant	Fizzy, but not as much as normal champagne.
Cru	A term for a specific vineyard's quality status, as in Burgundy's 1er Cru and Grand Cru and Alsace's Grand Cru. In these cases the individual name of the vineyard would be attached to the 1er or Grand Cru prefix, unless the wine was a blend of several 1er Crus, in which case it would just state 1er Cru (see the Burgundy section, page 125, for examples). The other meaning is 'growth', as in 1er Cru, 2ème Cru, down to 5ème Cru, translating as 1st growth, 2nd growth etc. This is a classification of Bordeaux top ranking Left Bank châteaux (see the Bordeaux section, page 111).
Cru Bourgeois	A Bordeaux classification for wines one level under that of Cru Classé.
Cru Classé	Literally, a classed growth, referring to a classification system covering the finest Left Bank Bordeaux châteaux.
Cuvée	The blend or a style of wine – a pretty uninformative term that only really differentiates the normal version of a wine from a slightly better one, as in Cuvée Spéciale, Grande Cuvée or Tête de Cuvée. Sometimes wine-makers write this on every wine they make, rendering the term meaningless.
Demi-Sec	Literally, half dry, therefore medium dry or off-dry.
Domaine	A winery that owns it own vineyards and makes its own wine.
Fût de Chêne	Matured in oak barrels.
Moelleux	Pudding wines use this term if they are rich and ripe rather than cloyingly sweet. Seen on Loire whites and Jurançon.

Mousseaux	Sparkling.
Négociant	A producer who buys in grapes or wine for vinification, bottling, labelling and selling.
Réserve	A meaningless term that implies a superior bottling, but in practice is used as often as Cuvée Spéciale (see above).
Sélection des Grains Nobles	The ultimate in sweet wine levels from Alsace or the Loire. Literally meaning 'a careful selection of noble-rot-affected grapes'.
Sur lie	On the lees, used for higher quality Muscadet and other white wines made in contact with their lees.
Vendange Tardive	Late picked or late harvested. Used for sweet wines.
Vieilles Vignes	Old vines. This should signify a superior wine, with a more concentrated flavour, although there is no recognised age at which vines become 'old'.
Vin Doux Naturel	Sweet wines and after-dinner drinks like Muscat de Rivesaltes, Muscat de Beaumes-de-Venise, Banyuls and Maury. Also written on some fortified wines, so watch out.

ITALIAN WINE LABELS

Abboccato	Medium sweet.
Amabile	Sweet.
Amarone	Dried grape wines.
Azienda Agricola	The equivalent of *Domaine*, where the grapes are grown and made into wine on the estate.
Bianco	White.
Casa Vinicola	The equivalent of a French *négociant*.
Castello	Castle, like the French term *château*.
Frizzante	Sparkling.
Passito	Wine made from dried grapes.
Recioto	A Venetian term for a strong sweet wine made from dried grapes.

Riserva	Indicates the pick of the crop that usually spends longer in oak barrels than the *normale* wines, and has higher alcoholic strength.
Rosso	Red.
Spumante	Sparkling.
Tenuta	Estate.
Vendemmia	The vintage.
Vigna	Vineyard.

SPANISH WINE LABELS

Abocado	Medium sweet.
Blanco	White.
Bodega	Winery.
Castillo	Castle, like *château*.
Crianza	Wine that has been aged for two years before release, one of which has to be spent in a barrel.
Generoso	Fortified.
Gran Reserva	Wine that has been aged for five years, of which a minimum of two is spent in a barrel.
Reserva	Wine that has been aged for three years, of which a minimum of one is spent in a barrel.
Tinto	Red.
Viña	Vineyard.

GERMAN WINE LABELS

Auslese	A selected harvest, meaning that the wine will be more ripe than normal; often, sweet.
Beerenauslese	A sweet style of wine made from individually selected over-ripe berries.

Eiswein	Made only in vintages where the grapes freeze on the vine, these are so concentrated in sugar they result in tooth-achingly sweet wines.
Halbtrocken	Half-dry, so one up from *Trocken*, and one down from *Auslese*.
Spätlese	A style that is late-harvested but not always sweet. More often less sweet than Auslese, and usually fermented dry to result in a higher alcohol more foody wine (see *Trocken*).
Trocken	Dry.
Trockenbeerenauslese	A mouthful in all senses of the word. Mega-sweet style of wine, made from noble-rot-affected grapes, usually shortened to TBA.

OTHER LABELS

Barrel-fermented	Any white wine that has been fermented in oak barrels resulting in a stronger oaky flavour than those wines just aged in oak barrels.
Botrytised/ botrytis affected	Unctuous, rot-affected, sweet wine.
Importer's details	A blatant advertisement, serving no purpose to the consumer whatsoever. I suppose it is good for the ego.
Late harvest/ late picked	Vines that are picked later than normal in the quest for extra ripe grapes with which to make sweet wines.
Miscellaneous terms	Either viticultural or vinification terms to help to add weight to the style of wine. E.g. 'Bush Vine' Grenache; Vat 65; Bin 12 or Old Vine Selection.
Unfiltered	Just that; a wine that is not filtered, probably with a more intense flavour. More likely to throw a sediment and may, in time, require decanting (*vin non filtré* in French).
Specific numbered bottles	Used to indicate the exclusivity of the wine, a bit like a personal number-plate. Only found on wines from relatively smart estates (there would be no point in Gallo using numbered bottles, as there would be no space on the label for any other writing).

Next time you are out and about in a wine shop, take a second or two to study all the information on a wine label. You will undoubtedly pick up more pointers to the taste of the wine than you would expect.

CHAPTER 5

WINE AND FOOD
the perfect combination

This section focuses on the combination of wine and food. It is totally up to you what you want to drink with your dinner, but some combinations really set off the wine and food partnerships perfectly. Unusually, instead of listing dishes and their ideal wines, I have organised this chapter in grape variety styles rather than food items. This might make you choose your wine first and then see what food is available at the market. Backwards, you say? Not at all. A different perspective will open up a broader understanding of flavour in both wine and food. Remember that wine and food are designed to go together. Very few wines are genuinely aperitif styles only.

RED GRAPE VARIETIES

BARBERA AND PINOTAGE

Both sharing a ripe fruit character but with an element of rusticity and acidity, they need meaty dishes like rabbit, duck or perhaps good quality sausages. Both can cope with red wine gravy and various roasted vegetables or pasta.

CABERNET FRANC, DOLCETTO AND FREISA

An unlikely trio, these grapes all share a high acidity thing. They are all relatively aromatic but not usually overly alcoholic. Cheeses like Sainte-Maure de Touraine or Port-Salut would work well, as would moussaka or classic roast chicken. My favourite combination with a young Cabernet Franc from the Loire is cauliflower cheese.

CABERNET SAUVIGNON

Cabernet Sauvignon is a versatile variety and, bearing in mind it comes in all shapes and sizes depending on the country or region, it can handle almost anything. Traditionally roast beef, Beef Wellington or roast lamb and claret (red Bordeaux) is a guaranteed success, making it a Sunday lunch regular. Game of all sorts could make a nice match; however do avoid anything that smells too 'gamey', as there are other varieties that do the job better. Cabernet Sauvignon loves cheese; try a young claret with Saint-Paulin, or any Old World Cabernet Sauvignon with Cheddar, Camembert and Saint-Nectaire. I say this because the juicier and fruitier the wine becomes in hot climates, the less suitable for cheese and the more classically 'meaty' it becomes. Toad-in-the-hole, beefburgers and rare steak are New World Cabernet winners.

GAMAY

Extraordinarily versatile, no wonder this grape is sold in practically every bar and brasserie in Paris. Beaujolais and Gamay de Touraine from the Loire have pure berry fruit and refreshing acidity making food matching relatively straightforward. Coq au vin, chilled for a curry, roast duck, roast chicken or turkey, ratatouille, steak and chips, croque-monsieur and 'meaty' fish like cod or hake all work well with Gamay. Cheese-wise, Vacherin du Mont d'Or is the unbeatable combination.

GRENACHE, CARIGNAN, CINSAULT, MALBEC AND MOURVÈDRE

The Rhône team, missing only a few members, are all on the spicy, firm side save for a few light-coloured Grenache wines that more than make up for it on hidden alcoholic power. Oxtail, toad-in-the-hole, cassoulet, goulash, shepherd's pie, Cornish pasty, steak and kidney pudding, casserole and any other beef options all work in this company. But things get exciting when cheese is mentioned. Cheeses like Saint-Marcellin and Chaumes love Châteauneuf-du-Pâpe, Gigondas or at the cheaper end, reds from the Côtes de Ventoux. Don't forget that Grenache has another side to its character: that of the sweet Vin Doux Naturel style. Blue cheeses like Roquefort and hard cheeses like Mimolette work well with both Vin Doux Naturels, Banyuls and Maury. These two wines also help out the age-old problem of chocolate. Rich chocolate puddings like Saint-Emilion au Chocolat, chocolate truffles or chocolate cake can all breathe a collective sigh of relief.

MERLOT

The in-built fruitiness of Merlot cannot be ignored when matching it to food. Beefburgers, roast duck and even chilli con carne wallow in the richness of fruity Merlot. But watch out when buying Merlots that you don't end up with a thin, green style, as it will not stand up to food as well as, say, a Chilean Merlot would. Cheeses like Brillat-Savarin and Gratte-Paille are Right Bank Bordeaux favourites.

NEBBIOLO

With a tannic, acidic monster like Nebbiolo, there are very few dishes that can really talk the talk. Cassoulet, venison, steak and wild boar would get through unscathed but if you have an older bottle of Barolo or Barbaresco, the fruit will have tamed down and then you can follow the Pinot Noir section below.

PINOT NOIR

Like Gamay, this grape variety loves food and rarely enjoys being drunk without. Inexpensive red Burgundy with raclette; light Chalonnais wines with roast chicken and coq au vin; bigger New World offerings and Côte d'Or village wines with game (well hung), beef (Boeuf à la Bourguignonne - Burgundy Beef!) and duck. Don't forget rosé champagne or red Sancerre with cheeses like Chaource. Back to the minerally Mâconnais and Chalonnais for Emmental, Tomme de Savoie, Brie de Meaux and Reblochon.

SANGIOVESE

What could be better than classic Italian cooking with the Chianti variety? Lasagne, spaghetti Bolognese or pizza - anything as long as it is not a seafood selection. Once again this variety has two sides to its character: that of the angry young rebel, needing big red meat dishes; but as Chianti and Brunello age, the other side emerges: the harmonious middle-aged gent that complements mushroom risottos and veal as well as Parmesan and Pecorino.

SYRAH/SHIRAZ

Another totally foody grape variety that can take on much heavier dishes. Best end of lamb, steak au poivre, cassoulet, Stroganoff, a traditional mixed grill, venison and old game birds: you name it, this grape is not scared. Brie de Meaux is the best cheese for the match.

TOURIGA NACIONAL

As this is the port variety, the classic winter combination is Stilton.

TEMPRANILLO

The Rioja variety behaves much like Pinot Noir when matching to food, so beef and lamb are the best places to start. The good thing about this grape is that it tends to have lower acidity than its Burgundian pal, so this time it doesn't need to be matched up to such demanding dishes.

ZINFANDEL

Chocolate once again finds a friend with dense fruit-packed styles of Zinfandel. If you are feeling less ambitious, duck, casseroles and any beef dish will work well. Follow the Sangiovese guidelines if you feel the need for a challenge.

WHITE GRAPE VARIETIES

CHARDONNAY

Another grape that has so many guises it can just about cover the whole menu single-handedly. Look no further than a crisp unoaked style to work with fish and chips. On the fish theme, fish cakes, all white fish like halibut and sea bass and also poached salmon are perfect matches for this versatile variety. Finer white Burgundies love lobster. Chablis and unoaked New World Chardonnays enjoy roast chicken and oaked wines, albeit not too dominant, like roast pork. The unlikely match is to cheese. Cheeses such as the stinky Epoisses like white Mâconnais wines, Vacherin du Mont d'Or can go for champagne and Beaufort loves a glass of Chablis. New World Chardonnays are often on the oaky side so make sure that the fish dish has enough sauce or at least some rice, pasta or potato to soak up some of this weight. Most chicken dishes enjoy a bit more power so oaked Chardonnays pose no problem.

CHENIN BLANC

In its dry, Old World form, the acidity is perfect for cutting through any fish dish; though New World Chenins, particularly South African versions, lack power and are really only up to light seafood or salads. When sweet, Chenin Blanc is honeyed and tropical and favours fresh fruit tarts, pastries and the unexpected classic French combination of a decadent liver pâté with toasted brioche.

GEWÜRZTRAMINER

The lychee-like spicy grape was tailor-made to take on the might of the Far East. Chinese food, unless it is too chilli-hot, goes well served with this refreshingly fruity, but beguilingly weighty variety. Dry Gewürztraminer is a good match with Pacific Rim dishes, and back home in Alsace it is matched up to all manner of fish dishes, terrines and savoury tarts. It also finds a natural partner in cheeses like Munster.

MANSENG

A special mention for these highly individual oddities, both Gros and Petit Manseng are stunning with fish dishes, fresh seafood and local cheeses like Tourmalet and Brebis.

MELON DE BOURGOGNE

The Muscadet variety would get the sack if it didn't complement its local industry – fishing. Oysters and *plateau de fruits de mer* including crab, langoustines, clams, prawns, crevettes, lobster, winkles and whelks fortunately go well with this relatively inexpensive white wine that also, thankfully, takes the sting out of the bill.

MUSCAT AND MUSCADELLE

Strawberries with freezing cold Moscato d'Asti, Orange Muscat with chocolate mousse, pear and almond tart with Muscat de Rivesaltes, liqueur Muscats for Christmas pudding and sticky toffee pudding – the huge Muscat family covers a load of bases on the pudding front.

PALOMINO AND PEDRO XIMÉNEZ

The two sherry varieties are real loners. Purists will tell you that dry sherry is a good match for various soups, whilst PX can only really be poured over ice-cream or sipped with a caffeine-laden espresso. I favour a bowl of really nice cashews or roasted almonds for the former and a stretcher for the latter.

PINOT BLANC/PINOT BIANCO

In the spirit of fair play the Pinot Blanc family does get some recommendations. Scallops and pork are my ambitious calls of the day, but they have to be twinned with good examples of the wines otherwise they just wouldn't work. If you can only find the light fresh styles, stick to salads and thin air.

RIESLING AND ALBARIÑO/ALVARINHO

Putting these two together will cause a stir, but Riesling at its lightest is not dissimilar to Albariño and is therefore a good seafood and fish match. Beyond that the similarity stops and Riesling gets into its stride. Chicken liver terrine, onion tart, duck pâté, Chinese food (although this goes better with Gewürztraminer), any creamy chicken dishes, chicken Kiev and an all-time favourite *assiette de charcuterie* (its English translation 'plate of meat' doesn't sound half as nice). Pork and veal are easily manageable. Sweet Rieslings like fruity puddings as well as, curiously, pâté again. But for my favourite, rhubarb crumble would win the award.

ROUSSANNE AND MARSANNE

The weighty, ponderous white Rhône varieties can handle a surprisingly wide range of food. Following in the footsteps of Chardonnay, but not quite as keen on the palate, these are main course wines that flounder a little. Chicken, pork and veal as well as a large range of fish dishes including fish and chips are all within their grasp. But lacking the fruit definition of Sauvignon Blanc, they are not particularly refreshing unless Viognier is in the blend, in which case they can match up to a cold chicken salad or a goat's cheese salad well. Speaking of cheese, they love Maroilles.

SAUVIGNON BLANC AND ALIGOTÉ

Sauvignon Blanc makes great food wine that revels in the chance to expose its acidic zip and fresh citrusy flavours. Aligoté lacks the varietal extremes of its friend but can almost keep up with the dishes. Prawn cocktail, Caesar salad, deep fried calamari, fresh asparagus and corn on the cob are all too easy. Chinese dishes, oysters, crab salad and Pacific Rim cooking with ginger and spices are perfect combinations. New

World Sauvignon Blancs, particularly from New Zealand, can really amaze the palate in their effortless handling of complex dishes. Sauvignon Blancs like Sancerre and Cheverny are the benchmark combination for goat's cheeses, like Crottin de Chavignol, Selles-sur-Cher and the good old favourite – a trusty cheese soufflé.

SÉMILLON

In dry, Old World form this grape behaves like Chardonnay and so covers much the same ground, although perhaps not quite as competently. New World Sémillon is a very different kettle of fish as it is far more tropical and lime-juicy (and works well with kettles of fish). The increased power and ripeness that the New World can offer, particularly as it is often blended with Chardonnay, means that Sémillon is a useful and good value versatile grape. In sweet form, Sémillon eclipses all others. Sauternes and the like from Bordeaux are spectacular pudding wines that can cope with everything from foie gras through terrines of all sorts, to every pudding under the sun (except belligerent chocolate). Another surprise is that botrytised Sémillon is a magical partner for blue cheese such as Roquefort or Fourme d'Ambert.

SYLVANER

This refreshingly dull grape variety really doesn't like to be troubled with anything too testing on the food front, preferring to have light-weight opposition. Waxy cheeses or barely whiffy offerings like Tomme de Montagne will work, otherwise you are banished to a life of salad obscurity.

TOKAY-PINOT GRIS/PINOT GRIS/ TOKAY D'ALSACE/PINOT GRIGIO

Think Gewürztraminer meets Riesling, gangs up on Chardonnay and has a fling with Sémillon. Well, that is what the first three grapes listed above can do in the food department (as they are all different names for the same thing). Pinot Grigio, a different prospect altogether, falls into the same category as Pinot Bianco (see above), in that it rarely has the texture or dominance to combat strong flavours; whereas Tokay-Pinot Gris/Pinot Gris/Tokay d'Alsace, the Alsatian cruiser-weight, loves smoked salmon, almost all starters, chicken, Thai food, creamy sauces, cheeses like Munster, all pâtés and countless other delights. In sweet form (*Vendange Tardive*), it relishes the opportunity to work with cheeses like Livarot and fresh fruit puddings.

UGNI BLANC/TREBBIANO

The Mr Boring of the wine world still manages to crack a smile with some dishes as the dryness and zingy character of both French Ugni Blancs and Italian Trebbianos are the mainstay café house wines in their respective countries. Good combos are asparagus, tomato salads, cold chicken, goat's cheese, and anything fresh and vegetabley.

VIOGNIER

The sultry diva Viognier, despite an actively aromatic nose, likes Asian-influenced dishes if not quite the genuine article, cheese like Pont-l'Evêque and fish dishes that don't test it too hard. An all-round lunch-time winner, this grape can only start to cope with bigger and more flavoursome dishes when it reaches its upper end of the price scale. Condrieu and the like from the northern Rhône are fiendishly expensive but are sublime with fish dishes. In the New World, Viognier is often blended with Chardonnay or Marsanne and Roussanne, where the weight of these three make it a bit more of an all-rounder.

CHAPTER 6

FRANCE

I will try not to sound too biased in my introduction to France, but if I had to make a list of my all time favourite ten wines, every one would be French. My very first tastes of wine were French and my cellar, albeit of the limited under-stair variety, holds a majority of French wines. Of the three hundred or so wines that I taste every week, over half of them are French. Why is this? Well for me, France is the spiritual home of wine-making. While I recognise that many other countries make outstanding wines (and I love drinking them), my wine brain always makes a mental comparison of any non-French wine to its French counterpart. I just can't help it. My palate has always been used to European levels of acidity and tannin in the make-up of a wine.

When you start to taste wine, you have to decide where in the world to kick off, and it is useful to have in your mind a definitive style, a sort of blueprint, for each grape variety.

It just so happens that most of my model grape variety flavours are French. If I gave you a glass of wine and asked your opinion, you would assess it in comparison to other wines you have tasted. I wonder which country's wine styles you would be using for your judgement?

I am not alone in this way of thinking. Leaving aside Germany, Italy and Spain as they have their own definitive grape variety styles, the rest of the wine-making world has always looked to the French classics for inspiration. Californian Cabernet Sauvignons try to shadow the great wines of Bordeaux; Australian Chardonnays strive for Burgundian longevity and New Zealand Sauvignon Blancs aim to capture the refreshing quality of the Loire Valley's finest. There seems to be a one-way rivalry between New World wine-makers and France. It is as if the young world of wine wants to play with old father France, but France just shrugs its shoulders and turns away. The French are usually caricatured as intrinsically arrogant, never showing any signs of concern about the wine challenges emerging from abroad; inwardly, I suspect that the French need this pressure and it is certainly clear that their wine technology and grass-roots viticultural skills have had an enormous collective kick up the derrière over the past ten years. This came about as a result of thousands of cases of varietally pure wines flooding the market from Bulgaria, Chile, Australia and elsewhere at low prices and high fruitiness with which the French could not compete.

Further proof of France's perceived wine-making superiority is also found in the celebrations that take place every time a fledgling New World wine beats glorious, venerable Château La Tour Eiffel in a blind-tasting. Personally, I think that this style of taste comparison makes no sense: surely wines should be considered like with like? I love finding out which is the best in a line up of Gevrey-Chambertins; but if a Carneros Pinot Noir was thrown into the tasting, it might sweep the board if the tasters identified with the atypical exceptional ripeness of fruit. These two styles are poles apart, the only similarity being the grape used. I would also like to balance the equation by conducting a similar tasting of Californian Pinots; then at least I would have the best of two different worlds. One wine is no better than the other and can't really be judged on the same playing field. Thankfully, after hundreds of years of New World wine-making, some gradually emerging Australians and Americans have realised that there is no need to try to beat the French, but to join them on the great wine lists of the world.

All wine-making countries have vastly different cultures and climates. The world's greatest wine-makers taste regularly and widely and have a passion for all things European but not an unhealthy jealousy. They like to drink the wines – don't we all – and the private cellars of some New World winery owners tell the tale. It is not unknown to find as many bottles of wine from France, Italy and Spain as well as the obligatory bottles of port as wines from their own country or estate, all resting together.

Aspirational young wine-makers travel to France to work with their heroes, hoping that some of the mystique will rub off as well as learning the ropes at the same time.

If some regions (California being the biggest culprits) stopped being obsessed with Bordeaux and Burgundy and made the kind of wines that they could really aspire to, we could see a day when French collectors scramble to get hold of New World wines to complete the balance of their own cellars.

Having said all this, the fact remains that the French have something much of the wine-making world has not and that is a true sense of place. They grow a vast array of grape varieties, each one focusing on its favoured area. These areas have been shown over centuries to extract the maximum potential and character from their chosen varieties.

The reason for this terrific sense of place is the strict application of French wine laws. The Appellation Contrôlée (AC) system was set up to preserve the regional character of the wines and is the envy of the entire wine world. I will touch on other countries' wine laws in due course, but for a country where the ACs can be anything from a tiny single vineyard to a whole region, the organisation and implementation is amazing. AC rules cover all of the exact vineyard plots allowed to be planted, their minimum vine density, pruning and training systems, maximum yields, wine-making processes (including alcoholic strengths and the permitted grape varieties) and incorporate a mandatory independent analysis by the region's enforcers. Irrigation is banned, as is the blending of multi-vintage wines to help boost the poorer years. Spain, Italy and Portugal all base their own systems on this model. Germany's own system is loose-knit and certainly less clear by way of a guide to its best wines. The AC system is by no means perfect, as the regulatory bodies seem to be a touch too lenient on some sub-standard wines that are awarded a seal of approval. The other problem is that AC laws are to some degree a strait-jacket on experimental wine-makers, forcing them to release any wines made from 'unacceptable' grape varieties under the lowly Vin de Pays classification, despite their obvious appeal. But there is no doubt that the overall idea is sound and the results speak for themselves. As in any governing body there are a number of anomalies, but this pioneering regulator works well enough to have influenced the rest of the wine-making world.

BORDEAUX

Our first port of call is just that: a port called Bordeaux, which gives its name to the huge surrounding wine region. Situated on the Garonne River that leads to the Gironde estuary on the west coast of France, Bordeaux is split into two parts, the Right and Left Banks. They each have distinctly different soils and produce different styles of wine.

Bordeaux is the biggest single wine region in the world, covering 115,000 hectares and producing 750 million bottles of wine per year. Claret, as all red wine from Bordeaux is known, is one of the mainstays of France's wine economy. However, the grand châteaux of the Médoc, Graves, St-Emilion and Pomerol only account for five per cent of the overall production. Some 13,000 producers struggle along, making this mighty region worth about a quarter of all of France's AC wine.

The immensely important grape varieties grown in this region are: for reds, Cabernet Sauvignon, Merlot, Cabernet Franc and Petit Verdot; for dry and sweet whites, Sémillon, Sauvignon Blanc and Muscadelle.

Here, blending is the key skill followed by maturation in oak barrels – a very classic style of wine-making.

The greatest advertisement for Bordeaux to the English must be that Richard the Lion-heart was a regular consumer of its wines. When Henry II married Eleanor of Aquitaine in 1152, Bordeaux became British for three centuries. King John actively encouraged shipments of *clairet* (pale red wine) to British shores on account of a favourable tax deal (nothing changes!). The consumption in those days was nothing short of outstanding. When the English left in 1453 and Gascony, including Bordeaux, reverted to French rule, wine was France's leading export and Britain its most important customer.

Britain remained a strong export market, even after the Dutch took over as the most important economic power in the seventeenth century. The Dutch brought an important skill to the low-lying banks of the Médoc: that of their home-grown talent for drainage. Dutch engineers cut the ditches that still criss-cross the Médoc today, allowing the marshy land to be reclaimed and exposing the famous gravel beds that form the basis of some of the world's greatest red wines. Meanwhile, in 1703, England signed a deal with Portugal called the Methuen Treaty. This raised taxes on French wines to exorbitant levels, favouring the wines of Portugal. However, the British, knowing a good wine when they tasted it, continued to access the finest wines of Bordeaux and built up a following in the cellars of the English aristocracy and the emerging wealthy industrial middle class.

The French Revolution was but a tiny disturbance for the Bordelais, and only a few rich château owners got the chop. The region was relatively unscathed and remained intact, only to be confronted by a double-whammy: in 1852, it was struck by a blight of oidium, followed by the demon *Phylloxera vastatrix* in 1869. By 1882 almost all of the vineyards had been destroyed. Only by the early twentieth century had everything reverted to normal, and Bordeaux entered the AC system in 1936.

Another point of interest is that in 1855 the Bordeaux Official Classification was drawn up. Sixty châteaux in the Médoc and one from Graves, as well as twenty-six Sauternes and Barsac châteaux were classified into two ranking systems, rather like football league tables. The reds were put into five classes or growths known as 'Cru', from 1st to 5th (Premier or 1er Cru to Cinquième or 5ème Cru). Sweet wines were divided into two classes, 1er Cru and 2ème Cru, although Château d'Yquem was elevated to its unique title of 1er Cru Supèrieure. These tables were created using the contemporary (1850s) market prices of the various wines. With only a handful of exceptions, they still have remarkable accuracy today. The Graves region was classified in 1959 and the Right Bank area of St-Emilion was classified in 1955, updated in 1985 and re-updated in 1996. Pomerol has no classification whatsoever.

In the Haut Médoc, below the classed growth system there operates another series of classifications. This splits up the remaining châteaux in terms of their 'Cru Bourgeois' status. From the top, they are Cru Grand Bourgeois Exceptionnel followed by Cru Grand Bourgeois and lastly Cru Bourgeois. This system is a bit of a mess, as there currently exist two versions of the same classification. These titles rarely indicate increasing levels of quality, although you would be advised to at least opt for a Cru Bourgeois grade wine when buying Médoc wines. For my part, I just think of them as one big classification – Cru Bourgeois.

THE LEFT BANK

MÉDOC

The striking aspect of Bordeaux is the sheer size of the region and its properties. Driving north-west out of Bordeaux up through the region of Médoc, the city gradually disappears and the châteaux gradually appear. At first the names seem a little obscure, but the further you progress along the main road, the grander the names and properties become. Unlike Burgundy, where a single domaine might produce 2,000 cases of wine covering seven or eight different labels, a large Left Bank château like Lafite-Rothschild produces 20,000 cases of its main wine and a further 20,000 cases of its second wine. Not only are these châteaux big but their wines are also expensive, making the Bordelais some of the richest wine producers in the world.

The Médoc is split into two parts, the Haut-Médoc and the Bas Médoc, or just plain Médoc. The Haut-Médoc is further split into several different 'communes'. Margaux, St-Julien, Pauillac and St-Estèphe are the big four, with two other less fashionable areas, Moulis and Listrac. A *commune* is a village and its surrounding land, and it is in the big four communes that almost all of the classed-growth clarets exist.

The Left Bank is sandwiched between two bodies of water, the Atlantic Ocean and the Gironde estuary, so its microclimate is maritime. The region gets mild winters and long, warm summers, and is protected from the harsh westerly Atlantic breezes by a line of pine forests that run between it and the ocean. All of the wines on this side of the river tend to be Cabernet Sauvignon dominant. Here the grape develops amazing blackcurrant, leather and cedarwood aromas, the international hallmarks of a great Cabernet Sauvignon.

MARGAUX

The biggest of the communes is home to its namesake Château Margaux, the extraordinarily pretty château and the first of the five 1er Cru wines that we come across. The style of the wines from this commune is said to be lighter and more 'feminine' (a tasting note I despise). That said, I know what the expression is supposed to mean. The classic Margaux hallmarks are a violet scent, 'rounder' fruit on the palate and less aggressive tannins on the finish than can be found in the meatier offerings from the neighbouring communes. Margaux has five little parishes: Labarde, Cantenac, Arsac, Margaux itself and Soussans, and they each have their own well-made château offerings. Just south of Labarde are two properties that are outside the Margaux appellation but whose wines I have always enjoyed, Châteaux d'Angludet and Cantemerle. Whenever discussing Margaux I automatically include them in the frame as they make similar styled wines and if there was ever a tweaking of the boundaries or a re-classification, I would vote for them as full-blown Margaux members with honours. Not only are their wines sublime, they would make it into my 'favourite châteaux' section below, if they were not already resplendent in the 'best value' section.

Favourite Châteaux: Brane-Cantenac, La Lagune, Margaux, Palmer and Rausan-Ségla.

Best value Châteaux: d'Angludet, Cantemerle, Ferrière, Haut-Breton Larigaudière, Kirwan, Monbrison and du Tertre.

MOULIS AND LISTRAC

These two little-known appellations are next door to Margaux, below St-Julien. They contain some remarkably good finds. Producing 600,000 cases of wine between them, of which eighty-eight per cent of Moulis and sixty-six per cent of Listrac is of Cru Bourgeois status, it would be foolish not to take a peek; and what you discover are some very good taste-alikes of the real thing farther up the road. If you are trying to get into classic claret but find that the prices are too punishing, then there is no better place to look than here, particularly in good vintages (see page 210). Generally these wines are a little lighter and earlier maturing than the classed growths, so they tend to be less expensive and more forward. It has to be said that some of these châteaux are proving to be reliable sources of very well-made wine and are beginning to step on the toes of one or two of the big names nearby.

Favourite Châteaux (they are all relatively good value): Chasse-Spleen, Fourcas-Dupré, Maucaillou and Poujeaux.

ST-JULIEN

Drive a few miles north out of Margaux up the D2, and St-Julien appears in front of you. This small commune is jam-packed with incredible names. Keep your eyes on the road as you pass the grand châteaux gates and your passengers shout out a constant stream of road signs indicating the impossibly famous properties. Here the wines have an elegance, balance and breeding not found in any other area of Bordeaux. St-Julien has a tangible feel of wealth and aristocracy in the air. In wine tastings, time after time, wine lovers prefer the charm and harmony of this commune's wines to any other. St-Julien seems to embody all of the other communes' best qualities, Margaux's subtlety and balance, Pauillac's power and longevity and St-Estèphe's old-fashioned blackcurrant and cigar-box nose. There are no first growth châteaux in St-Julien but a bevy of seconds, often referred to as 'super-seconds' on account of their concentration and excellence. There is also a run of third, fourth and Cru Bourgeois wines worth sniffing out. All of these properties make luscious gentleman's clarets with the classic hallmarks of leather, cassis, old library books and fresh tobacco on the nose. If you think I'm getting a little carried away, that's because this is my favourite commune in the whole of Bordeaux. St-Julien borders the heavy-weight commune of Pauillac and one château is worth giving a special mention as it treads the boards between the Moorish St-Julien style and the monster Pauillac character: Château Léoville-Las Cases, whose vineyards actually sit next to those of Château Latour. Léoville-Las Cases is an awesome wine, often needing a minimum of ten years to lose its tannic coating, but when up to racing speed this wine, to me, epitomises the global importance and enormous pleasure that Bordeaux wines can bring.

Favourite Châteaux: Branaire, Ducru-Beaucaillou, Gruaud-Larose, Lagrange, Léoville-Barton, Léoville-Las Cases, Léoville-Poyferré, St-Pierre and Talbot.
Best value Châteaux: Clos du Marquis (second label of Léoville-Las Cases), Gloria, Lalande-Borie and Moulin-Riche (second label of Léoville-Poyferré).

PAUILLAC

Magnificent texture, opulence and longevity are the Pauillac characteristics. Three of the five 1er Cru wines are from within these hallowed boundaries. Pauillac is the most famous of the Haut-Médoc appellations, with Mouton-Rothschild, Lafite-Rothschild and Latour its jewels in the crown. The wines, brutally tannic in their youth, are long-lived and exhibit cedarwood, blackcurrants and spice on the nose. They are generally deep, rich and full-bodied on the palate and monumentally long on the finish. Most of the châteaux are out of the price range of normal mortals, but there are some good Cru Bourgeois wines and second labels that can give a glimpse of what the commune can do. If, however, the chance to drink or even just taste one of the great 1er Cru or super-second Pauillac wines arises, drop everything and line up with a pint glass.

Favourite Châteaux: Grand-Puy-Lacoste, Haut-Batailley, Lafite-Rothschild, Latour, Les Forts de Latour (second label of Latour), Lynch-Bages, Mouton-Rothschild, Pichon-Longueville Baron, Pichon-Longueville-Comtesse de Lalande and Pontet-Canet.
Best value Châteaux: Haut-Bages-Libéral, Haut-Bages-Monpelou and Lacoste-Borie (second label of Grand-Puy-Lacoste).

ST-ESTÈPHE

At the end of the line of the famous communes is St-Estèphe. Just a few steps from the Pauillac vineyards of Château Lafite, the extraordinary-looking pagoda of Château Cos d'Estournel towers over the landscape. The wines of St-Estèphe have a reputation for being the leanest and slowest of the bunch to mature, with 'Cos', the snail, leading the pack. This may have been true in the past, but since the mid-eighties, the percentage of Merlot in this Left Bank Cabernet Sauvignon-dominant recipe has been increased a bit to soften off these brooding beasts. Not perceived as remotely commercial, St-Estèphe wines suffer from a sub-soil with a high proportion of clay. This makes the ripening process that bit more difficult and often results in wines with noticeably more acidity than the rest of the gravelly Médoc. Having said that, they tend to age gracefully and numerous Cru Bourgeois châteaux live much longer than is usually the case. This means that laying down cases of relatively inexpensive St-Estèphe clarets can be enjoyable and rewarding as the wines creep towards their long-awaited period of drinking. There are more underrated châteaux here than in any other commune; you just need patience to appreciate the wines.

Favourite Châteaux: Cos d'Estournel, Haut-Marbuzet, Lafon-Rochet, Montrose and Phélan-Ségur.
Best value Châteaux: Beau-Site, Le Boscq, La Haye, Lavillotte, Les-Ormes-de-Pez and de Pez.

HAUT-MÉDOC AND (BAS) MÉDOC

Lumped together in a single section, the two appellations Médoc and Haut-Médoc cover all the gaps in the Left Bank tapestry. They contain hundreds of properties that don't fall within the strictly controlled boundaries of the grander communes, so this is where the bargain hunter should look for up-and-coming, over-achieving properties. In good vintages the lower prices asked for these wines, lacking grand commune postcodes, are the best deals to be had in Left Bank Bordeaux. From the (Bas) Médoc, beyond the northern tip of St-Estèphe, all of the way back down to the outskirts of Bordeaux itself, this region covers some 22,000 acres of vines. There is no one particular style of wine produced under these two AC labels as the sprawl of châteaux cover such a vast array of soils and microclimates. One thing is for certain, and that is that the blend will favour Cabernet Sauvignon and the better the vintage, the better the bet.

Favourite Chateâux: Arnauld, Camensac, Caronne-Ste-Gemme, Citran, Haut-Peyrillat, Lamarque, Lamothe Bergeron, Lanessan, Liversan, Les Ormes-Sorbet, Patache d'Aux, Potensac, Sociando-Mallet, Tour du Haut-Moulin, La Tour St-Bonnet and Villegeorge.

GRAVES

The other main red and, for the first time, white wine region of Bordeaux's Left Bank is Graves. Situated south-east of the city of Bordeaux, it also has the fifth remaining 1er Cru château: Château Haut-Brion. In 1987, a separate appellation of Pessac-Léognan was created within the Graves area to encompass the most famous properties, lying on the best 'graves' (literally, gravel) soils. It is here that most of the finest wines are made. The dry white wines of Graves epitomise the power and poise of the classic Sémillon/Sauvignon Blanc partnership (sometimes including Muscadelle). Many red wine châteaux make a white wine, and these wines have started to be fashioned in a more Burgundian manner. By that I mean a pre-fermentation maceration, then a cool fermentation followed by a spell in new oak barrels (or indeed full-blown barrel fermentation). This change of tack has not only broken the mould but has also attracted world-wide interest in these wines that until now could best be described as dowdy. The red wines of Graves lack the power of the big four Médoc communes' wines, but make up for it with stunning texture and aroma. They tend to mature a little earlier and have a distinctive mineral character that truly reflects the composition of their gravelly soils.

Favourite red Châteaux: de Fieuzal, Haut-Bailly, Haut-Brion, La Mission-Haut-Brion, Pape-Clément, and Smith-Haut-Lafitte.
Best value red Châteaux: Bahans-Haut-Brion (second wine of Haut-Brion), Chantegrive, La Garde, La Louvière and Picque-Caillou.
Recommended white Châteaux: Carbonnieux, Domaine de Chevalier, de Fieuzal, Haut-Brion, de Landiras (Cuvée Suzanne), Laville-Haut-Brion and Smith-Haut-Lafitte.

SAUTERNES AND BARSAC

A forty-minute drive south of Bordeaux brings you to the capital of the world's sweet wine production: Sauternes. This area includes the five little communes of Sauternes, Barsac, Fargues, Preignac and Bommes. It accounts for the decadently sweet white wines that grace the most discerning dinner tables. It is bizarre that year after year, these properties pray for gloomy weather that brings on the onset of noble rot *(Botrytis cinerea)* which turns a regular late harvest into the nectar of the gods, albeit in minuscule proportions. The fact that these climatic conditions only really happen three years in ten means that the life of a Sauternes producer must be a stressful one. As Sauternes enjoys misty, mild, humid weather, the exact opposite of a red wine's wish list, it is not uncommon for Sauternes to have a great vintage when the rest of Bordeaux has a turkey. If you have never tasted a wine from these parts, I strongly urge you to track one down; it will, I promise, be worthwhile. Fashion plays a big part in the appeal of these wines and sadly, sweet wines seem not to have a regular slot on the menu. As a single half-bottle of this heavenly wine can serve eight people with a more than adequate glassful, it is a mystery to me why more people are not using Sauternes to finish off an evening's merriment. It seems so abrupt to end with a big red and just launch into coffee; I certainly need to wind down after the work-out a huge *rouge* gives my taste buds, and a glass of Sauternes is the vinous equivalent of a plunge pool.

Favourite Châteaux: Climens, Coutet, de Fargues, Gilette, Guiraud, Lafaurie-Peyraguey, Raymond-Lafon, Rieussec, Suduiraut, La Tour Blanche and Yquem (the greatest by a long way).

Best value Châteaux: Broustet, Doisy-Daëne, Filhot, Les Justices, Nairac, Rabaud-Promis and Rayne-Vigneau.

THE REST

Before we cross to the Right Bank, there are a number of miscellaneous areas that are worth a quick mention. Between the Right and Left Banks there are a few named regions that produce fairly simple wines that can provide an everyday style for Bordeaux-philes. Cadillac, Loupiac and Ste-Croix du Mont all make everyday sweet styles that rarely match even the most basic of Sauternes but can provide a nice summery wine for picnics or for big parties, such as Domaine du Noble. Entre-deux-Mers is the area between the Garonne and Dordogne rivers that separates the Left and Right Banks. This region is responsible for vast quantities of often bland red and white wines that usually go into supermarket 'own label' wines, or are used for house wines in bars and restaurants. Bordeaux and Bordeaux Supérieur wines account for the general appellation surrounding these smaller areas; the Supérieur label indicates a higher alcohol wine, made with stricter rules on yields. Here also we find the slightly more upmarket region of Premières Côtes de Bordeaux, where some properties make fairly useful reds and whites, particularly in good vintages. The trick with all of these wines is to try to angle a taste before you buy.

Recommended whites: Bauduc – Les Trois Hectares, Bonnet, Thieuley and La Tour de Mirambeau.

Recommended reds: Fontenille, Grand-Mouëys, Jonqueyres, Méaume, Plassan, Puy Bardens, Reynon, de Sours, Thieuley and de la Tour.

THE RIGHT BANK

ST-EMILION

This part of Bordeaux is really beautiful, unlike the flattish land of the Médoc. The town of St-Emilion itself nestles in the hills some twenty miles east of Bordeaux. The best vineyards in the area are perched on top of a limestone plateau and its surrounding hillsides, or on a gravel outcrop near the border with Pomerol. Here the classic Bordeaux *cépage* (blend) is reversed. Merlot is the dominant grape, followed by Cabernet Franc with Cabernet Sauvignon bringing up the rear. The wines of St-Emilion are widely enjoyed on account of their fleshy, forward fruit (high Merlot content) and lack of searing tannin in youth (low Cabernet Sauvignon content). The number of châteaux in this relatively small appellation is huge, producing some three million cases a year. The range of styles is fairly diverse as the differences in soil play a major part in the equation, so try to follow a property you like rather than simply relying on the appellation as a whole.

St-Emilion is also responsible for a new and fascinating trend in wine-making and that is the advent of micro-wineries. These wines are often made from single vineyard plots. They are harvested very late and at painfully low yields, giving rise to super-ripe fruit that inevitably, coupled with new oak treatment, results in awesomely impressive wines. The problem is that this phenomenon is relatively new and nobody can predict how these wines will age. Most of these fashion-victim wines have high Merlot content and show incredibly well when very young. They already command much higher prices than, say, majestic Château Ausone or the celestial Château Cheval Blanc (the top two estates in St-Emilion). It is remarkable that until the late eighties/early nineties nobody would have considered making such a ridiculously narcissistic style of wine. The American market, spurred on by a succession of good vintages, sought more and more over-the-top flavours similar to the naturally ripe wines of the Napa Valley and the like. One or two entrepreneurs obliged and now the trend is spreading like wildfire. I sound sceptical, because I am. The prices and allocations for single bottles of these wines sound like the equivalent case quantities from the old-fashioned estates. How long can it last before the honeymoon bubble bursts, and people buy with their palates as opposed to their wallets?

Favourite Châteaux: Angélus, l'Arrossée, Ausone, Cheval Blanc, Clos Fourtet, La Dominique, Figeac, Magdelaine, Monbousquet and Troplong-Mondot.

Best value Châteaux: Bellefont-Belcier, Chauvin, Dassault, Haut-Sarpe, Larmande, Quinault, Tour Baladoz, La Tour-Figeac and La Tour-du-Pin-Figeac.

THE ST-EMILION SATELLITES

Lussac St-Emilion, Montagne St-Emilion, Puisseguin St-Emilion and St-Georges St-Emilion are all tongue-twistingly named areas orbiting around St-Emilion itself. They offer wines of similar *cépage* to St-Emilion proper, but lack their impressive longevity. These wines are a good way of tasting the Right Bank style without paying ludicrous prices. They should usually be drunk over the first five to six years of life.

Recommended Châteaux: Bel-Air, Croix-Beauséjour, Durand-Laplagne, Haut-Bernat, Lyonnat, Montaiguillon, Roudier, St-Georges and Teyssier.

POMEROL

With no classification system, you might think it would be difficult to navigate your way around this tiny, exclusive region. But do not despair. There are but a handful of magnificent châteaux here making incredible wines, sadly in tiny quantities. The most famous of all is Château Pétrus, a byword for excellence. Pétrus is one of the only wines in Bordeaux to be made from ninety-five per cent Merlot, the balance being Cabernet Franc. Most Pomerols are very high in Merlot content, generally approaching eighty per cent. When the vintage is favourable, the wines cannot fail to be flattering, exuding exhilarating, plummy, chocolatey and spicy overtones. With such high proportions of Merlot, the wines tend to drink well when they are in their youth, so no matter how grand the wine it is always possible to enjoy a glass, even if the optimum drinking time might be a further ten years off. These wines are highly sought-after, and on account of the limited volumes the prices of Pomerols tend to be fairly punitive. Collectors line up every year, cap in hand, hoping for allocations. Once again, a chance to enjoy a top-flight Pomerol can be rare, but should never be passed up as this little region is single-handedly responsible for global Merlot fever!

Favourite Châteaux (and there are a few, as they are all small but perfectly formed): Bon Pasteur, Clinet, La Conseillante, l'Eglise-Clinet, l'Evangile, La Fleur de Gay, Le Gay, Gazin, Lafleur, La Fleur-Pétrus, Latour à Pomerol, Pétrus, Trotanoy and Vieux-Château-Certan.

Best value Châteaux: Beauregard, Certan-Giraud, Clos du Clocher, La Croix, La Croix St-Georges, l'Enclos, Feytit-Clinet, Gombaude-Guillot and de Sales.

LALANDE-DE-POMEROL

Like St-Emilion, Pomerol has a piggy-back appellation in the shape of Lalande-de-Pomerol. Lush styles lacking in true cellar potential which shape up early on in their lives are the wines to be found here. In top vintages the wines can be very intense but still manage to drink relatively young. With much lower prices than in Pomerol itself it's well worth keeping an eye on this part of Bordeaux. Perhaps the strangest fact about this region is that it is actually bigger than Pomerol.

Recommended Châteaux: Bel-Air, Belles-Graves, du Chapelain, Croix des Moines, La Croix-St-André, des Annereaux and Siaurac.

THE REST

Surrounding these main areas is a collection of lesser-known regions, all producing reliable versions of claret. **Canon-Fronsac** and **Fronsac** are areas several miles to the west of Pomerol, producing increasingly more competent wines. The style is a little more chunky and robust than their more famous neighbour, and in good vintages can resemble a more Left Bank-flavoured wine. The best reason to shop here is the price: very few châteaux have managed to command a regular global audience and so the price tags are refreshingly affordable.

Recommended Châteaux: Canon-Moueix, Fontenil, Mazeris, Moulin-Haut-Laroque, La Rivière, Rouet and La Vieille-Cure are well-made examples of these wines.

The **Côtes de Bourg** and **Blaye**, almost directly opposite Margaux and St-Julien on the other side of the Gironde, are two large, ancient areas of vineyards where several committed wine-makers make some very impressive wines. Once again, prices here are reasonable, but demand for the top wines will increase due to the huge prices rises in the more classic regions. The Côtes de Bourg is the finer of the two appellations and Roc des Cambes is worthy of a special mention. This property is owned by a talented St-Emilion wine-maker who, in his wisdom, recognised the huge potential of this unfashionable region. His wines are truly spectacular. Others will follow his lead; watch these areas closely.

Recommended Châteaux: Bel-Air La Royère, Fougas, Garreau, Haut-Bertinerie, Haut-Grelot, Haut-Sociando, Les Jonqueyres, Mondésir-Gazin, Peybonhomme, Roc des Cambes, Segonzac, Tayac and des Tourtes.

The **Côtes de Castillon** is situated east of Puisseguin St-Emilion and produces chunky, workhorse wines with relatively little complexity, but at a reasonable price. They tend to be Merlot-dominant, but have a fair degree of muscle and can often require a few years in the cellar to soften. Not pretty, but they do the job well.

Recommended Châteaux: de Belcier, Cap de Faugères, Lapeyronie, Pitray and Robin.

The **Côtes de Francs** is another of these little-known appellations, except that this time it is a relative newcomer. In the past it formed part of St-Emilion but now operates under its new name, the Côtes des Francs. Here, wealthy St-Emilion wine-makers have taken to buying run-down estates and, after injecting a bit of skill, in most cases make lovely wines.

Recommended Châteaux: de Francs, Laclaverie, La Prade and Puygueraud.

BURGUNDY

The next major French wine region to tackle is Burgundy. Compared to Bordeaux, this wine region is relatively small in production terms, making half as much wine. Take Beaujolais out of the Burgundy production figures and the volume of wine made plummets to only a quarter of that of Bordeaux. Its smaller size does not mean it is easier to get to know; far from it: for if Bordeaux has two dimensions, the château and the vintage, then Burgundy has three. Don't worry, it is relatively easy to get your head around. Imagine a mathematical graph representing Bordeaux: one axis lists the châteaux names, the other lists the vintages. When you next taste a wine from Bordeaux, you could run your finger down the side of the table and locate the château name, then run your finger across the table until you found its corresponding vintage, then write in your tasting note. It would be a large table and would certainly take several years of constant tasting to fill it in well. Of course, there would be the added problem that in a few years' time every wine would have to be re-tasted as they would all have aged and developed. (I promise I am not trying to create a monster here!) Burgundy's graph would have to have three dimensions. Once again, vintage would be on one axis, but on the other, instead of the château name, substitute the name of the specific vineyard or village the wine came from. The third dimension is the name of the producer who actually made the wine. Whereas in Bordeaux, Château Latour, for example, is from one estate owned by a single owner, a Burgundian vineyard like Echézeaux, is owned by no less than eighty-four smallholders. This is why Burgundy wines need a third dimension to include the owner or wine-maker that has access to the grapes from a specific *climat*, or plot in a vineyard. As in theory 1998 Echézeaux could be made by eighty-four different people!

So there, in a nutshell, is the beguiling and challenging aspect to this wonderful region. It is essential to get to know the individual *domaines* or producers who look after each separate plot of land, and that obviously takes some doing. But I will hopefully make it easier by recommending my favourites and giving you some solid pointers to the better areas and, of course, suggesting ways to remember this oh-so-complicated bastion of the wine world.

Situated in the centre of France, Burgundy's regions stretch all of the way from **Chablis** in the north (100 miles south of Paris), via the **Côte d'Or, Côte Chalonnaise** and **Mâconnais**, down to **Beaujolais** in the south, just a few miles north of Lyon. Unlike Bordeaux, it has a continental climate, with colder winters and cooler summers. Burgundy suffers from the awkward problem of spring frosts and unwanted October rain which can cause havoc at harvest. Undoubtedly the most complicated wine region in the world, it is the sort of place where local knowledge is worth its weight in gold. And within its boundaries the wines range from downright awful to mind-blowingly sensational. There are a number of rules to remember to help make sense of this region. But before divulging my hot tips, a few details regarding the history of Burgundy will explain why it is such a patchwork of small plots of land.

Prior to the French Revolution, most of the vineyards in Burgundy were owned by the Church. After the uprising, the Church lost out in favour of the people. Each delighted villager was given a plot of land to work and these plots further fragmented when new inheritance laws gave equal shares to all sons and daughters of the vineyard owners.

There were family agreements and the inevitable buying and selling of land but on the whole, very few families owned entire vineyards, just a few rows of vines here and a few more over there.

Ownership of these parcels of land only increased in size if one villager married another and they combined their little slices of land, and this still accounts for the predominance of double-barrelled names in Burgundy.

Some sites, like the white Montrachet and the red Chambertin vineyards produced such amazing wine that they became very well known. So well known, in fact, that villagers decided to borrow these names and tack them on to the name of their local village. This broadened the appeal of wines made from the whole village area and not just the famous vineyard itself. And so Puligny and Chassagne, two villages who both lay claim to the fame of the Montrachet vineyard, were henceforth known as Puligny-Montrachet and Chassagne-Montrachet. Lucky old villagers; this must have done them a favour when selling their wines. Likewise, the unknown hamlet of Gevrey became Gevrey-Chambertin, raising its street cred instantly. These double-barrelled versions at least let the outside world know that the style of the wine might in some way resemble that of the top quality, single vineyards. So in the end, Burgundy came to have a remarkably complicated ownership system and impossibly fragmented vineyards. On the up side, at least each vineyard has its own unique name.

The wines of Burgundy are classified into four different AC quality levels. Each and every vineyard belongs to one of these categories. These AC rules were set out in the 1930s and were awarded to each vineyard depending on its potential quality. The Côte d'Or region alone is divided up into over a hundred different appellations. The lowest level of Burgundy wines is known as **regional**. These wines are labelled Bourgogne Rouge (red Burgundy) or Bourgogne Blanc (white Burgundy). The grapes for these wines could come from anywhere within the boundaries of the entire region, and the variation in quality of these wines is understandably huge. A reputable producer will inevitably make a sound wine, whereas a cowboy company will invariably just bottle the dregs.

Almost every domaine makes this style of wine, usually used for home consumption or sold locally to restaurants. These wines generally contain below-par grapes that could have ended up in higher-quality wines but were deemed unsuitable, or grapes from outside the village boundaries.

However, an excellent domaine's duff grapes will often eclipse a duff domaine's best grapes, so there are bargains to be had once you know who's who. Other wines that fall within this category are more specific regional wines. These wines are made from grapes sourced from a number of approved villages within a specified area; for example, Beaujolais-Villages or Côte de Beaune-Villages and Côte de Nuits-Villages. Wines from more than one of the villages in Beaujolais, the Côte de Beaune or Côte de Nuits which are blended together are entitled to the -Village name. These wines are generally of higher quality than simple Bourgogne level as they focus on more precise areas within Burgundy as a whole. They should also reflect the flavour of the wines made from these sub-regions. Once again, the producer is the crucial factor when buying this style of wine.

Climbing up the quality ladder, the next level for Burgundy wines is the **village** classification. If a wine is made from grapes harvested within the boundaries of one village alone, not blended with grapes from further afield, it is entitled to use its village name. These wines' labels will indicate the village name and the Appellation Contrôlée designation, which also includes this village name as well. For example, a wine from the village of Volnay will state this village name and also say Appellation Volnay Contrôlée on the label.

Restricting the source of the grapes even further, the two remaining levels of classification refer to the individual quality status of wines made solely from specific named vineyards. Each plot of land is precisely mapped out and awarded its own quality status. *Village* level wines can be made from single vineyards, or blended between vineyards from one village alone. Some villages, however, have the next quality level of vineyards, that of **1er Cru** or **Grand Cru** status. Within the boundaries of the village of Meursault, vineyards such as Les Tillets and Les Luchets are classified as *village* status. While wines made from these vineyards can be labelled Meursault Les Tillets or Meursault Les Luchets, they are not 1er Cru status, just a specific vineyard-designated wine. The French term for this is a *climat* or a *lieu dit*. These wines are of an undoubtedly higher quality than, say, an ordinary, straight Meursault, but not as fine as a Meursault 1er Cru, from a higher-rated vineyard such as Les Charmes. Sometimes a village might possess several 1er Cru vineyards and even the highest level of all, a Grand Cru vineyard as well. The red wine village of Vosne-Romanée has no less than six Grand Cru vineyards, which need not include the reminder that they are in Vosne-Romanée on the wine label as their individual degree of fame is assumed. The only name needed on the wine label is that of the vineyard itself – of which La Romanée is predictably one of the six.

I have waited until now to introduce you to the Burgundy grape varieties and boy, are they famous.

The world-renowned white wonder, Chardonnay and its equally starry red companion, Pinot Noir, feature in the leading roles and are ably supported by the zingy white grape Aligoté and much-derided red Gamay. Remember, all Chablis, all Côte d'Or, Côte Chalonnaise and Mâconnais white wines are made from Chardonnay. The only exception to this will declare itself on the label and will invariably be the Aligoté grape. Similarly, all Côte d'Or, Côte Chalonnaise and Mâconnais reds are made from Pinot Noir, except for the wines of Beaujolais which use Gamay and a weird and wonderful blend called Bourgogne Passetoutgrains, that has to include a minimum of one-third Pinot Noir to two-thirds Gamay.

The word *domaine* is used in Burgundy to mean an estate. A domaine owns its own vineyards and makes its own wines. Look out for this word on a wine label, as it is an indication that the wine-maker has control over the growing of his grapes and didn't just see them for the first time when they arrived at the winery door. A domaine-bottled wine should be a sign of quality. A *négociant*, a French word meaning merchant, on the other hand, is the term used for a winery that buys in grapes from various different sources, blends them together, then bottles and sells the wine under their own label. The problem lies in the quality of the component parts of négociants' wines which often vary considerably in quality. Different farmers use different vineyard management techniques and this could give rise to superior and inferior crops. The blending of these grapes together rarely equal the sum of the parts. It is easy to understand why so many of Burgundy's wines are sold under the négociant umbrella as most of the smallholdings are too tiny to be able to afford wine-making equipment, so selling the crop is the easiest way to make some money. Négociants not only buy grapes, but can also undertake to blend finished wines together, as some small wineries lack the marketing skills or distribution network necessary to do this job on their own. Once again, the problem of blending together inferior wines can lead to dreary finished products.

Over the last twenty years, the word négociant has gone from a good reason to avoid certain bottles of Burgundy to a very good reason to reconsider certain négociant houses. As bad press was heaped on these merchants on account of their total lack of care over the wines they sold, some négociants introduced contracts with their growers. These contracts set out terms for tending the vines and ensured minimum levels of ripeness at harvest time.

The best négociants worked closely with their grape suppliers and this close contact led to a quantum leap in the quality of fruit, resulting in some outstanding wines being made.

Houses like Louis Jadot and Faiveley are at the forefront of this wave of new-found négociant confidence. Incidentally, both of these houses own their own vineyards as well as buying in grapes and their best wines are made from their own grapes bottled under domaine labels.

A relatively new 'old' trend is re-emerging in Burgundy, and that is the renaissance of the purist *éléveur*. In English, this means individuals who buy 'finished' wine and then take on the ageing responsibilities themselves, often in brand new oak barrels, bottling the wines without fining or filtration. Watch out for ex-pastry chef Dominique Laurent who kick-started this vogue, managing to capture enormous flavour and concentration in his wines. He now not only buys wines but is also buying grapes and acting as a normal négociant as well.

THE REGIONS (FROM NORTH TO SOUTH)

CHABLIS

Starting in the far north of Burgundy, Chablis is a region producing steely dry white wines made from the Chardonnay grape variety. Remember, Ch- for Chablis, Ch- for Chardonnay. It is easy to forget this, as a big, oaky Australian Chardonnay has no apparent similarity to these lean, focused beauties, but they are made from the same grape. I have heard many people in wine bars say, 'I don't want a Chardonnay, but I'll have some Chablis', unaware of their gaffe. It just goes to show how much climate can affect the flavour of a wine. Up in the far northern reaches of Europe's vineyards, it is very cold and frost is easily the biggest fear. In Chablis, one severe snap can ruin an entire vintage.

Chablis is a remarkably famous name in the wine world. In days gone by, the New World would use its name on any bottles of dry white wine. But today, Chablis guards its name and style of wine fiercely. Like other parts of Burgundy, it uses a 'Regional, Village, 1er Cru, Grand Cru' system established in 1938 to indicate increasing levels of quality. *Village* Chablis can vary from dull, insipid, watery white wine to green-hued, pinpoint accurate Chardonnay with invigorating, zesty and refreshing fruit. Once again, the domaine-bottled wines are worth favouring but there are some good négociants as well. Below *village* Chablis is the little-known Petit-Chablis appellation. These wines are usually lean, green and disappointing; and as Chablis is a relatively inexpensive wine, the amount of money saved by buying a Petit-Chablis isn't worth the drop in quality. Going in the other direction, of the forty famous Premier (1er) Cru vineyards, names like Fourchaume, Montée de Tonnerre (Thunder Mountain), Montmains, Vaillons and Vosgros among others have the ability to produce great wines. But like the rest of Burgundy, it is the responsibility and skill of the wine-maker that transforms the crop into a great wine. Premier Cru Chablis can live for anything up to ten years, getting more complex and developing more flavour nuances as time goes on. Only when you get up to Grand Cru level do the wines take on any sort of weight and structure. The seven Grand Crus to look out for are Blanchot, Bougros, Grenouilles (literally, frogs!), Les Clos, Les Preuses, Valmur and Vaudésir. All of these vineyards are grouped together on top of a hill overlooking the town of Chablis, hogging the best soil and sunlight. Grand Cru Chablis can happily last the course for fifteen years, although they usually get gobbled up long before they reach their peak.

Stainless steel is the order of the day when making these wines, although some producers use oak barrels to give them more flavour characteristics. The 'in' crowd frowns on this a little. However, on Premier and Grand Cru level wine the fruit can generally handle some oak, so, if it is in balance, then I do not see why wine-makers should not use it.

Favourite domaines: A. & F. Boudin, René & Vincent Dauvissat, Jean-Paul Droin, Jean Durup, Louis Michel and François & Jean-Marie Raveneau.

Before we move on to the rest of Burgundy there is a region called the Côte d'Auxerre stuck on the bottom of Chablis, where we find a village called St-Bris-le-Vineux which makes fantastic Sauvignon Blancs. It is a VDQS level area (one level lower than AC – see glossary, page 241) and makes a sort of cross between a Sancerre and a Chablis in style. The best wine-maker based here is Jean-Hugues Goisot, whose wines are incredibly good value. He makes a good Aligoté, a great Sauvignon de St-Bris and a stunning Corps de Garde Chardonnay. Also here is a village called Chitry, where Christian Morin makes lovely Chablis-style Chardonnays for a few pounds less. However, it is not all good news in this little region; ignore the nearby reds of Irancy as they are generally too thin and lean.

THE CÔTE D'OR

This is the collective term for the two main areas of vineyards situated at the heart of the Burgundy region, the Côte de Nuits and the Côte de Beaune. Stretching thirty miles from the vineyards of Marsannay in the north to Maranges in the south, the Côte d'Or is a near-continuous skinny slope of vineyards facing east. The village names you pass as you travel down the main road that follows this hill form a roll-call of the greatest Pinot Noirs and Chardonnays in the world. The finest vineyards are situated in the middle of the slope itself, and the lesser wines are made on the flatter land at the bottom, or on the hilltops. The patchwork of vineyards is mesmerising to look at. This is the most mystical and captivating wine region I have ever visited, somewhere the concepts of *terroir* (see glossary, page 215) and microclimate are felt in the soil, air and wines so clearly that all of the complexities of the region seem to make sense in an instant.

CÔTE DE NUITS

The Côte de Nuits, the northerly of the two main regions in the 'golden slope', is the red wine-dominant half. Here the Pinot Noir grape reigns supreme, making blockbuster styles from this sensitive variety. It is also here that all but one of the red Grand Cru vineyards are situated. Before I run through the villages themselves, it is worth noting the regional wines that can be found in this part of the Côte d'Or. Côte de Nuits-Villages comes from the vineyards on the northern (Fixin and Brochon) and southern (Comblanchien, Corgoloin and Prissy) extremes of the Côte de Nuits. These wines can offer very good value drinking, if you stick to reputable producers. Bourgogne Hautes-Côte de Nuits wines are made from the hills above and behind the Côte, where some fine estates (Naudin-Ferrand being a great example) have planted mainly red and a few white grapes to expand their production. These wines can be much cheaper than the Côte proper, but finding a good producer will guarantee expert wine-making and therefore a good wine.

The villages (north to south)

MARSANNAY-LA-CÔTE

Granted full AC status in 1987, the reds here can resemble Gevrey-Chambertin, and wine-makers based in nearby Gevrey often make the best versions of Marsannay. The wines are usually meaty and robust, often lacking in charm or elegance. Marsannay can be found in white and rosé form, but these wines are very rare.

Favourite producers: Charles Audoin, René Bouvier, Philippe Charlopin-Parizot, Bruno Clair, Fougeray, Géantet-Pansiot, Lucien & Alain Guyard and Denis Mortet.

FIXIN

Very hard fruit flavours from this blunt red wine making village. I have never tasted a charming Fixin (pronounced 'fiss-an' as opposed to 'fix-in'). There are some Premier Crus here, but they only make even more backward and muscular wines for the cellar owner to enjoy.

Favourite producers: Pierre Gelin and Lucien & Alain Guyard.

GEVREY-CHAMBERTIN

Burgundy proper starts here in Gevrey, the largest of the Côte d'Or villages (it's a small town really). These wines have the deepest colour of the red wines in the region, although there is a vast variation in the quality of Gevrey produced; so here, more than anywhere, the thirsty buyer must exercise caution. Gevrey has eight Grand Crus which I have listed in order of best and most intense to lightest and fruitiest: Le Chambertin itself, Chambertin Clos de Bèze, Mazis-Chambertin, Latricières-Chambertin, Charmes-Chambertin, Ruchottes-Chambertin, Griotte-Chambertin and finally, Chapelle-Chambertin (did you spot the link? no surprise that Gevrey hijacked the name). Gevrey also possesses some terrific 1er Cru vineyards. Les Cazetiers and Clos St-Jacques often out-perform the Grand Crus in the right hands. And finally, the charmingly named 1er Cru Craipillot is worth finding for dinner parties on account of its unrivalled comedy value.

Favourite producers: Claude & Maurice Dugat, Dujac, Dominique Gallois, Géantet-Pansiot, Philippe Leclerc, Denis Mortet, Ponsot, Roumier, Joseph Roty, Armand Rousseau and Serafin.

MOREY-ST-DENIS

Somehow not really setting the world on fire, Morey-St-Denis has suffered from being wedged in between two more famous neighbours. These wines seem to be lighter than Gevreys but more tannic than Chambolles. Waiting several years for the tannins to soften, only to find that the wines are a little lean, is always somewhat of a disappointment. However, some good domaines are making fleshier examples of these wines. Of the four Grand Crus here, I would favour the first two over the last two by some margin, with Clos de la Roche among the best red wines of the entire Côte d'Or. Clos de la Roche, Clos St-Denis, Clos de Tart and Clos des Lambrays are the four concerned, but Clos de Tart and Clos des Lambrays are soley owned by the Saier brothers and Mommessin respectively and I have rarely tasted an impressive bottle from either vineyard. The 1er Cru vineyards worthy of note are Clos de Monts Luisants, of which Ponsot make a bizarre white version, Clos de la Bussière and Clos des Ormes.

Favourite producers: Dujac, Hubert Lignier, Ponsot and Roumier.

CHAMBOLLE-MUSIGNY

The wines of Chambolle-Musigny are characterised by a sexiness and voluptuousness unlike any other red wines in the region. The scent of these wines is alluring (like crushed strawberries) and they tend to be approachable when fairly young on account of the layers of fruit. Underneath the stunning chassis, Chambolles have considerable power but are easier to appreciate than, say, the wines of neighbouring Vosne. It goes without saying that top domaines must be chosen for these hedonistic pleasures. Grand Crus in the village are Bonnes Mares and Le Musigny. Stunning 1er Crus are Les Amoureuses (which has to take the prize for the most romantic vineyard name) and Les Charmes (another beauty), as well as Les Beaux-Bruns and Les Fuées. Le Musigny makes some white wine, the only white Grand Cru outside of the Côte de Beaune, but I have never seen any! This village, for me, really shouts Pinot Noir from the rooftops, so perhaps is the place to start if you haven't encountered these wines before.

Favourite producers: Barthod-Noëllat, Pierre Bertheau, Comte de Vogüé, Dujac, Géantet-Pansiot, Ponsot, Daniel Rion and Roumier.

VOUGEOT

Clos de Vougeot is an enormous tourist-trap château with an accompanying large, walled Grand Cru vineyard owned by no less than eighty or so different proprietors. Given the diversity of ownership, it is not surprising that the quality of Clos de Vougeot wines ranges from dull to cosmic. Confusingly, alongside this plot of land is an area known as Vougeot which is Premier Cru rated, but often eclipses its grander namesake.

Favourite producers: Hubert Chauvenet-Chopin, Daniel Chopin-Groffier, Jean-Jacques Confuron, Méo-Camuzet, Roumier and Château de la Tour.

VOSNE-ROMANÉE AND FLAGEY-ECHÉZEAUX

These two villages have it all, from relatively inexpensive domaines all the way up to the extortionately priced but somehow reconcilable wines of Domaine de la Romanée Conti. From Bourgogne Rouge to Richebourg, this village covers a lot of ground on the palate. One thing is for certain: when tasting one of this village's Grand Crus, you have to remind yourself it is the medium-weight, aromatic Pinot Noir we have here. The wines are absolutely massive, with stunning aromas and structure only really reserved for grapes like Cabernet Sauvignon. The top producers' wines always amaze me, as they have the capability to age forever. First the big names: the Grand Crus, Romanée Conti and La Tâche are *monopoles* (vineyards exclusively owned by one domaine, in this case the aforementioned Domaine Romanée Conti); Richebourg, La Romanée, Romanée-St-Vivant, La Grande Rue are the others in Vosne. Echézeaux and Grands-Echézeaux are two Grand Crus situated in Flagey, where any *village* or 1er Cru level wines are sold under the name of Vosne-Romanée. Premier Crus worth looking out for are Les Beaux Monts, Les Brûlées, Les Chaumes, Les Gaudichots, Cros Parantoux and Les Suchots.

Favourite producers: Robert Arnoux, René Engel, Jean Grivot, Henri Jayer, Leroy, Méo-Camuzet, Mongeard-Mugneret, de la Romanée-Conti and Emanuel Rouget.

NUITS-ST-GEORGES AND PRÉMEAUX-PRISSEY

Nuits-St-Georges is a very long vineyard area (5 km) bisected by the town of Nuits itself. The vineyards are split into two distinct areas, and those closest to Vosne at the northern end have more elegance and fruit. The southern end of the vineyards, near the hamlet of Prémeaux, are planted on very stony soils that were once considered unfertile, but in fact give rise to lean, earthy, long-lived wines. Nuits has twenty-seven 1er Cru vineyards and not one Grand Cru. The best of the 1er Cru vineyards are Les Cailles (which translates as 'the stones'), Les Vaucrains (*vaurien*, literally 'good-for-nothing') and Les St-Georges itself at the southern end; and Aux Murgers, Aux Boudots, Les Damodes, Richemone and Aux Chaignots at the juicy Vosne end. The wines of Nuits are usually fairly robust and take several years to become approachable.

Favourite producers: Bertrand Ambroise, Jean Chauvenet, Hubert Chauvenet-Chopin, Robert Chevillon, Chopin-Groffier, Henri Jayer, Lecheneaut, Méo-Camuzet, Alain Michelot and Daniel Rion.

CÔTE DE BEAUNE

The Côte de Beaune section of the Côte d'Or runs south of the town of Beaune and is a further split into a red grape-dominant (Pinot Noir) northerly section and a white grape-dominant (Chardonnay) south. It is here that all but one of the white Grand Cru vineyards are situated. Before I run through the villages themselves, it is again worth noting the regional wines that can be found in this part of the Côte d'Or. Surprisingly, Côte de Beaune-Villages wines are all reds, despite being situated in a strong white wine region. These wines again offer good value drinking, but stick to well-known producers. Bourgogne Hautes-Côte de Beaune is also a red wine-dominant appellation, with the same rules applying as regards buying.

The villages

ALOXE-CORTON AND LADOIX-SERRIGNY

It is here that we find the remaining red Grand Cru vineyard, Corton. The wines of Corton tend to be more reminiscent of a Côte de Nuits style, having power and firm acidity in youth. They may not have the stuffing of a Vosne-Romanée, but are unlike the other fleshier red wines made in the Côte de Beaune. Corton can be simply labelled 'Corton', or can attach a named vineyard site to its title. The best *climats* within Corton to look out for are Clos du Roi, Bressandes and Perrières. Aloxe-Corton wines, both *village* and 1er Cru, are found on the lower slopes of the hill of Corton. These wines are scaled-down versions of the big red wine itself. The great white wine of this area is the Grand Cru, Corton-Charlemagne, which can be found nestling beside its red namesake on the panoramic hillside above the village. Austere, sturdy and mineral in youth, Corton-Charlemagne is the long distance runner of the white Grand Crus. They tend to broaden out after a few years, but if drunk too early seem to lack definition, despite their considerable weight. The wines of Ladoix are a mystery to me as I have tasted many bottles of this reputable village's red wines and have remained distinctly underwhelmed by them all. I suspect that most of this village's wines get sold under a Côte de Beaune-Villages label.

Favourite producers of Aloxe-Corton and Corton: Bertrand Ambroise, Louis Jadot, Tollot-Beaut and Michel Voarick.

Favourite producers of Corton-Charlemagne: Bonneau du Martray, Coche-Dury, Michel Juillot, Louis Latour and Maurice Rollin.

PERNAND-VERGELESSES

If you sneak around the hill of Corton to its north-west side and plunge down into the valley below, the vineyards of Pernand-Vergelesses lie in wait. Tucked away in a valley off the main Côte d'Or hillside, Pernand's problem is one of exposure as the hill of Corton blots out the sun for much of the day. The better vineyards on flatter land do receive adequate sunshine, but many of the vineyards in Pernand harvest late on account of their sunshine deficit and are consequently at the mercy of the elements in tricky vintages. I prefer the white wines of Pernand, as good examples have a 'baby-Corton-Charlemagne' feel about them, only you do not have to wait ten years to enjoy them. The reds often lack ripeness and fruit and like Ladoix, a lot of the wine here ends up sold as Côte de Beaune-Villages. However, in good vintages they can be very good value, so take advantage of one of the few bargains in this expensive region. The best 1er Cru vineyards to look out for are Ile de Vergelesses and Les Vergelesses (you could have guessed).

Favourite producers: Germain, Jean-Marc Pavelot and Maurice Rollin.

SAVIGNY-LÈS-BEAUNE

Here in Savigny-lès-Beaune, well-made white wines again resemble diminutive Corton-Charlemagnes in the mineral and nutty fruit they exude. In good years the reds can be sublime with the wines treading a taste tightrope between the flavours of Nuits and Beaune. My favourite growers make a vast range of styles of red Savigny, from light, fresh, strawberry cocktail *village* wines, via tight, mouth-watering, damson-infused 1er Crus like Maréchal and Tollot-Beaut's Les Lavières to brooding, monster 1er Crus like La Dominode from ever reliable Jean-Marc Pavelot.

Favourite producers: Claude Maréchal, Jean-Marc Pavelot and Tollot-Beaut.

CHOREY-LÈS-BEAUNE

Chorey is the forgotten village of the Côte de Beaune. Only awarded AC status in 1974 and without a single 1er Cru vineyard, this village is on the wrong side of the road and railway but is worth a mention because in good years the red wines have a pure red cherry appeal. They are precocious and require little cellaring. Stick to my recommended producers and you won't go wrong.

Favourite producers: Jacques Germain, Claude Maréchal and Tollot-Beaut.

BEAUNE

The capital of the southern section of the Côte d'Or, and once an encampment of Julius Caesar, Beaune's wines are almost all red and invariably form the Leslie Phillips of the red Burgundy charm school. Calm, collected, forward and fruity, these wines have style and yet rarely live as long as those of their two southerly neighbours, Volnay and Pommard. There are a huge number of 1er Cru vineyards in Beaune curling around the north-west corner of the town, and a small selection of the finest sites would include Les Bressandes, Les Marconnets, Les Grèves, Clos du Roi and Les Teurons.

Favourite producers: Drouhin (white Clos des Mouches only), Jacques Germain, Louis Jadot (domaine-bottled), Albert Morot and Tollot-Beaut.

POMMARD

Pommard is a few kilometres south of Beaune, but the wines could not be more different. I absolutely adore this style of Pinot Noir. Lacking in the brawn of the Côte de Nuits but possessing more structure and length than most wines from Beaune, Pommard is an attractive prospect for Pinot-philes. There are so many good wine-makers and vineyards in this village that if you combine the following 1er Crus with the producers below, the results are nothing short of epic. Les Pézerolles and Les Epenots on the Beaune side often have more power and require a few years to soften than Les Rugiens, Les Fremiers and Les Jarolières on the Volnay side, which have a silky, velvety dimension to the taste.

Favourite producers: Comte Armand's monopole Clos des Epeneaux, Jean-Marc Boillot, de Courcel, Girardin, Lejeune and Hubert de Montille.

VOLNAY

Volnays are sexy, silky-smooth, welcoming wines which somehow feel like red wines planted on white wine soil. In fact the Volnay vineyards touch the reds of Pommard on one side and the whites of Meursault on the other. The best Volnay domaines make heavenly wines that will appeal to all red wine lovers (and most white). No Grand Crus needed here as a host of outstanding 1er Crus do the job admirably. Les Taillepieds, Clos des Ducs, Champans, Clos de Chênes, Cailleret, Bousse d'Or and Les Mitans are all first class, and even a 1er Cru red vineyard in neighbouring Meursault is sold under the Volnay appellation: Les Santenots. *Village* level Volnay made by any one of the names below will always impress, and will give you a superb idea of what a classic Côte de Beaune red should taste like.

Favourite producers: Marquis d'Angerville, Blain-Gagnard, Jean-Marc Boillot, Réyane

& Pascal Bouley, des Comtes Lafon, Bernard Glantenay, Michel Lafarge, Roblet Monnot, Hubert de Montille and de la Pousse d'Or (particularly the monopole Clos des 60 Ouvrées).

MONTHÉLIE

Bordering Volnay and Meursault, one might expect this little village to make excellent wines; however, the reality is that the minuscule white production does not get anywhere near even moderate Meursault, and most of the red wine is presumably sold as Côte de Beaune-Villages. The best reds I have tasted have been notable but not amazing, but there must be more out there. There are eleven 1er Crus but I will not bother listing them as the domaine name is by far the most important factor.

Favourite producers: Boussey, Coche-Dury and Fichet.

AUXEY-DURESSES

Passing Monthélie and heading down a valley off the main drag, you come across Auxey. Like Pernand, being tucked up in a valley facing the wrong way has its ripening problems, but some vineyards have good aspects like the best 1er Cru, Les Duresses. A handful of famous domaines have vineyards here – Coche-Dury makes a good red – but the only local of note is M. Diconne, noted below. About a quarter of Auxey is white and it can do a passable impression of a Meursault in the right hands. The reds tend to be lean and green in youth, unlike their neighbour Volnay, needing a few years to iron out tannins. But do stick to good vintages otherwise the fruit will never ever appear. (Like Fixin, the x in Auxey is pronounced 'ss'.)

Favourite producers: Jean-Pierre Diconne and Claude Maréchal.

ST-ROMAIN

At the end of this valley sitting high up on a cliff is the town of St-Romain. I am not that keen on them, but in good vintages decent wines can be made.

Favourite producer: Christophe Buisson.

MEURSAULT

The first and largest of the serious white wine villages back on the Côte d'Or proper is Meursault. Some red Meursault is made, but don't bother about it. A utopian Chardonnay community, this village is a lovely place to stay on holiday, situated in the middle of a carpet of stunning old vineyards. There are no Grand Crus here, but a few 1er Crus of which Les Charmes, Les Genevrières and Les Perrières are the cream of the crop. Honey, nuts, lime, brioche, mouth-filling richness and heroic length are the hallmarks of great Meursault. This style of wine is the reason why Chardonnay is planted all over the world. Meursault is a village that uses a lot of *lieu-dit* names on bottles. These indicate the name of the vineyard the wine comes from, because even though it may not be a 1er Cru, it may have a track record nevertheless. *Village* Meursault is usually drinking two or three years after the harvest, making these wines the most forward of the three great white villages. Comtes Lafon and Coche-Dury are worth a special mention as they have made among three or four of the greatest white wines I have ever tasted.

Favourite producers: Michel Bouzereau, Jean-François Coche-Dury, Patrick Javillier, des Comtes Lafon, Marc Rougeot and Guy Roulot.

PULIGNY-MONTRACHET

This is the village that boasts the greatest concentration of white Grand Cru vineyards as well as no less than twelve 1er Crus. Chevalier-Montrachet and Bienvenues-Bâtard-Montrachet are in Puligny while Le Montrachet and Bâtard-

Montrachet have vineyards in Puligny and Chassagne. These tiny vineyards (Montrachet is only 100 yards wide) are supposedly the most expensive real estate in the world, including downtown Tokyo! As these wines are phenomenally expensive it is usually best to try to search out 1er Crus in order to get a glimpse of what the mighty wines taste like. Top 1er Cru vineyards are the superbly placed Le Cailleret and Les Pucelles (next to the big boys) and the rich, heady Les Folatières, Les Perrières, Champ Canet and La Truffière. It is hard to explain just how amazing these wines can be without lapsing into convoluted wine-speak and personal gibberish, except that there are few Chardonnays in the world that are just starting to drink well at ten years old, retain their freshness and complexity as well as layers of fruit flavours, and capture every element of your concentration and hypnotise your taste buds.

Favourite producers: Jean-Marc Boillot, Louis Carillon, Jean Chartron, Leflaive, Bernard Morey and Etienne Sauzet.

CHASSAGNE-MONTRACHET

Village Chassagne tends to be more impressive than *village* Puligny for some reason. Perhaps better value has something to do with it. Chassagne shares two Grand Crus with Puligny (see above), but also has one of its own, Criots-Bâtard-Montrachet. The white wines made in this village are superb and there are a number of fabulous reds as well. (About half of the wine made in this village is red, so always watch out when you are ordering Chassagne in a restaurant.) The 1er Crus once again hug the side of the hill, while the *village* or *lieu-dit* vineyards are on the flatter land. Good white 1er Crus are La Boudriotte, Les Chaumées, Les Caillerets, Les Champs Gains and Les Embrazées. Strangely, white Chassagne usually outlives red by a few years.

Favourite producers: Guy Amiot, Blain-Gagnard, Marc Colin, Colin-Deléger, Jean-Noël Gagnard, Gagnard-Delagrange, Bernard Morey, Michel Niellon, Paul Pillot and Ramonet.

ST-AUBIN

Like Chassagne, this little village is planted with white and red grapes. Tucked away behind Chassagne, St-Aubin's wine is often released as Côte de Beaune-Villages; but as more and more drinkers discover these Chassagne-style wines at much lower prices, the interest in St-Aubin is increasing. There are a handful of 1er Crus here, of which Sur le Sentier du Clou and Les Frionnes are the best reds and Murgers des Dents du Chien and La Chatenière, facing Puligny, and Le Charmois, abutting Chassagne, are the best whites. My favourite two producers of St-Aubin are both based in the village, but some outsiders make wines worth looking out for; Chartron & Trébuchet and Jadot are two excellent négociants and Domaines Bernard Morey, Marc Colin and Paul Pillot are based around the corner in Chassagne.

Favourite producers: Henri Prudhon and Gérard Thomas.

SANTENAY

The last main village on the 'golden hillside' is Santenay. Here, the charm and fruit that is found in the rest of the Côte de Beaune is somewhat lacking. Red Santenay is usually a rugged creature, lacking in elegance. Luckily, there are bargains to be snapped up from reputable domaines. I am only keen on Girardin as far as local talent is concerned (see below), preferring to look further afield for wine-makers who are used to handling finer fruit. White Santenay is a relative rarity and once again in the right hands can provide good, classy drinking for less cash than its near neighbours' wines. The best 1er Cru vineyards are La Comme, Clos de Tavannes, Les Gravières and Beauregard because they follow on around the hillside from the border with Chassagne.

Favourite producers: Vincent Girardin, Bernard Morey and de la Pousse d'Or.

MARANGES

This really is the last village (or rather, last three villages all sharing the name Maranges) on the Côte. Usually released as Côte de Beaune-Villages there are very few fine wines to be found in this outpost. Mainly Pinot Noir, only mercurial Morey manages to set my palate alight with enthusiasm. You are better off jumping over these three villages and heading into the Côte Chalonnaise.

Favourite producer: Bernard Morey.

CÔTE CHALONNAISE

Wedged between the Côte d'Or and the Mâconnais is a region known as the Côte Chalonnaise. Here, there are three distinct islands of vines set in rolling hills, starting just south of Santenay in the town of Bouzeron, where we find the other famous white grape of Burgundy – Aligoté. Bourgogne Aligoté de Bouzeron is the only appellation specifically set up for this refreshing, zingy white grape. A. & P. de Villaine make the finest version of Aligoté in the world and they achieve a surprising depth of flavour from this simple little grape. Just a few kilometres down the road is the village of Rully, where white and red grapes are grown. This time we are back in Chardonnay and Pinot Noir territory, but I have rarely seen juicy red wines from this appellation. Chardonnays are the order of the day and apart from the Château de Rully, I once again prefer to buy wines from outside producers. Chartron & Trébuchet make the stunning 1er Cru La Chaume, and Jean-Marc Boillot, based in Pommard, makes a 1er Cru called Grésigny. Both of these wines have finesse and will benefit from short-term ageing – and at half the price of a Puligny-Montrachet, they are worth searching for. Mercurey, the biggest village in the Chalonnaise, is the next on the list, dominated by the Pinot Noir grape. Years of tasting, showing fair play to all, have left me with only one domaine to truly recommend: that of Michel Juillot. Juillot makes a small amount of Corton-Charlemagne and uses these skills to fashion small quantities of stunning white *village* and 1er Cru wines. But his most famous wines are the age-worthy reds, from *village* and *Vieilles Vignes* cuvées to 1er Crus like Clos des Barraults and Les Champs Martins. All of his wines are packed with black cherry and leather fruit flavours, needing a few years to soften. Bargain-priced in comparison to the Côte d'Or, try to track these wines down.

There is then a break in the vineyards before coming to the village of Givry. Locals like Joblot and François Lumpp make fine reds that have less body than the wines of Mercurey but are preferable to gambling with red Rully. In this unfashionable village there is a small amount of white produced from Chardonnay, but I would wait until the exclusively white appellation of Montagny before choosing any wine. Montagny wines have Chablis-style acidity, with a depth and nuttiness more commonly associated with the Côte d'Or. The good news is that they are fortunately much cheaper than both of those regions. All of the wine from this village is classified as 1er Cru, as long as the alcohol level reaches 11.5 per cent.

Favourite producers: Bertrand and the multi-regional Jean-Marc Boillot make fine examples of this invigorating wine.

MÂCONNAIS

Neatly fitting like jigsaw into the southern end of the Côte Chalonnaise is the Mâconnais. This is 'white wine central' for Burgundy, as the Mâconnais pumps out three times more white wine than the rest of Burgundy put together. A quarter of the vines planted here are the red grape Gamay and there is a smattering of Pinot Noir as well. Ignore these wines! Red Mâconnais, pah; we have not yet got to Beaujolais where Gamay does its thing, and if you want Pinot Noir, go back up north: this is Chardonnay country.

There are three main types of Mâcon blanc; Mâcon plus a village name, Pouilly plus a village name and St-Véran. There are apparently forty-two villages that can attach their name to a Mâcon blanc, and here are but a few of the most well-known: Viré, Clessé, Lugny and Davayé. Pouilly, on the other hand, has only three: Loché, Vinzelles and the most famous Fuissé. St-Véran has only one: St-Véran, of course. One tricky point to pass on is the pronunciation of Pouilly-Fuissé. There are so many mangled English versions of this lovely wine it is now time to get it right once and for all: 'pwee-fwee-say'.

As with the rest of Burgundy, it is not where the vineyard is but who makes the wine that counts, and in this huge region there are a number of outstanding domaines. The beauty of the wines from the Mâconnais is that they range from crystal clear, rapier-sharp fruit to oaky, honeyed, decadent beauties. Most of these wines have the ability to age, although not as long as their Côte d'Or counterparts. The 'best-value Chardonnays in the world' is how many of my contemporaries rate this region. Stick to the estates below and that statement is not wrong.

Favourite producers (listed in order from drink young to lay down): Deux Roches, Robert-Denogent, Verget négociant (Guffens-Heynen is the domaine name), Daniel Barraud, André Bonhomme, Michel Forest, Jean Thevenet, Ferret and Château Fuissé (Domaine Vincent).

BEAUJOLAIS

Gamay is the grape of the region. This purple coloured, super-juicy red grape is responsible for the buffoonish Beaujolais Nouveau all of the way up to the most under-priced *grand vins* imaginable. This region makes approximately 15 million cases of wine per year against the rest of Burgundy's total of only about 9 million cases, so there is always enough to go around. The scary fact is that more than half of Beaujolais' production is sold as *Primeur* or Nouveau. There are three different styles of wine made here: Beaujolais, Beaujolais-Villages and Beaujolais Cru. 'Straight' Beaujolais is frankly worth avoiding as it could come from anywhere within the region, and most of this is sold as Nouveau. Beaujolais-Villages is a wine made from a blend of wines from two or more villages. This style of wine can be well-made, depending on the domaine or person that makes it. The third level is Cru Beaujolais, where the wine must be entirely made from within one of the ten approved villages' boundaries. It is said that each village has its own flavour nuances and style and this in part is true. But it is always up to the wine-maker whether or not the wine is light or heavy, forward or tannic, so I tend to follow wine-makers or domaines as opposed to village names. There is a tiny amount of white and rosé made in Beaujolais: skip the white as a Mâcon Blanc is a better bet, but a Beaujolais rosé can be delicious from a decent name. When on top form the red wines of Beaujolais can range in style from the chillable crushed red-fruit flavours so necessary on a picnic, to rich, gamey, blackberry fruit with pepper and spice on the nose, a worthy accompaniment to roast chicken or a beef stew. Beaujolais offers the most food-friendly, affordable wines in the world. The ten Beaujolais Cru Villages are St-Amour, Juliénas, Fleurie, Moulin-à-Vent, Brouilly, Côte de Brouilly, Régnié, Chénas, Chiroubles and Morgon.

Favourite producers: Champagnon, Michel Chignard, Coudert, Georges Duboeuf (domaine-bottled wines only), Henry Fessy, Pascal Granger, Louis Jadot (Château des Jacques), Paul Janin, Bernard Mélinand, Alain Passot, Jean-Charles Pivot and Vissoux.

CHAMPAGNE

Champagne is the one wine region where image counts above all. Victorious racing car drivers and the launching of ocean liners rarely involves actually drinking the stuff. You wouldn't get a Burgundy domaine to donate a single bottle of Le Montrachet for the launching of the new 'Mars and Venus Executive Class Space Shuttle', whereas champagne houses would be fighting over who had the rights to smash their finest on its titanium hull.

As you can probably tell, I am a slightly jaded champagne lover. The region and its wines split neatly down the middle. On one side sits the mass-produced, overpriced, mean-tasting fizz destined to be hosed down at parties, weddings and other functions, where the taste is secondary to the fact that it says 'Champagne' on the label. On these occasions I would rather drink some other sparkling wine, where at least there might be some flavour to mull over. On the other side are beautifully crafted, elegant wines with finesse and longevity, worth every penny of their not-inconsiderable price tags. I will concentrate on this latter category, but first I will deal with how to make this enigma and give you a run-down of the different styles found in the region.

Before we start, it is important to realise that the Champagne region is the most northerly of France's wine regions, so the grapes are barely ripe when harvested. The capital of Champagne, Reims, and the other main town in the area, Epernay, lie to the north-east of Paris. There would be no point making ordinary still wines here, yet this style of wine as a base for sparkling wine is fantastic – et voilà – the capital of the world's finest fizzy wines.

Champagne is made by firstly crushing the harvested grapes, quickly removing the skins from the must. The wine is usually made from Chardonnay, Pinot Noir and Pinot Meunier, so the two red grapes might colour the juice if there were any delay.

The must is then fermented in stainless steel tanks, or occasionally oak barrels. Alcoholic fermentation is followed by malolactic fermentation in an effort to soften the high levels of acidity. This results in a bone dry, searingly acidic, rather unpleasant white wine. It is now that the magical blending process occurs. 'Non-vintage' champagne is not only a blend of up to three different grape varieties and many different vineyard sites, but also of different vintages of wine (hence *non-vintage:* 'not one vintage'). The most skilled job in this region is that of the blender, who assembles infinitely variable combinations of base wine into a completed cuvée, or blend. The aim is to produce a 'house style' that remains the same despite any variations in vintage. Non-vintage Taittinger, for example, should always taste the same: if you like it once, you should like it again. Once the blend is determined, the second fermentation takes place in the bottled wine. A small amount of *liqueur de tirage* is added to each bottle. This contains sugar, yeast and still champagne. The bottles are sealed with a cap, like a beer bottle, and banished to the cellars for the second fermentation. The carbon dioxide generated from this fermentation is trapped in the bottle and dissolves into the wine, later to be released in the form of bubbles when the day of uncorking arrives. The next process, *remuage*, is a gradual twisting and jiggling of the bottle in order to shake the lees (dead yeast cells) in the bottle down to the neck behind the cap. This is done by stacking the bottles in an A-frame wooden contraption, drilled on both sides with sixty holes. The neck of the bottle is put into this *pupitre* (desk), with the bottle lying horizontally. Over the course of eight or so weeks a man called a *remuer*, with wrists like a gorilla, gradually twists and turns the bottles into an upright position, with the sediment ready to be ejected. The bottles are plunged into a frozen brine solution and the neck of the bottle freezes, capturing the sediment in a champagne ice cube. This ice cube is gently popped out of the bottle *(dégorgement)* and replaced with a *liqueur d'expédition*, a wine with a touch of sugar, depending on the style. A cork is banged in quickly, wire is fastened around it to prevent any unwanted explosions and the bottle is labelled, ready for the off.

Sounds easy? It is hardly surprising that champagne is a fairly expensive wine style as the wine-making process is complicated, the equipment costs a bomb and the wine must be aged for a minimum of one year with the best houses usually aiming for three.

CHAMPAGNE STYLES

NON-VINTAGE

As noted above, this style is blended across different vintages, endeavouring to capture a 'house style'. Non-vintage champagne accounts for three-quarters of all champagne produced. It ages well in the short term, and most wines will improve after a year of extra cellaring. This is the least expensive style of champagne, one that marketing managers strive to get their customer to remain 'brand-loyal' to.

VINTAGE

This style of champagne is made in particularly good vintages where the wine is made entirely from one year's harvest and tends to be more expensive than non-vintage wines by about half as much again. This can lead to unscrupulous houses releasing a vintage as often as possible, which is not the point; but reputable houses tend to stick to the five or so years in ten when the weather is favourable and the wine worthy.

ROSÉ

Non-vintage or vintage style, these wines are made by blending a little red wine with white. Most rosé champagnes also have a higher percentage of red grapes in the blend to help marry the tastes together. The rosé style tends to suffer from fashion trends and sadly usually only gets consumed on Valentine's Day or summer sporting events. Its unique flavour does in fact complement many dishes well and shouldn't be restricted to seasonal consumption.

BLANC DE BLANCS

This style can also be made in non-vintage and vintage form, and as the name suggests, is white wine made from white grapes only; as we are in Champagne, that means one hundred per cent Chardonnay. Usually much tighter on the palate and needing some time in the cellar to soften, these wines can be amazingly concentrated with very long finishes.

BLANC DE NOIRS

'White wine from black grapes', in this case the two Pinots, Meunier and Noir. A rare style of wine that can have a pink tinge to its colour, Blanc de Noirs are much more fruity than other styles, perhaps even (shut your eyes) tasting red! Non-vintage and vintage styles can be found.

CRÉMANT

Crémant is a very rare style that is so called on account of its 'creaming' or frothing character, which means the wine is less aggressively fizzy than normal champagne. It is usually made from the finer Chardonnay grape.

PRÉSTIGE CUVÉES

The top of the ladder, these styles are usually vintage wines, although there are some notable exceptions. The finest vineyards' crops are put aside in excellent vintages, then hand-crafted into these beautiful wines. It is not unknown for this style of champagne to last for twenty or thirty years, making them some of the longest-lived dry white wine styles. Super-expensive, usually drunk by secret agents and the like, they should always reward the consumer with unbeatable complexity and heroic length.

As always, it is necessary to follow certain houses over others, and here is my list of the greatest champagnes around. Please don't waste your money on cheap champagne: for just a few pounds more, the experience can be ten times as pleasant. This list contains inexpensive non-vintage wines all the way up to the summit of perfection. Find your preferred style and stick to it!

TOP CHAMPAGNE HOUSES AND THEIR FINEST CUVÉES

Billecart-Salmon	**Non-vintage:** Brut, Demi-Sec and Rosé.
	Vintage: Cuvée Nicolas-François Billecart, Elisabeth Salmon Rosé, Grande Cuvée and Blanc de Blancs.
Bollinger	**Vintage:** Grande Année, R.D. (*récemment dégorgé*, or recently disgorged) and Vieilles Vignes Françaises Blanc de Noirs.
Gosset	**Non-vintage:** Brut Excellence and Grande Réserve Brut.
	Vintage: Grande Millésime Brut.
Jaquesson	**Non-vintage:** Blanc de Blancs.
Krug	**Non-vintage:** Grande Cuvée.
	Vintage: Clos du Mesnil.
Laurent-Perrier	**Non-vintage:** Cuvée Rosé Brut.
	Vintage: Grand Siècle 'La Cuvée'.
Moët & Chandon	**Vintage:** Cuvée Dom Pérignon Brut.
Pol Roger	**Non-vintage:** Brut 'White Foil'.
	Vintage: Brut Vintage and Cuvée Sir Winston Churchill.
Louis Roederer	**Non-vintage:** Brut Premier.
	Vintage: Blanc de Blancs, Brut Millésime, Cristal.

Ruinart	**Vintage:** 'R' de Ruinart Brut and Dom Ruinart Blanc de Blancs.
Salon	**Vintage:** Blanc de Blancs.
Taittinger	**Non-vintage:** Brut Réserve.
	Vintage: Comtes de Champagne Blanc de Blancs.
Veuve Clicquot	**Non-vintage:** Brut 'Yellow Label' and Demi-Sec.
	Vintage: Vintage Réserve, La Grande Dame Brut, La Grande Dame Rosé.

ALSACE

I said that Champagne was a long way up north in wine-making terms. Well, Alsace is up there too, and ought to suffer with the same climatic and ripening problems, but it doesn't. There is one reason why: the magnificent Vosges Mountains, which form a classic rain shadow (remember geography lessons at school?). This results in some of the lowest rainfall statistics in France, coupled with superb sunshine hours. So it is not all doom and gloom in Alsace. Twelve million bottles of mainly dry white Alsace wine are produced in a good year. The only real obstacle as far as Alsace wines are concerned is the public perception of the wines themselves. The wine trade's love of these wines has never quite crossed over to the consumer. Perhaps it is because the wines are bottled in the traditional flute-shaped bottle – looking dangerously German! Or maybe the grape varieties written on the wine labels are not that familiar. Whatever the reason, the only way to bring these uniquely delicious wines to the attention of the drinking public is to talk about them and increase communication channels. So here we go.

Alsace is one of France's easier regions to understand. The rules and regulations are relatively straightforward, and the wines are all AC quality level. If the grape variety appears on the label, the wine must contain one hundred per cent of the variety stated. Similarly, if the wine does contain one hundred per cent varietal fruit, this grape variety will be noted on the label. If it is blended, then a brand name may be used or else the term *Edelzwicker* will be mentioned. Some sparkling wines are made using the traditional method and these are known as *Crémant d'Alsace*.

The best fifty vineyards in Alsace have been designated Grand Crus, and when the grapes from one of these vineyards have been used, the label will read *Alsace Grand Cru* followed by the name of the vineyard and the grape variety. Only four of Alsace's grape varieties have Grand Cru quality status: Riesling, Gewürztraminer, Tokay-Pinot Gris and (for some reason) Muscat. Other grapes used for making Alsace wines are Sylvaner, Pinot Blanc and Pinot Noir.

Vendange Tardive and *Sélection des Grains Nobles* styles can be made, weather permitting, by leaving the grapes on the vines late into the picking season, then harvesting them with higher than normal sugar levels, or when they are botrytis-affected. These two styles of wine are generally very rich in style and usually sweet. *Vendange Tardive* styles last in bottle for ages, gradually drying out as time marches on. *Sélection des Grains Nobles* usually remain sweet and can be very syrupy and decadent.

That is it. I absolutely adore the wines from this region. They act as thirst-quenching aperitifs, skilful food-matching wines, from pâtés, salads, all fish dishes, chicken, Chinese, Asian, French, English – whatever; plus standing up to puddings and working beautifully as after-dinner sippers – oh, they do everything, and they are such good value. The one golden rule is, as always: it's not the grape variety, or the vintage, or which Grand Cru vineyard the grapes came from that matters, but *who made the wine!*

Favourite producers: Bott-Geyl, Marcel Deiss, Schoffit, Weinbach-Faller, Zind-Humbrecht, Schlumberger, Hugel, Ostertag, Rolly Gassmann and Trimbach.

THE LOIRE VALLEY

Starting on the Atlantic coast in the town of Nantes, then slicing eastwards through over 600 miles of verdant French countryside, the Loire river and its tributaries cover a myriad of soil types and dozens of microclimates. In fact, this one region has it all, from light aperitif sparklers, through all manner of whites (including some superb sweeties), to Beaujolais-challenging, fruit-driven gluggers, ending at dark, deep, brooding, cellar-demanding red wines. The greatest single incentive as to why you should demystify this region above all others is that for some reason the wines made here lag a long way behind the other classic regions in terms of price. It is nearly impossible to spend more than £15 on a bottle of Loire wine and most can be snapped up, including the top domaines' wines, for between £5 and £10. So save some cash and prepare for a taste bud challenge. (Oh, there are some great châteaux there as well . . .)

The four main regions in the Loire are (starting on the coast):

Nantes

The *Pays Nantais* or Nantes countryside is famous for one main white wine: **Muscadet.** You might think this an inauspicious start to our tour, but the best wines in Muscadet are so inexpensive and so thirst-quenching that they are worth sniffing out. The Muscadet grape (also known as *Melon de Bourgogne*) is at its best in the Sèvre-et-Maine region, south-west of the town of Nantes. There are two rules to remember when buying Muscadet. First make sure that the label specifies that the wine comes from the superior sub-region of Sèvre-et-Maine; second, that the style of wine made is *sur lie*, meaning that the wine sits on its lees, or sediment, resulting in more flavour and depth to the wine. Drink these wines as young as possible, with salads, seafood or in the garden on a hot summer's day.

Favourite producers of Muscadet: André-Michel Brégeon, Château de Chasseloir, Vincent & Sébastian Chéreau, Marquis de Goulaine, Luneau-Papin and Domaine de la Mortaine.

Anjou-Saumur

This is a large region covering the land between the towns of Angers and Saumur. Forget Anjou Rosé, the watered down cranberry juice of the wine world; this fine region sports the champion white grape of the Loire, Chenin Blanc. Remarkably age-worthy, dry Chenins are made in this region, the finest of which are **Savennières**. One or two domaines here produce wines that can live for twenty or thirty years, so perfect are their balance and acidity. The other styles of Chenin Blanc made here are the sweet wines of **Coteaux du Layon** (which can add any one of six village names to the label), **Coteaux de l'Aubance, Bonnezeaux** (pronounced Bonzo!) and **Quarts de Chaume**. Late picked and often botrytis-affected, the wines are unctuous, oily and dripping in honeyed fruit. The Chenin Blanc grape does not let us down as again, these wines can live for as long as top Sauternes, but represent much better value.

Saumur is the capital of the sparkling wine industry in the Loire Valley, where traditional method wines are made from Chenin Blanc, Chardonnay and Cabernet Franc. It is said that Chenin makes a lumpier, sweeter style of fizz than its noble northern French competitors; however, with the Champenois owning several properties here and a much lower price tag, these wines are worthy of a place in your wine rack.

The first glimpse at the red wines of the Loire comes in the shape of **Saumur Rouge** and the superior **Saumur-Champigny**. Here, where the Vienne river meets the Loire, the gravel soils are perfect for the Cabernet Franc grape to thrive. The top estate here is Domaine Filliatreau where they make several cuvées, from a light, purple-coloured, blackberry-scented Saumur, Château Guiraud, to an ancient Saumur-Champigny *Vieilles Vignes* selection that needs five years to be approachable and is a perfect example of Cabernet Franc's depth of fruit and black-cherry infested finish. This wine is only about the same price as a bottle of supermarket own-label champagne!

Favourite producers of Savennières: Domaine du Baumard (Clos du Papillon), Domaine du Closel (Clos du Papillon), Nicolas Joly (Clos de la Coulée de Serrant) and Pierre Soulez (La Roche-aux-Moines).

Favourite producers of sweeties: Domaine des Baumard, Château Pierre Bise, Château de Fesles, Vincent Lecointre, Moulin Touchais, Didier Richou and Domaine des Rochettes.

Favourite producers of sparklers: Domaine des Baumard, Bouvet-Ladubay – in particular their Cuvées Saphir and Trésor (owned by Champagne Taittinger) and Gratien & Meyer (associated with Alfred Gratien Champagne).

Favourite producers of reds: Domaine Filliatreau and Langlois-Chateau.

Touraine

Touraine, around the town of Tours, has both some of the Loire's best-known wines and some of its best-kept secrets. With its western end bang next to Saumur, the region starts with three heavyweight reds (these are the last big reds in the entire region). **Chinon, Bourgueil** and **Saint-Nicolas-de-Bourgueil** are meaty Cabernet Francs that generally drink well between two and six years old. With concentrated, rich blackberry fruit in good vintages, these wines are good claret substitutes as they are always good value and can have considerable complexity. They are delicious chilled in warm weather. The famous white wines of **Vouvray** can be dry (sec), medium-dry (demi-sec) or sweet (moelleux), and once again the Chenin Blanc grape fulfils these tasks admirably. The only criticism of dry Vouvrays are that in youth they have considerable acidity and need food badly to balance the dryness. **Montlouis** is the little-known next door neighbour to Vouvray, copying its styles and often offering even better value for money.

Surrounding these river-hugging regions is the Touraine countryside, where two bargain wines can be found. **Sauvignon de Touraine** and **Gamay de Touraine** are a white and red double-act that are best drunk young, and give a cut-price Sancerre or Beaujolais taste beloved of Parisian cafés. Stick to the best producers and you can't go wrong. Finally, two sneaky, secret areas called **Jasnières** and **Cheverny**. In hot years, Jasnières can give Savennières a run for its money at half the price; and white Cheverny, made from Sauvignon Blanc, can out-perform many Sancerres for a fraction of the cost.

Favourite producers of Chinon: Couly-Dutheil, Charles Joguet and Olga Raffault.
Favourite producers of Saint-Nicolas-de Bourgueil: Lamé-Delille-Boucard, Jean-Paul Mabileau and Joël Taluau.
Favourite producers of Bourgueil: Pierre-Jaques Druet, de l'Espy, Lamé-Delille-Boucard and Joël Taluau.
Favourite producers of Vouvray: Bourillon-Dorléans, Gaston Huet, Daniel Jarry and Philippe Foreau.
Favourite producers of Montlouis: Michel & Laurent Berger, Délétang and Dominique Moyer.
Favourite producer of Sauvignon de Touraine: Alain Marcadet.

Favourite producer of Gamay de Touraine: Henry Marionnet.

Favourite producers of Jasnières: Joël Gigou and Jean-Baptiste Pinon.

Favourite producers of Cheverny: de la Gaudronnière and Salvard.

Central Vineyards

This is surely the most fashionable section of the river as it includes the mega-famous villages **Pouilly-Fumé** and **Sancerre** whose wines feature in every media lunch and catwalk launch, as well as the less well-known (and often much better value) **Quincy, Menetou-Salon** and **Reuilly**. Of the last three, Menetou is the finest Sancerre taste-alike, with Reuilly and Quincy being a little more rustic. We are so far along the Loire that we are within spitting distance of Chablis, where the climate is far from maritime and more continental. This is the world-wide home of the Sauvignon Blanc grape variety. With chalky soils and Sauvignon Blanc as far as the eye can see, these five villages produce variations on a theme. And that theme is fresh, dry, zippy, citrusy, green, tangy, nettles, crisp, floral, elderflower, asparagus and gooseberries.

This famous quintet of villages acts as the role-model for all of the Sauvignons on the globe, and if you follow the list below, you will see why. Once in a while, ambitious wine-makers use oak barrels to augment the flavour of their Sauvignon Blancs. One of these mavericks is eccentric M. Didier Dagueneau. His Pouilly-Fumé (*fumé*, meaning 'gun smoke', often found on the nose of the wine) Cuvées Silex and Clos des Chailloux have a strong oak element. I find these wines interesting, expensive and unusual, but rarely does the dominant oak flavour knit well with the freshness that Sauvignon Blanc embodies.

Rosés and reds are made from Burgundy's Pinot Noir grape, resulting in a cross-dressing style of wine: definitely Pinot underneath, but sporting a sheer, floaty, off-the-shoulder number on top. A good way of tasting well-made, feather-light French Pinot without having to spend Côte d'Or prices.

Favourite producers of Sancerre: Sylvain Bailly, Bailly-Reverdy, Philippe de Benoist, Henri Bourgeois, Cotat, Vincent Delaporte, André Dézat, Henri Natter, Vacheron and André Vatan.

Favourite producers of Pouilly-Fumé: Didier Dagueneau, Jean-Claude Chatelain, Château du Nozet (de Ladoucette) and Château de Tracy.

Favourite producers of Menetou-Salon: de Chatenoy, Henry Pellé and Jean-Jacques Teiller.

Favourite producers of Reuilly: Henri Beurdin and Gérard Cordier.

Favourite producer of Quincy: Jacques Rouzé.

MISCELLANEOUS

There are a handful of outlying areas that fall under the Loire jurisdiction, many of which are closer to other wine regions, but it just goes to show how long this river really is. My picks of the group are the VDQS region **Haut-Poitou**, fifty miles south-west of Tours, around the town of Poitiers, making Bordeaux-blend reds and some useful Sauvignon Blancs and Chardonnays. **Saint-Pourçain** is a VDQS region whose best wines come from the local co-operative Union des Vignerons. Gamay blended with Pinot Noir forms the red, and Sauvignon, Chardonnay and Aligoté the white, giving us some idea that this region is between the Loire and Burgundy. Lastly, the AC region of the **Côtes Roannaises**, which despite being on the Loire, is only one range of hills west of Beaujolais! Gamay is the call of the day, similar to Beaujolais in style and taste, only much cheaper. This region and its wines are making a comeback after an apocalyptic decline in business in the early twentieth century.

THE RHÔNE VALLEY

Situated in the south-east corner of France, this hot region stretches 200 kilometres from Vienne in the north to Avignon in the south. There is a lot of talk about the value afforded by the fabulous wines made in this region. Sadly, some of the best wines are getting out of reach; but if it is spicy, meaty reds you are after for under £10, this is still the place to be. Split neatly into two distinct regions, the northern and southern Rhône, I'll deal with the area from north to south.

THE NORTHERN RHÔNE

The bruiser of the red grape varieties, Syrah, dominates all of the red wines of the northern Rhône. By way of a change, the whites favour the Cinderella grape, Viognier and its ugly sisters Marsanne and Roussanne. The northern Rhône Valley is a craggy, steep-sided, narrow strip of vineyards following the river south. The climate is continental despite the mistral, a bitter wind that whistles down the valley at over 100 kmph, endangering shoots and leaves without warning. The great wines of this region sit firmly at the top of the world's best lists, with Syrah and Viognier rarely bettered outside of this collection of famous appellations.

The villages

CÔTE-RÔTIE

Some of the most monumental wines I have ever tasted have come from this relatively small appellation. Up on the hillside, where the English translation 'roasted slope' really hits home, the vines cling to the terraces by the skin of their grapes. One man, Marcel Guigal, is single-handedly responsible for making these wines so famous. His vineyards, or cliffs of vines, are situated in an amphitheatre-shaped hollow above the town of Ampuis. Single vineyard bottlings of La Turque, La Mouline and La Landonne are indefinably majestic, as is his latest acquisition of the Château d'Ampuis, represented by another cuvée in his cellar. Côte-Rôtie can be made with the addition of up to twenty per cent Viognier, tempering the violets and spice on the nose and calming slightly the roar of Syrah's cassis, smoke and leather on the palate. Côte-Rôtie can usually live happily for up to twenty years, with Guigal's wine managing even longer.

Favourite producers: Pierre Barge, Bernard Burgaud, Clusel-Roche (Les Grandes Places), Yves Cuilleron, Marius Gentaz-Dervieux, E. Guigal's entire portfolio, J.-P. & J.-L. Jamet and René Rostaing.

CONDRIEU

Moving from one of the most impressive red wines to one of the most celestial whites, Condrieu is an exotic concoction made from the beguiling Viognier grape variety. Very few serious white wines demand to be drunk young, but Condrieu doesn't want to waste any time and hits the ground running – or, should I say, sashaying. The opulent peach kernel, nutmeg and apricot blossom characters make this wine one of the most attractive white grape varieties on the nose. The lack of mouth-drying acidity makes it all too easy to drink. This is the wine that made Viognier world-famous, but there is one factor that naturally slows the sales down: the price. Condrieu tends to be as expensive as Côte-Rôtie, and that is a lot to fork out for a puppy-fat white wine. The only bargains to be had in this part of the world are the 'de-classified' Condrieus made from young vines, reject cuvées or vines grown above the officially permitted AC altitude.

Favourite producers: Yves Cuilleron, Pierre Dumazet, Pierre Gaillard, E. Guigal, André Perret, Georges Vernay and François Villard.

CHÂTEAU-GRILLET

This preposterously overpriced, tiny, single-estate AC (the only one in France) is supposedly the pinnacle expression of Viognier. Blame Thomas Jefferson: he started it all off; and whereas his claret tastes were clearly exemplary, he got this one wrong. Apparently it ages well, but I have tasted many vintages of dull, confusingly variable wines. Ignore it and save yourself a fortune.

ST-JOSEPH

Both red and white wines are made in this appellation and they offer a good value alternative to both red Hermitage, Cornas and Côte-Rôtie and white Hermitage. The reds are made from Syrah with the addition of up to ten per cent of the white grapes Marsanne and Roussanne. The white wines are Marsanne and Roussanne blends. The style is that of a slightly more rustic version of the grander names, lacking finesse, but making up for it in presence. Both styles should be drunk within six years of the vintage. I love these two styles of wine as they are honest, have chunky fruit, and they really do represent a genuine taste of the region (goût de terroir).

Favourite producers: Jean-Louis Chave, Yves Cuilleron, Bernard Faurie, Pierre Gaillard, Jean-Louis Grippat, André Perret.

HERMITAGE

Hermitage is a tiny appellation that includes the most famous of the northern Rhône's red wines. A small amount of Marsanne and Roussanne may be added to the red wines of Hermitage, but they are usually one hundred per cent Syrah. They have deep, plummy, chunky, peppery fruit with a full-bodied ripe and gripping finish. The white wines from Hermitage are fairly 'bosomy' numbers, with Marsanne and Roussanne bursting out everywhere in the form of peachy, nutty, oily fruit. Of all of the northern Rhône whites these last the longest (5–15 years). The reds age at a snail's pace and rarely show their full hand until at least five years old and can survive happily until twenty-five.

Favourite white Hermitage producers: Chapoutier's Chante Allouette, Jean-Louis Chave, Grippat and E. Guigal.
Favourite red Hermitage producers: Chapoutier (particularly Le Pavillon, it's a stonker), Jean-Louis Chave, Grippat, E. Guigal, Paul Jaboulet Aîné (La Chapelle is a legendary wine) and Henri Sorrel.

CROZES-HERMITAGE

Scaled down versions of Hermitage are available in the form of Crozes-Hermitage, both in red form and white, made from the same grapes. Situated around the town of Tain, this largish appellation (ten times that of Hermitage) requires a careful hand when selecting fine wines. Best drunk young and even chilled in the summer, the red wines can be unbelievably peppery on the nose and very juicy and fleshy on the palate. White Crozes-Hermitage needs only to be one year old to reach its peak, then use it to wash down some grilled or poached fish, or a goat's cheese salad.

Favourite producers: Albert Belle, Dumaine, Alain Graillot (particularly the La Guiraude cuvée), Paul Jaboulet Ainé and Domaine Pochon (Curson).

CORNAS

Only red wines are made here, coming entirely from Syrah. Unapologetically full-bodied, these wines can be over-intense in their youth. Lacking finesse and quite often balance, they require a few years to soften before summoning up the courage to attempt the huge fruit on offer. These powerful, tannic wines can last for up to fifteen years in a good vintage. Representing good value on wine shop shelves, put your seatbelt on and go for it.

Favourite producers: Thierry Allemand, Auguste Clape (a hero), Jean Lionnet, Robert Michel, Stéphane Robert, Noël Verset and Alain Voge.

ST-PÉRAY

A white wine-only village with some fizz produced as well, this is the last in a line of appellations from the northern Rhône. Don't even bother: the Loire makes better sparkling wine and we've already had some cracking whites.

While we are on the subject of wines to give a miss, there are two regions at the bottom of the northern Rhône that you can cross off your shopping list as well. Clairette de Die, a sparkling wine made from the unspeakably dull white variety of the same name, and the reds and whites of Chatillon-en-Diois. If you have to drink some to say you've at least tried it, then have a go at Clairette de Die Tradition, a fizzy Muscat-dominant wine that is France's answer to Italy's Moscato d'Asti. On second thoughts, don't bother; I am only trying to be nice.

THE SOUTHERN RHÔNE

Where the northern Rhône relied on Syrah to do the legwork, the southern Rhône is a heavily blended region, with Grenache grabbing the lion's share of most of the reds. This region is huge in comparison to the northern Rhône and has a much more Mediterranean climate. The mistral is still present, but does help occasionally to dry out the vineyards when conditions are too humid.

This is the land of **Châteauneuf-du-Pape**, **Gigondas**, **Vacqueyras**, **Lirac** and gallons and gallons of **Côtes-du-Rhône**, a generic appellation covering the entire Rhône region, although the vast majority of the wine comes from the southern end. There is also an enormous variation in quality of these wines, from disgraceful, chemistry-set reds to baby-Châteauneuf-style wines; but as ever, the best are always from well-known producers. There are seventeen villages in the southern Rhône that are allowed to use their names on the label if the contents of the bottle comes exclusively from within their boundaries. These wines are known as Côtes-du-Rhône-Villages, of which the best known are Gigondas, Vacqueyras, **Cairanne**, **Rasteau**, **Valréas** and **Sablet**. These wines are a big step up in quality over basic Côtes-du-Rhône as the permitted yields are lower, and the minimum alcoholic strength is 12.5 per cent. In 1971 Gigondas broke away from the -Villages list and became an appellation in its own right; Vacqueyras followed in 1990. These two represent the finest wines to come out of the southern Rhône save for Châteauneuf itself.

The red wines from this region are complex blends, and can include anything up to thirteen varieties (as in the case of Châteauneuf). Grenache, Mourvèdre, Cinsault and Syrah always grab the first places on the bus, with Picpoul, Terret Noir, Counoise, Muscardin, Vaccarèse, Picardin, Clairette, Roussanne and Bourbelenc usually somewhere behind. The last three of those, incidentally, are white. Very few wine-makers actually follow the letter of the law and use all thirteen, most relying on the first four.

Most southern Rhône reds are drunk between two and eight years old, although Châteauneuf-du-Pape should be allowed three years to become approachable and can last for twenty.

White wines are made from Grenache Blanc, Clairette and Viognier, with the reliable Roussanne variety often lending its weight to the blend. Châteauneuf-du-Pape

Blanc is the only really serious white from down here, and it is very rare. Rosés are popular, especially the over-rated **Tavel**, whose tannin and alcohol levels are quite something.

Sweeties are produced in the southern Rhône from the Muscat Blanc à Petits Grains grape via the Vin Doux Naturel process. These light, fresh wines are reminiscent of peaches, coconut, apricots – and grapes! Drink very cold in order to appreciate them fully, as they get a little sickly when they warm up.

Favourite Côtes-du-Rhône (and -Villages) producers: Auguste Clape, Coudoulet de Beaucastel, Domaine Gramenon, E. Guigal, Rayas (Fonsalette), R. & J.-P. Meffre, Pelaquié, Piaugier, Rabasse-Charavin, Richaud, Renjarde, Emmanuel Reynaud (Château des Tours) and Château du Trignon.
Favourite Lirac producers: A. & R. Maby and de la Mordorée
The best Gigondas producers: Edmond Burle, Font-Sane, R. & J.-P. Meffre (Saint Gayan), Piaugier, Santa-Duc and Château du Trignon.
Favourite Vacqueyras producer: Emmanuel Reynaud (Château des Tours).
Favourite Châteauneuf-du-Pape producers: de Beaucastel, Chapoutier, Clos du Caillou, Clos des Papes, Clos du Mont Olivet, de la Mordorée and Rayas.
Favourite Muscat de Beaumes-de-Venise producers: Chapoutier, Domaine du Durban and Paul Jaboulet Ainé.

There are a host of miscellaneous regions tacked on to the bottom and sides of the Rhône. Here is a summary of what to hit and what to miss. The **Côtes du Ventoux** on the south-eastern fringes of the southern Rhône between the **Coteaux du Tricastin** and the **Côtes du Luberon**, makes light quaffing reds in a mini-Côtes-du-Rhône style. The best labels to look out for are La Vieille Ferme and Claude Fonquerle's Château Valcombe. The aforementioned Tricastin makes chunkier wines than Ventoux and the finest estate is Domaine de Grangeneuve, owned by the indomitable Madame Odette Bour. Both of the areas were promoted to AC status in 1973. The **Côtes du Vivarais** is situated opposite Tricastin in the Ardèche region. I would give this a miss in favour of the previous two regions. And finally to the **Coteaux de Pierrevert** and the Côtes du Luberon where the wines are again made in a Rhône style but leave me a little bored.

FRENCH COUNTRY

French Country is a catch-all term for any wines not already covered in the classic regions. I have split this into five short sub-sections, featuring my favourite areas and recommended estates. Here we find some of the best bargains on the French wine scene, capturing that essential *goût de terroir*.

JURA AND SAVOIE

These two wine-making regions make classic examples of holiday wines – they taste great when you are skiing or walking in the Alps, but distinctly dull back home. Situated in south-east France on the border with Switzerland, not far from Geneva, the wines of Jura and Savoie are a classic example of wines that do not travel too well. However, if you fall for the peculiar salty, nutty, sherry-like flavour of the Savagnin (not Sauvignon!) grape, then there are a few estates to follow. If you are keen to taste **Vin Jaune**, the yellow wine, then Château-Chalon's producer, Henri Maire, makes a good example. **Vin de Paille**, a masochist's version of Vin Jaune where the grapes are dried before becoming sherried, is a taste I have never acquired, although some people go into raptures. Domaine de Montbourgeau and Château de l'Etoile are the star performers (no pun intended) in the appellation of l'Etoile, where Savagnin again is the weird white grape in charge. **Arbois** makes Chardonnay and yet more Savagnins (including Jaune and Paille styles) in a slightly more commercial fashion and the reds can be made of Pinot Noir, resembling weak and feeble Côte de Beaune rouges. The other two strange red varieties are Poulsard and Trousseau; like the detectives in Tintin, they are chaotic and rarely get the job done.

Roussette de Savoie can be a nice change from the lean whites found in this area. Prieuré Saint-Christophe makes my favourite example. Other whites of Savoie, **Crépy, Apremont, Abymes, Chignin** and **Chignin-Bergeron** (the best of the bunch) are usually fresh, light, insignificant creatures that spend only a few seconds on the palate before disappearing. The reds, using grapes like Pinot Noir, Mondeuse and Gamay are all light and dry and only really worth it when you are on the piste. Do yourself a favour: book a skiing holiday, drink and be merry, but don't bring any back home.

SOUTH-WEST FRANCE

Scattered across a vast area of land in the south-west corner of France are some amazingly diverse and exciting wines. To the east and south of Bordeaux, all of the way down to the Pyrenees, there are some superb reds, whites and sweeties worth hunting for, as value for money is built in to these little-known wines. **Bergerac** makes Bordeaux-style reds and whites using the same grape varieties, and often outclasses many of Bordeaux's cheaper wines. Châteaux de la Jaubertie, Calabre and La Tour des Gendres, made by Luc de Conti, are the leaders here. **Monbazillac** and **Saussignac** are two best Sauternes-style sweet wine-producing areas within Bergerac. Here, Domaine de l'Ancienne Cure, Château la Borderie and Château Richard make great value wines, which often replace Sauternes at cunning dinner parties without ever being found out. **Cahors**, made from the gutsy red grape Malbec (also known as Auxerrois or Cot), used to be known as 'black wine' on account of its soupy texture and teeth-staining tannins, although nowadays the wines are often softened with a slice of supple Merlot. Châteaux du Cèdre, de la Grezette and Clos Triguedina make terrific Cahors – just make sure you have a steak big enough to cope.

South-west from Cahors towards Spain we come across some of the most amazing of the French Country wines. **Pacherenc du Vic-Bilh**, a white wine made using Gros and Petit Manseng, Arrufiac, Petit Courbu and other varieties is a prettier name for what is, to all intents and purposes, Madiran Blanc. It has lovely crushed white fruit aromas with a very dry finish. The sweet version, a *moelleux* style, can be very exotic; Domaine Berthomieu makes a classic example. The great red wine **Madiran**, made from the Tannat variety, often tempered with a touch of Cabernet Franc, is a chewy monster of a wine. Somewhere between a St-Estèphe and a Gigondas, this wine has not attended finishing school and will certainly not endeavour to be charming in public. The finest brutes come from Châteaux Montus, d'Aydie, Boucassé and Domaine Pichard.

The next region we come across is **Jurançon** where Clos Lapeyre, Domaine Cauhapé, Clos Uroulat and Domaine Bellegarde all make stunning dry (*sec*) and sweet (*moelleux*) wines from the Petit and Gros Manseng grapes.

Haunting flavours of pineapple, spice and honey make these wines nearly as sought-after as Viogniers. They are immensely fashionable aperitif or pudding wines for those in the know.

Gros Manseng tends to make the dry wines whereas Petit Manseng, late harvested and partially dried on the vine, makes the sweet ones that can rival the greatest sweet wines in the world, when on form.

LANGUEDOC-ROUSSILLON

The vineyards of the Languedoc-Roussillon form an enormous continuous crescent shape on France's Mediterranean coast. With the bookends of the Pyrenees on the south-west side and the mouth of the river Rhône on the north-east, this collection of vineyards is one of the largest in the world. For most of its two-thousand-year vine-growing history, this part of France has underperformed shockingly. It took the New World's assault on the global wine market in the late eighties to kick-start it into action. We now have some epic wines filtering out of this huge mass of villages and towns, helped in no small part by New World wine-makers themselves, often on work experience tours of the globe.

The two main types of wine found down here are spicy Rhône-style reds, to give Châteauneuf-du-Pape a rest, and sweet and fortified wines for after-dinner enjoyment. Here is a list of the best areas and the wizards behind their success. Remember that that these wines are startlingly good value, so look here for everyday drinking favourites.

Corbières can thank Château de Lastours for its reappearance on wine shop shelves. Along with **Fitou**, these two ACs make chunky Carignan-heavy reds that are designed for short-term gratification. Other good estates here are Château Le Palais, Château Etang des Colombes and Château Vaugélas, all in Corbières; and Domaine des Gautier in Fitou.

Minervois is home to some excellent reds but very few whites at all. Châteaux de Gourgazaud, d'Oupia and Fabas (in particular the Cuvée Alexandre, made from loads of old vine Carignan) will warm you up on a winter's day.

The Languedoc is a vast area including two prime villages, **St-Chinian** and **Faugères**, who were both awarded their AC status in 1982. Again, Rhône grapes are used for these meaty reds. Star estates in the Languedoc include Gilbert Alquier and Château des Estanilles in Faugères; Domaine de Coujan in St-Chinian; Mas de Daumas Gassac and La Granges des Pères in the **l'Hérault** region; Mas Jullien,

Abbaye de Valmagne, Château La Sauvagéonne and Mas Champart in the Coteaux du Languedoc; and Mas Brugière, Lascours and Domaine de l'Hortus coming from the famous area of Pic St-Loup. Châteaux Grand-Cassagne, Belle-Coste and de Campuget in the **Costières de Nîmes** are making stunning wines, of which the rosés represent good value and can even out-perform Tavel.

The best estates in the Côtes de Roussillon are Mas de la Garrigues owned by Marcel Vila in St-Esteve, and Château de Jau. In **Collioure**, a small appellation just south of the Côtes de Roussillon, some Mourvèdre and Grenache heavy southern Rhône blends are made. Domaine de Mas Blanc, Château de Jau and Mas Amiel make stunning reds here as well as some incredible Vin Doux Naturel red wines called **Banyuls** and **Maury**. A good substitute for port, these wines are Grenache-dominant and can be chilled – delicious with chocolate puddings. Other sweet wines from this region are **Muscat de Rivesaltes, Muscat de Lunel** and **Muscat de Frontignan**, in that order of preference. These wines are fruity and innocent, and often smell a little too bubble-bathy for my liking. Other Vin de Pays estates to track down are Chemin de Bassac, Domaine d'Aupilhac, Domaine Capion and Domaine de Baruel from the Cévennes.

PROVENCE

Situated on the eastern side of the Rhône delta, running all the way up the Italian border, this is another great undiscovered region full of sumptuous wines. Sad to think that most of the loaded luvvies who spend their holidays gambling and attending film premières down here probably drink claret and Burgundy when there are so many great wines nearer to hand.

Bandol, made predominantly from Mourvèdre, with Grenache and Cinsault included, is the noblest red wine of the region. These wines have spicy, plummy, chocolatey fruit and drink well from five to ten years old. The best estates are Pradeaux (Vieilles Vignes), Mas de la Bégude, Domaine Tempier (Cuvées La Tourtine, La Migoua, Cuvée Spéciale and Cabasseau), Domaine de Pibarnon and Mas de la Rouvière. These estates have all made wines that have blown me away. In fact, I would claim that Tempier is one of the greatest wines on the entire planet.

Bellet is a tiny appellation behind Nice, where a few estates like Château de

Crémat and Domaine de la Source make unusual and intriguing wines. Whites are often made from the Rolle grape, rosés from Braquet and the reds from Fuella: weird and wonderful is the order of the day! A little expensive as production is minuscule, it is worth tracking one down if only to cross it off your list.

Palette is a twenty-hectare appellation, of which fifteen hectares are owned by Château Simone. Grenache, Cinsault and Mourvèdre are used in their red (so far so good), but so are grapes like Manosquan(!), Castet(!!) and Branforquas(!!!), according to owner René Rougier. These reds age like clockwork, but are a bit on the dear side. His white sticks to well-trodden varieties like Ugni Blanc, Clairette, Grenache Blanc and Muscat.

The pretty fishing village of **Cassis** is our next stop where for once the reds take a back seat and the whites, made from Ugni Blanc, Clairette and Bourbelenc, take over. These wines have a liquorice, herb and spice character under the honeyed fruit that is very attractive. The nicest wines are from Clos Ste-Madeleine.

The **Coteaux d'Aix-en-Provence** is a huge area where one man has captured the palates of the entire wine-loving world. In Les Baux, Eloi Dürrbach from Domaine de Trévallon has planted Cabernet Sauvignon and Syrah in the most barren, rocky terrain, and over the last few decades has made stunning red wine. Breaking the AC laws by planting Cabernet Sauvignon (and presumably upsetting neighbours with his magnificent creations), he has been forced to label his wines Vin de Table! I have tasted every wine that this estate has ever made and this is one of the very few occasions when I can wholeheartedly say that the entire range is incredible, capturing explosive black fruit flavours with a Provençal bouquet of rosemary, thyme and dried herbs. Other estates making fine wines from Aix are Château Vignelaure, Château des Gavelles, Terres Blanches and Mas de Gourgonnier.

The famous rosés from this part of France come from the **Côtes de Provence** area. Carignan is the main red grape with Cinsault, Grenache and Mourvèdre again filling in the gaps. I have never really been taken by Domaine Ott, the most expensive and well-known of the wineries in this region, but Domaine de Rimauresq, Domaine Gavoty, Domaine de St-Baillon and Domaine Richeaume are all my pick of the crop.

CHAPTER 7

ITALY

With over a thousand grape varieties, an appalling, meaningless classification system, gallons of poor wine to avoid, but hundreds of awesome wines to find, Italy ought to be a nightmare chapter destined to be skipped over. But this country produces a quarter of the world's wine, and it's worth sorting out the good from the bad. I have divided the country into five sections detailing the best estates, avoiding the Fiat 126s and concentrating on the Ferrari Maranellos.

THE NORTH-WEST

Piedmont (or Piemonte) is the most important region in this corner of Italy. South-east of Turin, near Alba, the noble red wine **Barolo** is made from the Nebbiolo grape variety. This tremendously powerful, shudderingly tannic creature must be carefully chosen. Poor Barolo is lean, stewed and hollow; great Barolos last for decades and pack so much black cherry, leather and tobacco fruit into the bottle you might think it has a black hole. **Barbaresco** is made in a similar way to Barolo but is usually lighter and less tannic. **Spanna** and **Gattinara** are two other strangely disappointing wines made from Nebbiolo that are rarely spotted outside Italy. All wines made from Nebbiolo have an in-built tannic and acidic factor, and should also be very rich in fruit. There is no optimum time to drink these wines, as with a carefully chosen menu they can be enjoyable after only five years of life. But should you get the opportunity to taste an old one, then aim for a twenty-year-old – just don't expect the tannins to be soft! Also in Piemonte, the red **Barbera** grape is vinified by most estates and can result in plummy, blackcurrant fruit with much lower tannin levels than Barolo. **Dolcetto** is another red variety that has a peculiar scent of rubber and blackberries; drunk cool, it makes a grown-up equivalent to Cru Beaujolais. The last red grape to watch out for is the red cherry-scented Freisa. Made by a good producer, this grape can be invigorating and rewarding.

There are four main white wines of the region: **Arneis**, a rich-flavoured, zesty wine with a unique scent and fine length; **Gavi**, made from the Cortese grape, a restaurant favourite on account of its fine acidity and honeyed, citrus palate; **Erbaluce di Caluso**, a beautiful wine made from the grape of the same name, the finest example of which comes from Orsolani; and Moscato, the grape used to make the refreshing sparkling Moscato d'Asti and **Asti** (Spumante). All of the whites should be drunk as young as possible.

Favourite producers of Piedmontese reds: Elio Altare, Bruno Ceretto, Michele Chiarlo, Domenico Clerico, Aldo Conterno, Giacomo Conterno, Angelo Gaja, Elio Grasso, Giuseppe Mascarello, Luciano Sandrone, Paolo Scavino and Roberto Voerzio.
Favourite producers of Moscato: Fontanafredda and La Spinetta.
Favourite producers of Gavi: Nicola Bergaglio (La Minaia), La Chiara and La Giustiniana, La Scolca.
Favourite producers of Arneis: Marcello Ceretto and Carlo Deltetto.

There are three more regions in north-west Italy. **Lombardy (Lombardia)**, north-east of Piemonte, around Milan, has an interesting red wine called **Franciacorta**, the best example of which comes from Ca' del Bosco. The finest white is a wine called **Lugana,** made on the shores of Lake Garda from the Trebbiano variety, the best version of which is Brolettino by Ca' dei Frati. Forget the wines in the other two areas: the best thing to do in the **Valle d'Aosta** is ski and in **Liguria** is sunbathe.

NORTH-EAST

There are some amazing wines made in the Tyrolian third of north-east Italy at the foot of the Dolomites. In **Trentino-Alto Adige**, which stretches north-south between Bolzano and Verona, most of the vines are planted on mountainsides and produce some of the purest single varietal wines in the world. White grapes include Chardonnay, Pinot Grigio, Pinot Bianco, Traminer (Gewürztraminer), Sylvaner, Muscat, Riesling Renano, Sauvignon Blanc and many other Italian varieties like Nosiola, and Goldmuskateller and Rosenmuskateller which make extraordinary sweet wines. Just take your pick and follow a good producer. It is the same with the reds – Cabernet Sauvignon, Cabernet Franc, Merlot, Pinot Nero (Noir), and three stunning indigenous varieties: Lagrein, Teroldego and Marzemino. Most styles drink well young. There is no doubt that Trentino-Alto Adige is in a period of enormous expansion and wine-makers are brimming with self-confidence. Watch out for this region, as the wines are becoming world-class.

Favourite producers in Trentino: Endrizzi (Teroldego Rotaliano), Grigoletti (Marzemino), The Wine Institute of San Michele, Vigneto Dalzocchio (run by the dynamic Dr. Elisabetta Dalzocchio who makes a sensational Pinot Noir), Letrari, Pojer & Sandri, Elisabetta Foradori, Tenuta San Leonardo, Conti Bossi Fedrigotti (incredible Fojaneghe Bianco made from Chardonnay and Traminer) and the sublime sparkling wines from Ferrari (particularly the Giulio Riserva).

Favourite producers in the Alto Adige: San Michele Appiano, Santa Maddalena, Hofstätter, Franz Haas and Alois Lageder.

VENETO

Around the towns of Padova, Vicenza and Venice, this region is famous for two wines that have actually had pretty grubby reputations in the past. **Soave** and **Valpolicella** are responsible for upsetting more palates than Liebfraumilch ever has. But Soave at its best is oily, nutty and honeyed, with a long finish and is just about the most scrumptious glass of chilled white wine I could hope for on a picnic. These days a handful of committed wine-makers have dragged this wine, made from the dull Garganega and Trebbiano varieties, up to speed. Valpolicella is made from Corvina, Rondinella and Molinara, and ranges from a fresh Beaujolais-style glugger to a very impressive beast indeed. There are two unusual styles of Valpolicella made, **Recioto della Valpolicella** and **Amarone della Valpolicella**. The Recioto style has a sweet taste and the Amarone style has a very rich, but dry flavour. This results from semi-drying the grapes (passito) until the water evaporates and the sugar content is raised, then fermenting the must until dry for Amarone or leaving some residual sugar for Recioto. Soave is also made in a Recioto style, resulting in a delicious sweet wine. The Lake Garda's **Bianco di Custoza** (white) and **Bardolino** (red) use exactly the same grape varieties as Soave and Valpolicella, but in both cases are much lighter and less memorable than our two comeback kids. (Avoid the rosé form of Bardolino called Chiaretto.) A very dry sparkling wine is made in Veneto from the Prosecco variety, called **Prosecco di Valdobbiadene**. The best producer of this summer fizz is Ruggeri, with their Santo Stefano. Maculan, based in **Breganze**, makes a sweet wine from semi-dried Vespaiola grapes called Torcolato, a type of Recioto aged in oak barrels. They also make a botrytised version called Acininobili. All but the top Valpolicellas and sweet wines drink beautifully young. Amarones can last for up to twenty years.

Favourite Soave producers: Roberto Anselmi (try his Recioto, I Capitelli), Gini (single-vineyard Soave, Frosca) and Leonildo Pieropan (the king: try La Rocca, Vigneto Calvarino and Recioto Le Colombare).

Favourite Valpolicella producers: Allegrini (his La Grola and Palazzo della Torre are amazing, as is his Amarone and his La Poja – 100% Corvina), Dal Forno (Amarone) and Giuseppe Quintarelli (barking mad styles of Amarone).

FRIULI-VENEZIA GIULIA

On the far north-eastern Italian border, white wines are the order of the day. Wine-makers again favour the single varietal styles, making it easy to select varieties that you like. The Colli Orientali del Friuli and the Collio Goriziano (shortened to Collio) are the finest vineyard areas. Look out for Ribolla Gialla, a lemony, floral variety that makes crisp, mouth-tingling wines; Tocai Friulano, a broad-flavoured interesting variety that can be fairly weighty; Malvasia, that makes weird-scented, mineral and honeyed whites and Picolit, which makes over-priced sweeties. All of the old favourites are planted as well, with Pinot Grigio, Pinot Bianco and Chardonnay producing the best wines. Very few producers use oak barrels as the style of whites from Friuli is one of freshness, youth and up-front fruit flavours. I have rarely been enamoured with the reds from this region as they tend to taste a little green, lack weight and have intrusive acidity.

Favourite producers: Miani, Ronco del Gnemiz, Sergio & Mauro Drius, Vinnaioli Jermann (whose famous white Vintage Tunina is a complex blend of Chardonnay, Sauvignon, Ribolla Gialla, Malvasia and Picolit), Mario Schiopetto and Vittorio & Giovanni Puiatti (whose motto is, bizarrely, 'Save a tree, drink Puiatti') in particular their Archètipi range).

CENTRAL EAST

There are four wine regions in this long, thin stretch of vineyards on Italy's eastern Mediterranean coastline. Situated between the Apennines and the Adriatic coast, listed from north to south, the first is **Emilia-Romagna** whose infamous stars are **Lambrusco** and the spectacularly over-rated white, **Albana di Romagna**. My favourite wine of the area is made from a clone of the Chianti Sangiovese grape, known as **Sangiovese di Romagna** – try one made by producer Fattoria Zerbina.

The next region is **Marches (Marche)** where **Verdicchio dei Castelli di Jesi** is made – Italy's answer to Muscadet; and in the right hands, it can be refreshing and equally as delicious with seafood. The best producers are Coroncino, Brunori and Umani Ronchi. The finest red wine of the area is **Rosso Conero**, made from the Montepulciano grape variety. Again, Umani Ronchi lead the pack: their San Lorenzo is the finest and best-value version. They even make a super cuvée called Cùmaro which, despite being more expensive, is undoubtedly the greatest red of the region and really shows the potential of the Marche.

Abruzzi (Abruzzo) is the next region heading south, where only two decent wines are made: **Montepulciano d'Abruzzo** (red) and **Trebbiano d'Abruzzo** (white). Almost all of these wines fall into ordinary-at-home, fun-on-holiday category, except for Valentini's Trebbiano which has so much depth and richness it bears no resemblance to any other Trebbiano I have ever tried. No surprise that wine-maker Edoardo Valentini is known as the 'Lord of the Vines'. There are two Montepulciano producers that you could search out, Monti and Cornacchia, whose wines will show you what this grape can do in the right hands.

Molise is the last of the regions in this sweep down the coast, where only one solitary wine is worth a try, from an area on the coast called Campomarino: a Rosso from Di Majo Norante's Montepulciano grape variety.

CENTRAL WEST

Tuscany (Toscana)
Family estates here have been making wine for centuries: Ricasoli started in 1141, Antinori and Frescobaldi in the 1300s. This historic land is Sangiovese country and the home to a large number of Italy's best red wines. There are a few grand whites made in these regions which tend to be light and fresh styles, with one exception: the decadently sweet Vin Santo, of which more later.

Tuscany is home to an impressive roll-call of red wines like **Chianti, Brunello** di Montalcino, Carmignano and Vino Nobile di Montepulciano. Brunello is a Sangiovese clone, as is Prugnolo, the predominant red grape in Vino Nobile; so Sangiovese has very much a controlling interest here. In a good vintage Sangiovese has a richness and plummy character with fresh herb and tobacco on the nose. Almost always a food wine, Chianti and its Sangiovese partners can happily live for ten years, with the best Vino Nobiles and Brunellos continuing for a further ten. With Brunello, watch out for **Rosso di Montalcino**, the earlier-drinking, earlier-released wine that can often be superb. One last point concerning these reds: the best estates are often very expensive, and Riserva cuvées can be very dear. With Chianti, the best estates' normale (non-Riserva) wines will be stunning and often better than a poor estate's top-of-the-range wine.

Vernaccia di San Gimignano made from the white Vernaccia grape is the finest of the local white wines. Usually possessing a nuttiness and floral character with trademark Italian zippy acidity, these wines complement seafood and salads, as well as Parmesan and Pecorino. Trebbiano is the most widely planted white grape, making fairly ordinary wines; although Pomino from Frescobaldi, a blend of Trebbiano, Pinot Bianco and Chardonnay, can be well made.

Vin Santo is the heavenly pudding wine made from drying Trebbiano and Malvasia grapes and then crushing and fermenting the sugar-laden raisins, then ageing the wine in small barrels. The finished wine is a cross between a Fino sherry on the nose and Sauternes on the palate.

Now we are in Tuscany, it is time to introduce you to the ugly topic of the Italian wine laws. Trying to copy the success of the French AC system, the Italians introduced a DOC (*Denominazione di Origine Controllata*) equivalent to AC, and DOCG (*Denominazione di Origine Controllata e Garantita*) further guaranteeing the quality of specific 'controlled' élite regions. Zones were mapped out, maximum yields calculated, vinification methods outlined and vine varieties decided upon. But whoever thought this up was obviously receiving a few free *calzones* down at the local pizzeria and possibly a villa on Capri. DOCs were handed out like flyers and regulations not only acted as strait-jackets stifling innovation, but also encouraged sky-high yields, resulting in a dilution in the overall quality of many wines. Regional boundaries were relaxed, totally blurring localised geographical differentiation and missing the point of the French concept of *terroir*, so well protected by their AC system.

The first five DOCGs were given to Barolo, Barbaresco, Chianti, Brunello di Montalcino and Vino Nobile di Montepulciano. This had a beneficial effect on these regions by reviewing yields and wine-making practices. Then the dodgy decision to award a DOCG to the previously mentioned Albana di Romagna was put down to a political move that did nothing to convince sceptics of the validity of this classification. Eight more DOCGs have been handed out since, mostly to worthy regions.

However, another big problem existed which affected some of the best wines in Italy. *Vino da Tavola* (table wine) was the classification awarded to wines using any grapes outside DOC law. Thus Tignanello, the very first 'Super-Tuscan', fetching astronomical prices for an Italian red wine and upsetting traditionalists, was lumped in with rocket fuel as far as the authorities were concerned. Why? It was made using some Cabernet Sauvignon and small French *barriques* instead of large Italian *botti* (barrels). The often lean Sangiovese was boosted with this fully ripe blackcurrant-flavoured grape and created some monumental wines. Ornellaia, Sassicaia, Solaia and countless others followed, boosting the region like never before. The authorities created a new level – IGT – to give these extraordinary Vino da Tavolas some credibility. Not that they needed it, as they already had the kudos. *Indicazione Geografica Tipica* may or may not succeed as a style but at least it attempts to acknowledge the efforts of thirty years of hard work and passion spent breaking the wine laws.

As always, in order not to get tripped up by unscrupulous wines with famous names, follow this guide to the best estates.

Favourite producers of Chianti: P. Antinori, Berardenga, Carobbio, Felsina, Fontodi, Isole e Olena, Querciabella and Selvapiana.

Favourite producers of Brunello di Montalcino: Altesino, Argiano, Case Basse, Costanti, La Gerla and Lisini.

Favourite producers of Vino Nobile di Montepulciano: Dei, Il Macchione and Poliziano.

Favourite producers of Carmignano: Ambra and Ville di Capezzana.

Favourite producers of Super-Tuscans: Altesino (Palazzo Altesi), L. Antinori (Masseto and Ornellaia), P. Antinori (Solaia and Tignanello), Argiano (Solengo), Castello dei Rampolla (Sammarco), Falchini (Campora), Felsina Berardenga (Fontalloro), Fontodi (Flaccianello della Pieve), Isole e Olena (Cepparello), Le Macchiole (Paleo Rosso), Marchesi Incisa della Rochetta (Sassicaia), Poggio Scalette (Il Carbonaione), Le

Pupille (Saffreddi), Tenuta del Terricio (Lupicaia and Tassinaia), and Villa di Capezzana (Ghiaie della Furba).

Favourite producers of Vernaccia di San Gimignano: Falchini, Montenidoli, Pietraserena and Teruzzi & Puthod.

Favourite producers of Vin Santo: Isole e Olena and Selvapiana.

UMBRIA

After Tuscany's vast range of wines, you might think Umbria seems a bit dull, and you'd be right. **Orvieto** is the lone white of interest and the biggest maker of it is Luigi Bigi. Despite Orvieto being light, dry and rarely inspiring, there is one white wine worth a go. Made on Antinori's estate at Castello della Sala, a fabulous white called Cervaro della Sala from Chardonnay and the local Grechetto is by far the most captivating white of the region (no surprise that under Italy's shocking wine laws it is classed as a Vino da Tavola!). The lone red wine holding fort in Umbria is called Rubesco, made by Lungarotti. The best version of this wine, a Sangiovese blended with the ancient Tuscan grape Canaiolo, is the Riserva called Monticchio. It attracted such good press that the local region of **Torgiano** was raised from DOC to DOCG on the back of this wine alone.

LATIUM (LAZIO)

On south to Rome and Latium, where we find the ridiculously named **Est! Est!! Est!!!**, an insipid white wine made from Trebbiano and Malvasia. Another wine that has been ridiculed in the past is **Frascati**. There is no doubt that this variable wine can be dry, lean and tasteless, but new-style Frascati is around the corner. Spearheaded by Castel De Paolis, the dull Malvasia and Trebbiano grapes have been introduced to small percentages of Viognier which has resulted in some of the finest white Italian wines I have ever tasted. One of the top cuvées, Vigna Adriana, is nothing short of sensational. Classic Frascati estates I recommend are Villa Simone and Fontana Candida's Santa Teresa.

THE SOUTH

Apulia (Puglia), Campania, Basilicata and Calabria

There are very few wines at the boot end of Italy worth sniffing out. The baking hot temperatures and lack of rain make light whites impossible to produce and although there are a handful of funky reds, there is nothing so cheap or so unmissable as to divert you away from the regions already mentioned. I will list my best selection of wines in the hope that you use them for medicinal purposes only.

whites: Fiano di Avellino from Feudi di San Gregorio or Mastroberardino in Campania; Greco di Tufo from Feudi di San Gregorio in Campania.

reds: Copertino Rosso from Masseria Monaci in Apulia; Salice Salentino Riserva, Brindisi Rosso Patriglione and Notarparano from Cosimo Taurino in Apulia; Salice Salentino, Aleatico and Cappello di Prete from Francesco Candido in Apulia; Montevetrano from Silvio Imparato's estate Montevetrano in Campania; Aglianico del Vulture from Paternoster in Basilicata; Aglianico del Vulture and Canneto from Fratelli D'Angelo in Basilicata; Cirò, Duca San Felice and Gravello from Librandi in Calabria.

THE ISLANDS

Sicily (Sicilia) and Sardinia (Sardegna)

Sicily, home to the unfashionable fortified wine Marsala, is in a current stage of enormous expansion. Flashy new estates are popping up, using consultant wine-makers and making impressive wines, and two names to follow closely are Planeta and Regaleali. If you want to taste a slice of history, you will find it in the shape of De Bartoli's Bukkaram, a fortified *passito* Moscato made with grapes from the volcanic island of Pantelleria. It tastes like a wicked, boozy marmalade.

Sardinia's wine trade is also expanding at a rate of knots. Rhône varieties are very important here. The red Cannonau variety (Grenache) is transformed by Sella e Mosca into a spicy heavyweight beast. Carignan, known as Carignano, is quite stunning in Santadi's Carignano del Sulcis. They also make Rocca Rubia, a Riserva version of the Carignano del Sulcis and a Vino da Tavola, Terre Brune.

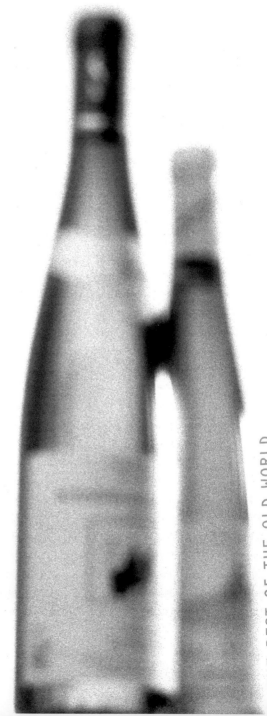

CHAPTER 8

GERMANY

The two driving forces behind German wines are skill and passion. You certainly need both in a northern European country where wine-making is a serious business and viticulture a constant challenge as the elements are against you (and, come to mention it, so is most of the wine trade).

But the Germans love a challenge and, like the Italians, have rather a lot of work to do to convince the wine-buying public that their wines are back on form.

Germany has suffered from a similar problem to the DOC fiasco in Italy, when bulk-blended Liebfraumilch (Black Tower and the like) flooded the market, forcing prices and expectations to spiral down. These wines were classified as QbAs but bore no resemblance to any other wines of this quality level, and in fact were often nowhere near as tasty as many Tafelweins. If you have ever tasted one of these wines (and judging by the millions of cases sold every year you probably have) then forget it: wipe it from your taste memory banks. Great wines have always been made in Germany; Liebfraumilch was just an awful experiment that blew up in their faces.

Firstly, the classification system. The Germans grade their wines by the most difficult criteria, of course: the natural sugar levels in the grapes at harvest (which actually makes sense in chilly Germany). The naturally sweeter the wine, the finer the grade. This may seem excruciatingly difficult, but German wine-makers are so brilliant at selecting varieties, ripening grapes and capturing the perfect balance of fruit and acidity that these on-the-surface delicate white wines can outlive the biggest, butchest Chardonnays by a decade.

In ascending level of importance, the grades are Tafelwein (Table wine) Landwein (equivalent of French Vin de Pays), QbA, then QmP, which includes Kabinett, Spätlese, Auslese, Beerenauslese and Trockenbeerenauslese. In addition to this, there are Trockens (dry wines), Halbtrockens (half-dry or fruitier wines) and Eisweins (made when the grapes freeze on the vine). Grapes used to make these wines are as follows, in order of importance: Riesling, Müller-Thurgau, Scheurebe, Gewürztraminer, Rülander (Pinot Gris), Sylvaner and a lone red Spätburgunder

(Pinot Noir). Refer to the grape variety section (see page 5) and the glossary (see page 213) for more details on grapes and classification terms.

Finally, the wine label on a German bottle will tell you a number of things: the vintage (e.g. 1997); a 'Grosslage' or collective site area (e.g. Kiedricher – from the village of Kiedrich); an 'Einzellage' or single-vineyard name (e.g. Gräfenberg); the grape variety (e.g. Riesling); the quality level (e.g. QmP plus which QmP level – e.g. Kabinett); the region (e.g. Rheingau) and the producer (e.g. Weingut Schloss Groenesteyn). This wine would be listed in a wine list as 1997 Kiedricher Gräfenberg, Riesling Kabinett, Rhiengau, Schloss Groenesteyn.

THE BEST REGIONS

The **Mosel** is full of steep slate slopes running down to the river itself, where Riesling makes some of its greatest wines. Characterised by a finesse and elegance, Mosel Rieslings are racy, refreshing and ripe. The upper reaches of the Mosel is where the **Saar** tributary flows in from the south. Here, where the climate is cooler, Riesling makes tighter, dryer styles of wine. The **Ruwer** (another tributary of the Mosel) again grows Riesling, with remarkable ageing potential. The **Rheingau** is regarded as one of the finest regions in the entire German wine-making scene, producing rich wines with less biting acidity than the Mosel. The **Rheinhessen** is Müller-Thurgau, Scheurebe and Sylvaner country; this is where a lot of Liebfraumilch, Blue Nun and Niersteiner Gutes Domtal comes from. The **Rheinpfalz** is the warmest district where the meatiest whites come from, made from Riesling, Müller-Thurgau, Rülander and Scheurebe. The **Nahe** region makes distinctively perfumed, smooth wines with some weight. **Franken** is where the dumpy bottles come from that won't fit into bottle banks!

Favourite producers: J.B. Becker, Dr. Bürklin-Wolf, J.J. Cristoffel, Fritz Haag, Weingut Kerpen, von Kesselstatt, Koehler-Ruprecht, Franz Künstler, H. & R. Lingenfelder, Dr. Loosen, J.J. Prüm, Willi Schaefer, von Schubert-Maximin Grünhaus, Selbach-Oster and Dr. H. Thanisch.

SPAIN

A huge wine-producing country with relatively few world-class wines is the honest truth regarding the Spanish wine industry. But they are playing catch-up at a blistering pace. There is a new wave of stainless steel tanks, clean, fresh whites and under-oaked as opposed to over-oaked reds. This is welcome news as in the early seventies, ninety-five per cent of Spanish wine left Spain in a tanker! While the rest of the world embraced modernisation and deft vinification techniques, Spain just carried on using dirty old barrels. Oxidised whites and stewed reds are at last becoming a thing of the past, and indigenous Spanish grape varieties are being allowed to flex their muscles and show their talents to the rest of the world. OK, some of them are dull, like the white Airen which covers nearly a third of the country's vineyards; but the Albariño is a stunning white grape destined to feature on connoisseurs' tables around the world in the not too distant future. Spain is a great value country, well worth considering when classic French and Italian wines are out of reach.

But what prompted this change and woke the industry up? One man, Miguel Torres, who had the audacity to enter a Catalonian Cabernet Sauvignon – 1970 Torres Gran Coronas Black Label – in the Cabernet class of the 1979 Gault-Millau 'Wine Olympics'. He walked off with the gold medal, leaving Châteaux Latour, Pichon-Lalande and La Mission Haut-Brion with their not-inconsiderable noses out of joint.

Red grapes found in Spain include Garnacha Tinta (Grenache), which behaves much the same as it does in France, boosting blends; although in Priorato it really sings. Tempranillo, also known as Ull de Llebre, Tinto Fino and Cencibel, is the king of Rioja and Navarra, as well as being Cabernet's partner in the terrific wines of Ribera del Duero. Cariñena (Carignan) is planted extensively and used for lower quality reds, whereas Cabernet Sauvignon flourishes, lending class and complexity to indigenous varieties. Monastrell is another useful red grape that is generally tucked away in blends.

Whites are less exalted save for the aforementioned captivating Albariño, the world-famous Chardonnay, the world infamous Viura, the fizzy wine twins Xarel-lo and Parellada, and the underrated Malvasia.

Spanish wine laws are relatively straightforward, but do not expect to see many of the first three examples unless you are on holiday. *Vino de Mesa* is a blended table wine from unclassified vineyards; *Vino Comarcal* is a regional table wine; *Vino de la Tierra* is the equivalent to French Vin de Pays; DO, or *Denominación de Origen*, is the equivalent to French Appellation Contrôlée; DOC, or *Denominación de Origen Calificada*, is the highest grade. The equivalent to Italy's DOCG, Rioja was Spain's first region to qualify in 1991.

The styles are all concerned with oak ageing. *Crianza* is a term for a wine that has been aged for two years before release, of which a minimum of one year is spent in a barrel; *Reserva* is used for a wine that has been aged for three years before release, of which a minimum of one year is spent in a barrel; *Gran Reserva* describes a wine that has been aged for five years before release, of which a minimum of two years is spent in a barrel.

The Regions

RIOJA AND NAVARRA

Rioja is Spain's most famous red wine, with sweet vanilla oak, plummy fruit and a mellow red cherry palate. It is still one of the best-value mature red wines available. Rioja far outshines Navarra in terms of great wines, although the styles of production are the same. Usually over seventy per cent of a red Rioja is made from Tempranillo, with Garnacha, Graciano and Mazuelo providing the balance. Viura is the dominant white grape in Rioja Blanco, with Malvasia making up the numbers. Rioja is split into three areas, the best two being the Rioja Alta and Alavesa, with the Baja area just a bit too hot to produce grapes with fine acidity.

Navarra, which overlaps the Rioja Baja, tends to make wines with less complexity and longevity; but if you want round, tangy, plummy reds with a touch of liquorice and oak on the nose, then you are in the right place. Just watch out for old-fashioned whites as they are unbelievably oaky and not to everyone's taste.

Favourite producers of Rioja and Navarra: CVNE (Viña Real, Imperial and Contino), R. López De Heredia (Viña Tondonia), Marqués de Murrieta (Reserva Especial), Muga

(Prado Enea only), Navajas, Ochoa (Navarra), Principe de Viana (Navarra), Remelluri and La Rioja Alta (Reserva 904).

CATALONIA

The most famous style of wine from this north-eastern Spanish region near the city of Barcelona is Cava, Spain's answer to champagne. Made from rather dull grape varieties, Xarel-lo, Parellada and Macabéo (the local name for Viura), these wines are made in the traditional method and if needed, are often boosted with Chardonnay. I have not really come to terms with these wines, preferring to look to the Loire for cheaper fizz, but some producers make nice enough wines. **Penedès** is the most important region in Catalonia where Cava is made. It also happens to be Torres's base! The undisputed leader of the pack, the Torres range of wines is stunning, from Esmeralda and Viña Sol up to Spain's best Chardonnay Milmanda, as well as the entire red portfolio. The only other name to look out for here is Jean León. Inland, to the south-west of Penedès, is the parched, mountainous region of **Priorato**. Here, Garnacha and Cariñena are used to fashion thunderous reds like the wines of Clos de l'Obac, Clos Mogador by René Barbier and Scala Dei. Keep this region to yourself as I predict some awesome wines will be made here at reasonable prices. A short distance south-east of Priorato is the region of **Terra Alta**, where one property called Bàrbara Forés, is making incredible reds. (Once again, do not shout about it as I am keeping this one to myself.)

Other Spanish regions of note are the Rias Baixas in **Galicia**, in the far north-west corner of Spain. Here the Albariño variety is carefully being made into Spain's answer to Viognier. The estates to follow are Pazo de Barrantes, associated to Marqués de Murrieta in Rioja; and Lagar de Cervera.

South of Madrid, **La Mancha**, in the centre of Spain, is the biggest source of bulk red and white wine. This is where Don Quixote used to roam, and he would be pleased with the wine-making efforts of Almansa and Hermanos Morales as well as Señorio de Los Llanos from the finest sub-region of La Mancha, **Valdepeñas**.

Saving the best till last, **Ribera del Duero** is the jewel in the crown of Spanish red wine production. This is where the most expensive red wine of Spain is made,

Vega Sicilia's Unico Reserva. Cabernet Sauvignon and Merlot have found their way into the vineyards here and the result, combined with Tempranillo, known locally as Tinto Fino, are spectacular and incredibly long-lived. The best producers of Ribera del Duero (apart from Vega Sicilia) are Cillar de Cilos and Pesquera. If you find these wines far too dear to buy – and they cost a fortune – then Vega Sicilia make a more forward style called Alion, and Pesquera make Condado de Haza. Luckily hardly anyone has come across Cillar de Cilos yet.

SHERRY

Sadly, sherry is a deeply unfashionable drink that really doesn't deserve to be. Perhaps this time it is the fault of the British, whose taste for cream sherries has taken our eye off the real, quality styles made in Jerez de la Frontera, inland of Cádiz in southern Spain. Sherry is a wine made principally from the Palomino grape variety. Pedro Ximénez (PX) is another variety that is used to sweeten sherry, and also makes an intense pudding wine in its own right.

To make sherry, the Palomino grapes are harvested and then de-stalked and pressed. The must is then acidified with the addition of 'yeso' (gypsum) or tartaric acid.

Fermentation takes place to total dryness in oak barrels or stainless steel tanks. The bone-dry white wine is then put into casks to mature, leaving an air space at the top. It is now that the magical yeast-strain known as flor may or may not appear in the maturing sherry casks.

Flor, or *Saccharomyces beticus*, is a filmy scum that forms on top of the wine, feeding off the oxygen in the butt (or barrel) and the alcohol in the wine. Butts that don't attract flor are fortified immediately. These casks have now had their fate decided and are fortified with a grape spirit called *aguardente*, destined to be Olorosos. Olorosos are fortified to eighteen per cent. Finos (see below for styles) are fortified to alcohol levels of between fifteen to fifteen-and-a-half per cent, as the precious flor is killed above sixteen per cent. Flor-infected casks are tasted and monitored to decide upon which style of sherry the wine will be released as. Once the style has been established, the wines are put into a fractional-blending system called a *solera*. This ensures a constant taste of each *bodega*'s (producer's) brand of sherry every year, rather like the constancy of non-vintage champagne. A sherry solera is made up of a number of groups of butts known as *criaderas*. Up to one-third of each barrel from the oldest criadera is drawn off for each bottling, the space being filled with a younger wine from the next oldest criadera. This refreshing of the Fino butts keeps the flor alive for anything up to ten years. There can be as few as four or as many as fourteen criaderas in a system, and the bottling and topping up process usually occurs two or three times a year.

So why drink sherry? I believe it is a spectacular aperitif, and a stunning after-dinner tipple. Try a Fino instead of a gin and tonic or glass of champagne before a meal and an old Oloroso with coffee after. Stick to the top bodegas and avoid cream sherry at all costs. Here below are the different styles available:

Manzanilla is made in Sanlúcar de Barrameda on the coast and is the lightest and driest of the styles. It tends to have a salty tang from the sea air. Drink as soon as the bottle is opened.

Fino is the best-known style and is light, dry, delicate and cleansing. Again, drink as soon as the bottle is opened.

Amontillado is an aged Fino style that loses its flor. It will be at least eight years old with a deeper, amber colour and a tangy, nutty taste. Keep it in the fridge after opening.

Oloroso styles have higher alcohol than Finos and are made from casks that did not attract flor. These wines have raisiny, burnt-toffee flavours with a dry and complex finish, and the alcohol levels can reach twenty-four per cent as evaporation occurs in older butts. Keep them in the fridge after opening.

Palo Cortado is a rare style between Oloroso and Amontillado in taste. Again, keep it in the fridge after opening.

Two miscellaneous wines of note are **Málaga** and **Pedro Ximénez**. These styles are sweet and chocolatey with a nutty, almost liquidised-Christmas-pudding flavour.

Favourite bodegas: González Byass, Lustau and Valdespino.

PORTUGAL

Portugal is home to port and Madeira, two of the most classic and stunning fortified wines in the world. Less distinguished are some of the Portuguese rosés (no, I'm not going to mention the brand), some dry light whites like Vinho Verde and some earthy, tannic, headachy reds. But, like Spain, they are in all-change mode and as every day goes by, cleaner fresher wines are being made.

PORT

Situated in the Douro valley in the north of Portugal, the grapes for port are grown on some of the most spectacular terraces in the wine world. There are over eighty grape varieties that can go into port, but wine-makers usually select from about ten or twenty, the best of which are Touriga Nacional, Tinta Roriz (Tempranillo), Tinta Barroca, Touriga Francesa and Tinta Cão. There are two distinct styles of port: wood- or cask-aged and bottle-aged. Wood-aged ports are generally ready to drink on release, as the wood softens the tannins in the wine over time. Bottle-aged ports have spent a short amount of time in wood but are bottled without filtration or fining and need to age for a long period in the bottle for the same softening of tannins to occur.

In the production of port, the grapes are harvested and instead of being trampled underfoot (that was in the old days) they are crushed, macerated and fermented. After only two or three days fermenting, when a sufficiently high level of alcohol is achieved (about six to eight per cent), about one-fifth of neutral grape spirit, *aguardente*, with a strength of seventy-seven per cent is added to the must. This kills the active yeasts and raises the alcohol to about nineteen per cent, preserving the remaining sugars in the wine. As the fermentation process is relatively short-lived, the maceration process is frenzied, extracting as much colour and tannin as possible – hence the reason for treading in the old days. The wine is matured in oak barrels and assessed to determine what quality level of wine has been made. In the second year after the harvest, and only then, the decision is made as to whether a vintage will be declared or not. Samples will be sent to the Port Wine Institute along with details of quantities of wine made. Only after the nod has been given will the wine be bottled for sale. The wine then waits to be sent away to someone's cellar, only to languish there for a further twenty to fifty years.

There are several styles of port available, as follows:

White port should not be drunk unless you are on holiday. Try as I might, and that is pretty hard, I cannot see the point to this style. It is supposedly a nice aperitif, but you'll never get to the food if you have a few of these.

Ruby is the fruity, raw and most cherry-like of the styles of port. This wine is aged in bulk and is the youngest released style. It is sometimes drunk chilled as an aperitif by the French, or with lemon by the British!

The genuine **Tawny** style, as opposed to just a light, weak port, is aged for extended periods in oak barrels, resulting in the deep red port colour leaching out into the wood and ending up with a tawny hue. Tawny port styles are categorised by age: 10-year-old, 20-year-old, 30-year-old and so on, and can be stunning.

Late-Bottled Vintage, shortened to LBV, is supposedly the best way to enjoy vintage flavours for less money and without having to wait twenty-five years for the wine to age. These wines should be ready to drink upon release, as they spend between four and six years in oak barrels softening the tannins. But I think they rarely manage to harness the full richness of a vintage port.

Single-Quinta wines are usually made in years when a vintage style has not been declared. A single *quinta* is a single estate or vineyard, and connoisseurs who want to enjoy a wine earlier than would be possible for a vintage style favour this type of port. Reputable port houses make this style in a vintage mould and then keep it back for bottle ageing, only releasing the wines when they are ready to drink. The best are Warre's Cavadinha, Dow's Bomfim, Graham's Malvedos and Taylor's Vargellas.

Vintage port, the big daddy, is only made in first-rate vintages, when a port house will declare their intention to do so. Vintage port is only usually made four years out of ten. It is the most expensive style, requiring extended bottle-ageing as the time spent in oak during the production process is relatively short. Most vintage ports should be left for a minimum of fifteen years before drinking, but it is not unusual for them to only start to drink perfectly from thirty to fifty years old. They will throw a sediment and require decanting.

Favourite houses: Taylor, Warre, Fonseca, Dow, Graham, Quinta do Noval and Quinta do Noval Nacional.

MADEIRA

Made on the volcanic island of the same name 600 kilometres west of the Moroccan coast, Madeira is an institution amongst wine drinkers.

> These wines are the longest lived of all. Think nothing of taking a 200-year-old bottle of Malmsey from your cellar and drinking it: it will be fine. Like port and sherry, Madeira rarely seems to be in fashion, but who cares: there are only small amounts made and that leaves all the more for us to enjoy.

In the late 1600s, trading ships on their way to the Far East would stop at Madeira and pick up casks of local wine. In order to help it get to its destination in one piece, the wine was fortified to make it more stable. The onward journey would involve travelling through the tropics, encountering temperatures as high as 45°C. The cargo was heated up during this time and then cooled down as the ships arrived at their destination. Only when the Madeira wine-makers had an opportunity to taste some wine that had been returned unsold did they realise that the flavour was greatly enhanced. They determined that the improvement in flavour had come about not by the rolling and pitching of the ships, but by the heating and cooling process. So a baking process was introduced during the production of Madeira.

Nowadays, cheaper, bulk styles of Madeira are put into the equivalent of a large kettle and heated to high temperatures by means of a coil. The temperature is kept between 40°C and 50°C for three months. Finer styles of Madeira are placed in 600-

litre wooden casks in warm rooms. These rooms are heated to between 30°C and 40°C for six months. The very best Madeiras are produced without artificial heating and are stored in casks in the eaves of the Madeira lodges, naturally heated by the sun. They usually stay like this for twenty years or more before being bottled. These three types of production all use the so-called *estufagem* or heating process. Drier styles are fortified before *estufagem*, sweeter styles after. Then the wines enter a solera system, similar to sherry.

Styles of Madeira include the following (each style is also the name of a grape variety): **Sercial**, which is pale, dry, with a light body and good acidity; **Verdelho**, which is golden-coloured, medium-bodied, tangy and medium dry; **Bual**, a darker-coloured, fuller-bodied, smoky, fairly sweet wine; and **Malmsey**: rich, raisiny, full-bodied and very sweet.

Favourite producers: Cossart Gordon and Henriques & Henriques.

OTHER PORTUGUESE WINES OF NOTE

Made in the Minho region on the coast north of Porto, **Vinho Verde** should be a searingly dry white wine as it is picked early (*Verde* translates as green) to preserve as much acidity as possible. Bring your ladder for harvesting, as the grapes are trained on eight-foot high trellises; the best producer is Palácio da Brejoeira. Good red wines are made in the **Douro** alongside port; try those from producers Quinta de Gaivosa, Quinta do Crasto and Quinta de la Rosa. South of Porto, **Dão** and **Bairrada** are widely thought of as two of Portugal's best red wines, made predominantly from Baga and Touriga Nacional respectively. Caves São João and Luis Pato make the best Bairradas, while Conde de Santar makes a meaty Dão. The single best Portuguese red wine I have ever tasted is a Dão called Quinta dos Roques, who make a straight Touriga Nacional and a Reserva using Touriga Nacional and another obscure variety, Alfrocheiro Preto. Further south, **Bucelas**, a weird white wine in need of major surgery, is worth avoiding until some form of technology helps it out. **Alenquer's** star is Quinta de Pancas whose plantings of Cabernet Sauvignon soften the local red grapes. In **Setúbal** near Lisbon, José-Maria da Fonseca makes reds Periquita, Pasmados and Quinta de Camarate as well as **Moscatel de Setúbal**, a fortified

Muscat with all the charm and poise of a gorilla – people love it. In **Colares**, vineyard workers sport baskets on their heads to prevent the three-metre-deep sandy trenches in which the vines are planted from falling in and suffocating them. These reds last for ages and the central co-operative makes interesting, if unusual wine.

GREAT BRITAIN

In support of our hard-working vineyards, I am writing a short entry for English wine. There are 2500 acres of vines in the UK and we all ought to at least taste one of their wines. With the climate not quite up to Bordeaux standards, it is no surprise that it is hard to get grapes to ripen. But the Germans manage, and so to Germany we have gone in search of early-ripening varieties that can cope with the chilly climes. Huxelrebe, Reichensteiner, Optima, Seyval Blanc, Kerner, Schönburger and Müller-Thurgau are some of the chosen bunch. With skilful viticulture and vinification, Germanic styles of wine can be made and even Sancerre wannabes are produced. Some reds are grown in plastic tunnels, but surely the best style of all is sparkling wine. After all, we have the chalky soils and a Champagne-like climate. The greatest problem is that equipment is expensive, but I think sparkling wine is the way forward for British wine-making – consider how much Cava we wouldn't need to import. Chapel Down in Kent makes a very good traditional method wine that is already captivating consumers. They have even secured a spot in a few supermarkets for other styles as well.

> With something like a hundred and twenty wineries active in England, the least you can do is encourage them by visiting and tasting their wines. You never know what might happen, the way global warming is going.

THE REST OF THE OLD WORLD

The remainder of the Old World covers another twenty or so countries or regions that make wine. Some are amazing, like Austria's dry Rieslings and sweet Beerenauslese and Trockenbeerenauslese wines made by Opitz and Kracher; Hungary's decadent sweet wine Tokaji, a cross between Sauternes and a top flight sherry; and Bulgaria's spicy red grapes Mavrud and Gamza, worth tasting for an often-needed change of flavour. Serge Hochar's fantastic Château Musar, a blend of Cabernet Sauvignon, Syrah and Cinsault from the Bekaa Valley in the Lebanon is definitely worth a try. Others are not so great, like Swiss reds, Greek wines, the output from Luxembourg, Cyprus, Corsica, Malta, Turkey, Egypt, Israel, Jordan and Russia. But we can only keep on tasting to see if this will all change.

And if you think that the Old World gets a rough ride on the rejects, I'm not going to do Mexico, Uruguay, Peru, Bolivia, Colombia, Brazil, Paraguay, China, India or Japan. (I bet you didn't know they even made wine. . .)

CHAPTER 9

THE NEW WORLD

With reference to wine, the term 'New World' refers to wine-making countries outside Europe and the Mediterranean, as opposed to the term 'Old World' for the countries covered in the previous few chapters in this book. The Old World widely established vines by the fourth century, whereas the New World countries had another thousand or so years to wait before they had a go (Chile in the middle of the sixteenth century, South Africa in 1659, California in 1782 and Australia in 1788). What New World wine-makers lack in history and tradition they more than make up for in a willingness to embrace technology, a lack of prejudice, a dedication to quality and, of course, enviable climates.

SOUTH AFRICA

Try as I might, I am still not utterly convinced about South African wines. There are nice wines made, but they are not really as serious, on a world scale, as they should be. The best regions like **Stellenbosch** and **Paarl** have perfect growing conditions – almost too good – so what is holding them back, apart from everybody's expectations? Since they re-established themselves on the world market in the early nineties, they have struggled to make a big impact. Cabernet Sauvignon, Merlot, Shiraz and the indigenous Pinotage in the red camp and Chenin Blanc (known as Steen), Sauvignon Blanc and Chardonnay in the white are all working well. Some top estates are all performing admirably, but none of them have hit the heights attained by some of the wines in other New World countries. I'm sure it is only a matter of time before this happens. Keep an eye on South Africa, and in the near future there should be a wholesale increase in overall quality and a subsequent resurgence in popularity. Until then, try some of these recommended estates wines in order to establish a base for yourself from which these wines will surely soar.

Favourite producers: Thelema, Warwick, Delheim, Hartenberg, Simonsig, Bouchard Finlayson, Hidden Valley, Jordan, Vergelegen, Hamilton Russell, Steenberg, Klein Constantia, Linton Park, Muratie, Wildekrans, Whalehaven, Neil Ellis, Boekenhoutskloof and Grangehurst.

USA

CALIFORNIA

It is perhaps not surprising that there is a touch of Hollywood about Californian wine-making. Big budget releases feature alongside art-house or boutique creations. Wine-makers are as famous and charismatic within the wine industry as film stars are on the silver screen.

This is very much Cabernet Sauvignon and Chardonnay land. The Californians were sensible enough to select the two most powerful and universally appealing varieties with which to mount an assault on the world of wine. Merlot, Syrah, Pinot Noir and the stunning indigenous Zinfandel, as well as various Rhône varieties (grown by 'Rhône Rangers'), play a supporting role for the reds. Sauvignon Blanc, some Rhône varieties, Riesling and others make up the cast and extras on the white side. But make no mistake: Cabernet and Chardonnay are headlining this show, and they can be blockbusters.

Extending over nearly 1000 kilometres of vineyards from north to south, this state produces the sixth-largest amount of wine in the world, and over ninety-five per cent of America's quality wine. The styles of wine made are usually rich, pure, varietally correct wines, with texture and fruit levels corresponding to the climate. Regions within California vary from Germanic chilliness to Saharan heat. Generally, the better areas take advantage of moderating ocean breezes and the cooling effect of early morning fogs. Californian wines are often ready to drink on release, as the tannin levels in reds and the acidity levels in whites are usually in balance from the word go. Some estates, however, make long-lived wines, and I have been lucky enough to taste several thirty-year-old reds that were holding up well.

In North America, if a wine has a grape variety stated on the label, it must contain a minimum of seventy-five per cent of that grape in the bottle. If it states a vintage then it must contain ninety-five per cent from the said vintage, and if it mentions an AVA, then eighty-five per cent must come from that AVA. An AVA (or Approved Viticultural Area) is a rudimentary equivalent to a French Appellation Contrôlée. Unlike the French or Italian systems, the AVA system imposes no vinification parameters, yield limits or rules on varieties planted. But, in time, it should enable wine-makers to concentrate on soil types and microclimates in order to focus on the most suitable varieties to plant within given AVA boundaries. As the region as a whole is only really thirty years old in serious wine-making terms, it will take some time before these laws can and will be tightened.

The **Napa Valley** is surely the best-known of the Californian wine regions. It starts, at the cool end, in the San Francisco Bay area and ends up, at the baked end of the valley, in Calistoga. Cabernet Sauvignon holds court here, producing arguably the greatest reds of all California. Most of the grapes are grown on the valley floor around the towns of Yountville, Rutherford, Oakville and St. Helena, although the trend now is to head to the hills for improved drainage and aspect: Howell Mountain and Mount Veeder are two of the most successful areas. **Carneros** is a region overlapping the southern ends of the Napa Valley and Sonoma County. It is here that some of the best Chardonnay and Pinot Noir is grown on account of its proximity to the bay and the foggy, cooler temperatures. **Sonoma County** includes the famous sub-regions of the Russian River, Dry Creek, Knights and Alexander Valleys. These are homes to wineries like Kistler, Matanzas Creek and Nalle. This is a quieter, less under-the-spotlight region, fragmented into particular soil types and microclimates. Its AVA regions and the notion of *terroir* make more sense here than many other areas of California. The ever-present Cabernet Sauvignon is grown here, but I favour the Zinfandels, Chardonnays and Merlots. Further north are **Mendocino County** and **Lake County**. These two areas are cooler and grow Zinfandel, Sauvignon Blanc and of course Cabernet Sauvignon. In Mendocino's chilly Anderson Valley, Chardonnay and Pinot Noir are grown for sparkling wines, with Champagne's very own Roederer Estate making some fine wines.

East of San Francisco in the first of the Central Coast's regions is the **Livermore Valley**. A small AVA, Livermore is a prime site for Sauvignon Blanc and Sémillon, but unfortunately they are not planted nearly as widely as they should be. To the south, the **Santa Clara Valley** (otherwise known as Silicon Valley) and the **Santa Cruz Mountains** have a small number of useful vineyards: Bonny Doon and Ridge are the big names here, growing Zinfandel and Rhône varieties. Other areas dotted around this northern end of the Central Coast include **San Benito**, where Calera make Pinot Noir on Mount Harlan; **Chalone, Arroyo Seco** and the **Carmel Valley**.

The south Central Coast has some excellent wineries. It is here, in **Santa Barbara**, where two famous AVAs are to be found. The **Santa Maria Valley** and the **Santa**

Ynez Valley make awesome Chardonnays and Pinot Noirs, and Rhône varieties respectively. Top producers Au Bon Climat and Qupé are based here. **San Luis Obispo County** also has two fine AVAs: the baking hot **Paso Robles**, where Zinfandel flourishes, and the cooler **Edna Valley**, home to Chardonnays.

Inland, the vast **Central Valley**, including the Sacramento and San Joaquin Valleys, is responsible for bulk wines and some lesser labels accounting for nearly three-quarters of all wine made in California. R.H. Phillips and Mondavi's Woodbridge labels are among the better wines made here.

Favourite Cabernet Sauvignon/Merlot producers: Beringer (Private Reserve, Chabot Vineyard and Bancroft Merlot), Bernardus (Marinus), Caymus (Special Selection), Corison, Dalle Valle, Dominus, Etude, Harlan Estate, Havens (Reserve Merlot), Justin Vineyards (Isosceles), Matanzas Creek (Merlot), Robert Mondavi (Reserve and Opus One), Moraga (Bel Air), Newton, Paradigm, Joseph Phelps (Insignia), Quintessa, Ridge (Monte Bello), Shafer (Hillside Select), Spottswoode, Stag's Leap (Cask 23, SLV and Fay), and Viader.
Favourite Chardonnay producers: Arrowood, Au Bon Climat (Bien Nacido, Sanford & Benedict, Nuits-Blanches and Talley), Beringer (Private Reserve), Chalone, Kistler (entire range), Matanzas Creek, Robert Mondavi (Reserve) and Trefethen.
Favourite Pinot Noir producers: Au Bon Climat (Isabelle and Sanford & Benedict), Calera (Jensen, Mills and Selleck), Etude, Kistler and Saintsbury (Reserve).
Favourite Rhône Rangers: Au Bon Climat (Cold Heaven Viognier), Bonny Doon, Jade Mountain (entire range), Qupé (entire range) and Sean Thackrey (entire range).
Favourite Zinfandel producers: Cline (Bridgehead), Elyse, De Loach (O.F.S.), Doug Nalle, Ravenswood, Ridge (entire range) and Turley.

PACIFIC NORTH-WEST

Oregon has long been labelled the perfect place to grow Pinot Noir on account of its similar climate to Burgundy; but as we already know how Burgundians can be made to suffer at the hands of the weather, it was always going to be a struggle in Oregon. Since the early seventies, Pinot freaks have attempted to emulate the wines of the Côte d'Or. The Willamette Valley is the centre of this activity and over the last few years they seem to have been nearing the target. These estates tend to be tiny, so production is always limited and they may be hard to track down, but they are definitely worth the trouble as they will certainly give you another angle on the tricky Pinot Noir variety. They make some nice whites here as well. Chardonnays can be fine with elegance and good acidity and Pinot Gris, only superb in Alsace, can be excellent.

Washington State also makes wine, and often at much better value than either California or Oregon. Cabernet Sauvignon, Merlot and Chardonnay are the most successful varieties here. I have been mightily impressed with many of these wines, in particular the India Wells Vineyard from Ste-Michelle. By the way, you can forget the wines of **Idaho**.

Favourite producers in Oregon: Amity, Adelsheim, Bethel Heights, Domaine Drouhin (run by the daughter of the famous Burgundian family), Elk Cove, Evesham Wood, Eyrie and Ponzi.

Favourite producers in Washington: Château Ste-Michelle, Columbia Crest, Leonetti and Woodward Canyon (from the gorgeously named Walla Walla Valley).

CANADA

Canada has two main wine-making regions, **Ontario** and **British Columbia**, and while very few examples of Canadian wine are readily available outside Canada, some do creep on to our shelves. Steer clear of red wines in general as they tend to be green and lack fruit. Light whites are well made, particularly Chardonnays and Pinot Blancs, and ice wines are a particular favourite. Unlike Germany, where the climatic conditions only happen in certain vintages, the icy weather in Canada arrives like clockwork. Don't go for the Vidal grape variety; stick to Riesling.

Favourite producers: Burrowing Owl, Inniskillin and Mission Hill.

SOUTH AMERICA

The two main wine-making countries in South America are Chile and Argentina. None of the others even come close; but believe me, they all have a go. The amazing fact about these two fairly similar countries is that they both have superb, almost too perfect, weather. They are also both allowed to irrigate. With a good understanding of the classic grape varieties they plant, both countries are beginning to embrace technology and new wine-making skills with open arms. Chile and Argentina enjoy inviting Italian, French, Californian, Australian and New Zealand wine-makers to show them how it's done. The Argentinians also have the dubious honour of not only being the fifth-largest wine-producing country in the world, but also of consuming inhuman amounts of the stuff themselves. Perhaps this is why they are lagging behind Chile a few paces in terms of exports; but pound for pound, if I had to choose, I would say that Argentina has the best red wine potential, Chile the best white. But what is the downside to all of this? There is none, apart from the fact that the wines will inevitably get more expensive as time goes by. There is no doubt that as our consumer palates begin to demand more complexity and finesse in the wines, these two countries will be discovering how to achieve it. So sit tight and take advantage of the last two bargain wine countries in the world.

CHILE

Chile is split into three regions: the Northern, Central and Southern Zones. In the Northern Zone it is too hot and dry; in the Southern, too wet; but surprise, the Central Zone is perfect. The Central Zone is further split into wine regions. From north to south, the **Aconcagua**, one hundred miles north of Santiago, is the prime site for Cabernet Sauvignon. This is where Errazuriz make their mega-expensive Seña, in partnership with the Californian wine guru Mondavi. **Casablanca**, on the coast near Valparaiso, attracts cool early morning Pacific Ocean fog that makes it perfect for Sauvignon Blanc, Gewürztraminer and Chardonnay, rather like a Chilean version of Carneros. The **Maipo**, just south of Santiago, is half-red, half-white, with Cabernet Sauvignon, Sauvignon Blanc and Sémillon all sharing the work. **Maule**, which includes the Curicó and Rapel Valleys, plants Cabernet Sauvignon, Sauvignon Blanc and Sémillon again. The last remaining region is **Bío-Bío**, where much of the bulk wine is made for local consumption.

Favourite producers: Caliterra, Casa Lapostolle, Concha y Toro, Errazuriz (whose Seña and Don Maximiano wines are simply outstanding), Miguel Torres, Montgras, Valdivieso, Viña Cousiña Macul and San Pedro.

ARGENTINA

Argentina's wine regions are even easier to understand. There is only one really good one: **Mendoza**. Watch out for amazing Malbecs, as better Malbec is grown here than anywhere in France. Tempranillo, the Rioja variety, also loves the hot climate and irrigated water in the evening. The best Chardonnays are made by Catena, and since they have a Californian consultant, the wines are Californian-style and a lot cheaper. Weinert is the most famous estate and their Merlots and Cabernets are world-class. Look out for their Carrascal label, a blend of Merlot and Malbec.

Favourite producers: Bodegas Weinert (entire range), Catena, Finca El Retiro, La Agricola (the 'Q' range), and Valentin Bianchi.

AUSTRALIA

Gone are the days of Aussie 'port' and 'sherry': we are now in a new era of skilful 'light' wine production, aided by in-depth knowledge of soil and climate, clones and training techniques. One of the world's foremost wine colleges, Roseworthy in Adelaide, has fuelled the wine business with a huge number of graduates, some of whom have become 'flying wine-makers'. These gun-slingers are responsible for raising global standards of wine-making and have catapulted Australia to the top of the New World's list of fine wine countries. The new Australian wine industry of nearly eight hundred estates has never been fitter, and the selection of Australian wines on wine shop shelves is increasing by the day. Australians are now obsessed with a 'sense of place' theory. Like the French concept of *terroir*, rather than slapping any old vine in anywhere, the understanding of microclimates and soil profiles has led to specifically chosen varieties flourishing in the most suitable sites. The idea that regions have their ideal varieties makes the public understanding of Australian wines easier to grasp. We are already talking about Coonawarra Cabernet, Barossa Valley Shiraz, Margaret River Chardonnay and Clare Valley Riesling, so we are only one step away from a complete understanding of Australian wine: focusing on the best producers. But first of all, the regions.

WESTERN AUSTRALIA

With a superb climate, somewhat cooler than the rest of Australia but hot in European terms, Western Australia is a wine drinker's paradise. Split into three main regions, the hottest and driest is the **Swan Valley**. Situated inland of Perth, several wineries make good value wines here, with Evans and Tate being my favourite. But the real quality comes from the **Margaret River**, an area 150 miles to the south of Perth with a unique climate. Jutting out into the ocean with bodies of water on three sides, the microclimates here range from positively hot in the north to chilly and windy in the south. Most of the wineries are planted within five miles of the coast, around the various brooks that flow into the sea. Margaret River's climate is often mistakenly compared to that of Bordeaux. But as Denis Horgan of Leeuwin Estate puts it, 'The heat gets turned on earlier, and off later'. This supposedly cool region is warm enough to make some of the nicest Cabernet Sauvignon, Shiraz and even Zinfandel I have ever tasted. As far as whites are concerned, Sémillon and Chardonnay do well. The forty-six boutique wineries in Margaret River make up less than one per cent of Australia's wine production, but in quality terms, this is possibly one of the finest wine regions in the entire world.

The **Lower Great Southern** area of Western Australia has four particularly fine sub-regions: **Mount Barker, Pemberton, Frankland** and **Albany**. Cooler and producing tense, nervy wines, Riesling does well here, as does Pinot Noir in Albany. Chardonnay and Shiraz can also hit the heights. All in all, a region to follow.

Favourite producers: Amberley (Sémillon), Brookland Valley (Chardonnay and Sauvignon Blanc), Cape Mentelle (Sémillon/Sauvignon Blanc, Shiraz, Cabernet Sauvignon and Zinfandel), Château Xanadu (Sémillon and Reserve Cabernet Sauvignon), Cullens (entire range), Devil's Lair (Chardonnay and Cabernet Sauvignon), Evans and Tate (Sauvignon Blanc/Sémillon and Margaret River Shiraz), Howard Park (entire range), Leeuwin Estate (entire range, but their Art Series Chardonnay is epic), Moss Wood (Cabernet Sauvignon and Chardonnay), Plantagenet (Shiraz), Vasse Felix (Sémillon and Heytesbury labels) and Wignalls (Chardonnay and Pinot Noir).

SOUTH AUSTRALIA

Over half Australia's wine production comes from the state of South Australia, as well as being the headquarters of most of Australia's largest wineries. The climate varies from region to region, with Riverland at one extreme being very hot, and Coonawarra and Adelaide much cooler. **Clare Valley** in the far north of South Australia is our starting point, where lime-juice style Riesling is made. These are my favourite of all Australian Rieslings, as they tend to be magnificently balanced and age-worthy.

The **Barossa Valley** is a warm region that produces powerful, spicy red wines with a good capacity for ageing. The favoured grape here is the meaty Shiraz. This is where Grange Hermitage is made, Australia's most expensive wine. Grenache and Mourvèdre are also grown in the Barossa, making it a veritable Mecca for Rhône lovers. In Barossa there are still some very old vineyards, some with one-hundred-year-old vines. These vines are the prized possessions of specialist wine-makers, and unlike France where very few Syrah vines get that old, it is possible to taste the results here.

The **Adelaide Hills** region and the adjoining **Eden Valley** are rapidly becoming one of the best cool-climate regions in Australia. Tim Knappstein at Lenswood, Adam Wynn at Mountadam and Jeffrey Grosset are all making great wines here. This is Chardonnay country at high altitude, where the cooler climate leads to a longer ripening period. Pinot Noir is also grown up here and the Riesling from Pewsey Vale is delicious. **McLaren Vale**, with its moderating maritime influence, makes juicy Shiraz and Cabernet Sauvignon. Further afield, **Coonawarra** has a cooler climate and famous 'terra rossa' soil which is perfect for growing top-quality Cabernet Sauvignon and Shiraz grapes. Intense blackcurrant flavours and a eucalyptus and mint nose are the hallmarks of Coonawarra Cabernet. **Padthaway**, north of Coonawarra, is slightly warmer and makes excellent Chardonnay, Sauvignon Blanc and Riesling. Irrigated **Riverland** is where the bulk grapes come from that account for over thirty per cent of the nation's wine.

Favourite producers: Tim Adams (Fergus and Sorby), Jim Barry (Armagh), Coriole (Lloyd Reserve), Henschke (entire range), Elderton (Command Shiraz), Grosset (Piccadilly Chardonnay and Gaia Cabernet Sauvignon), Knappstein Lenswood (Pinot Noir), Peter Lehmann (Stonewell Shiraz), Lindemans (Limestone Ridge and Pyrus), Charlie Melton (Nine Popes), Mountadam (entire portfolio), Mount Horrocks (Riesling and Chardonnay), Parker (Terra Rossa), Penfolds (Grange Hermitage and Bin 707), Pewsey Vale (Riesling), Primo Estate (La Magia botrytised Riesling and Joseph Amarone), Rosemount (Traditional, GSM and Balmoral Syrah), Shaw & Smith (Reserve Chardonnay), St Hallett (Old Block Shiraz), Torbreck (Runrig), Wynns (John Riddoch), Yalumba (Signature, Menzies, Octavius), Nepenthe (Riesling and Pinot Noir), Hollick (all), Penley (all), Rouge Homme (all), Katnook (all) and Mildara (Peppermint Pattie).

NEW SOUTH WALES

Sémillon is the star of the **Hunter Valley**, eighty miles north of Sydney. The climate here is hot and humid, and can be annoyingly rainy at harvest time. Big, sweaty Shiraz and succulent, rich Chardonnays are made with good results. All these wines have remarkable ageing capabilities, especially the Sémillons. **Orange** is a cooler region further inland which produces stunning Chardonnay and Cabernet Sauvignon fruit. **Mudgee** (Aboriginal for 'a nest in the hills') is due west of the Hunter Valley and has become a favourite region for Cabernet Sauvignon and Shiraz. All of these areas are championed by the superb family business Rosemount Estates, standing head and shoulders above all other producers in the region, with Roxburgh Chardonnay being one of the finest wines in Australia. Their latest foray into Mudgee has resulted in a Cabernet Sauvignon/Shiraz blend called Mountain Blue which is set to become one of Australia's flagship wines. The bulk producing area of **Riverina** is bag-in-box-wine country, a hundred miles or so further south-west. Only one single wine of note is made here in the **Murrumbidgee Irrigation Area** (MIA), and that is De Bortoli's sensational Sauternes-style botrytised Sémillon, Noble One.

Favourite producers: Brokenwood, Rosemount (Mountain Blue, Show Reserve, Giant's Creek, Roxburgh and Orange Chardonnays) and Rothbury.

VICTORIA

North-east Victoria, centred on **Rutherglen** and **Milawa**, is the centre of super-sticky Liqueur Muscat and Liqueur Tokay production. South-west of Melbourne we find the **Geelong**, where Scotchmans Hill make a fine Riesling, and Bannockburn and others' Pinot Noirs and Chardonnays are also favoured on account of the relatively cool maritime climate. The **Mornington Peninsula** is where T'Gallant make a cult Pinot Gris, and some elegant Pinot Noir is also produced. The **Yarra Valley** grows Pinot Noir, with Mount Mary's being a fine example; a honeyed Marsanne from Yeringberg; and Yarra Yering's stunning 'Dry Red, Nos. 1 and 2', a huge Bordeaux blend and Shiraz respectively. Tarrawarra also make a big, toasty Chardonnay here.

    Central Victoria includes **Great Western**, the **Goulburn Valley**, **Bendigo** and the **Pyrenees**. Dalwhinne, Redbank and Taltarni are the big three in the Pyrenees, also home to Mount Langi Ghiran's impressive, peppery Mount Arrarat Shiraz. Michelton also experiment with Rhône blends; Salinger, one of the nicer sparkling wines of Australia, is made by Seppelts; and a world class Chardonnay is made by Giaconda.

Favourite producers: Baileys (Liqueur Muscats), Campbells (Liqueur Muscats), Giaconda (Chardonnay), Mount Langi Ghiran (Shiraz), Yarra Yering (entire range), Yeringberg (Marsanne), Yarra Burn, Coldstream Hills (Reserve Wines), Domaine Chandon (fizz), Diamond Valley (white label and close planted Pinot Noir) and de Bortoli.

TASMANIA

Its beauty is often compared to that of the Welsh valleys, this cool-climate island is perfect for the growing of Pinot Noir and Chardonnay for sparkling wine production. Several champagne houses have come a-calling: Louis Roederer stayed, in the form of Heemskerk, but only one estate really does it for me.

Favourite producer: Pipers Brook (Chardonnay, Pinot Noir and sparkling wine – Pirie).

NEW ZEALAND

I had never tasted any New Zealand wines before my very first day in the wine trade. Very few New Zealand wines had even been shipped into England until the mid-eighties. However, two wines stuck in my mind and they still have the same high standards today as they did back then: Montana and Cloudy Bay Sauvignon Blancs. They immediately put New Zealand on the map. Forget about the lean Chardonnays and the weedy reds that followed: no one had ever tasted Sauvignon Blanc like this. It was as if Sancerre had been given a makeover, become more sociable and perhaps, dare I say it, a little risqué. These wines had tropical fruit flavours like mango and guava, but remained gooseberry-like and retained Sauvignon's trademark zippy acidity.

Much has changed since then with respect to their Chardonnays and reds! New Zealand wine-makers and viticulturalists are regarded in the wine world as some of the greatest geologists and technicians in the business. Nor did it take long to crack the *terroir* thing. Suddenly Martinborough was Pinot Noir country, Marlborough was for Sauvignon Blanc and Gisborne was for Chardonnay – all sorted in only a few years. Prices are creeping up, but the majority of New Zealand wines are still available for less than £10.

NORTH ISLAND

Auckland, at the northern end of the North island, is home to wineries like Matua Valley, Selaks, Collards and most importantly, Kumeu River with its Mates Vineyard – my favourite New Zealand Chardonnay. **Gisborne** on the east coast is Chardonnay territory, despite running second to the deeply unfashionable Müller-Thurgau in terms of planting. Here Chardonnay picks up a creamy, tropical fruit texture and flavour, with a luscious character that is almost uniquely Gisborne's own.

Hawke's Bay Sauvignon Blanc has a fatter, fleshier feel than more classic areas like Marlborough, and Chardonnays lack the richness of Gisborne. But Hawke's Bay's talent lies in reds. Cabernet Sauvignon and Merlot love the gravelly soil here and Awatea, Te Mata's superb blend, shows what this area is capable of.

Martinborough and **Wairarapa** sit at the southern end of North Island near Wellington and make some fantastic reds, particularly from Pinot Noir. Ata Rangi's Pinot Noir is New Zealand's best, and Palliser, Dry River and Martinborough Vineyards also make fine versions.

SOUTH ISLAND

Nelson, on the north-west tip of South Island, is where Redwood Valley makes fabulous sweet Rieslings and stunning Chardonnays. It is cooler and wetter here than around the corner in **Marlborough**, which is situated on the north-eastern tip of the South Island. This is where Cloudy Bay is grown and made, so I do not need to tell you that it is Sauvignon Blanc countryside. Chardonnay is the second most important variety here.

Canterbury, on the eastern side of South Island, is cooler and dryer with Pinot Noir and Chardonnay the most planted varieties. **Central Otago** is home to the world's most southerly grapevines, and that is the most interesting thing about it. Actually, there is a cracking winery called Felton Road here making excellent Pinot Noir and Chardonnay.

Favourite producers: Ata Rangi (Pinot Noir), Cloudy Bay (Sauvignon Blanc, Chardonnay and Pelorus – fizz), Collards (Rothesay Chardonnay and Cabernet Sauvignon), Dry River (Pinot Noir), Esk Valley (Chenin Blanc and The Terraces), Felton Road (Pinot Noir and Chardonnay), Kumeu River (all Chardonnays), Martinborough Vineyards (Pinot Noir), Palliser Estate (all wines), Redwood Valley (Chardonnay and Rhine Riesling), Selaks (Sauvignon Blanc), Te Mata (Elston and Awatea), Vavasour (single-vineyard Sauvignon Blanc) and Villa Maria (Reserve level).

CHAPTER 10

VINTAGE

a ripe old age

A vintage is the year in which a wine is produced and the word also encompasses the characteristics of that year. Most of the world's vineyards are situated in variable climates. Weather patterns change; frosts, thunderstorms, droughts and hail can affect the quality of the harvest. In cooler climates, sunshine hours are the all-important currency, and pickers try to shepherd in the crop before any untimely downpours. Some parts of the world don't suffer as badly as others, and in these, vintage variation in wines can generally be ignored. One thing is certain, though: great wine-makers tend to make great wines in bad vintages as well as the good ones, and mediocre wine-makers only fare well when the weather gives them a boost. Throughout this book I have recommended the world's best châteaux, domaines, wineries and estates – the kind of people and operations who can make something out of nothing. I can safely say that even in difficult regions like Burgundy, wine-makers like Lafon or Mortet make stunning wines every year. In the best years, their wines are sublime, but in the 'worst', the difference in quality is barely noticeable. If anything, the wines just tend to lack longevity and for that reason drink earlier – not necessarily a bad thing. In Bordeaux, perennial over-achiever Château Latour can be relied upon even in sopping vintages, so I feel that on balance, vintage is a secondary consideration to who makes the wine and where they have their vineyards.

The international wine press trumpet better vintages and slate 'bad' ones. Producers shout 'vintage of the century' at every given opportunity. I don't blame them, as they want to sell their wine. But one thing that hype surrounding top vintages attracts is high prices. As a consumer who is not given to laying down wine for a prolonged period of time, I generally want to buy wine to drink, so I find myself willing the expensive regions large, average-quality vintages, in the hope that prices will be affordable and wines will drink early. Given the precious knowledge of the best producers, I am rarely let down. Don't get me wrong: I love superb vintages as much as the next drinker, but I do not set all of my store in relying on them to find great wines.

For those of you who revel in the knowledge of the wine world's perfect climatic conditions, here is a guide to some of the best vintages of the twentieth century. You may be able to find somebody's birth or anniversary year here and spoil them with a thoughtful present. Remember that the biggest, richest years last for the longest, but don't gamble with wines that are too ancient as they may have fallen to bits in the meantime. All wines should be considered within the context of their styles.

FRANCE

RED BORDEAUX The top wines from the best châteaux can live happily for thirty or forty years; beyond that, cross your fingers: 1945, 1947, 1948, 1949, 1953, 1959, 1961, 1962, 1964, 1970, 1982, 1983, 1985, 1986, 1988, 1989, 1990, 1995, 1996.

SAUTERNES With the sugar levels in this style of wine, it can last for ages 1945, 1949, 1955, 1959, 1967, 1971, 1975, 1976, 1983, 1986, 1988, 1989, 1990, 1996, 1997, 1998.

ALSACE Only Vendange Tardive and Sélection des Grains Nobles styles live for more than fifteen years: 1971, 1976, 1983, 1985, 1988, 1989, 1990, 1992, 1993, 1994, 1995, 1996, 1997, 1998.

BURGUNDY Try to drink earlier rather than later, as Pinot Noir and Chardonnay show well up to fifteen years old: 1969, 1971, 1972, 1978, 1980, 1985, 1988, 1989, 1990, 1995, 1996, 1997, 1998.

CHAMPAGNE Surprisingly long-lived if kept in good conditions: 1964, 1966, 1971, 1976, 1979, 1982, 1985, 1988, 1989, 1990, 1992, 1995, 1996, 1997.

LOIRE SWEET WINES With Chenin Blanc's acidity, these wines are amazingly age-worthy: 1947, 1949, 1959, 1962, 1969, 1976, 1983, 1985, 1986, 1988, 1989, 1990, 1995, 1996, 1997, 1998.

NORTHERN RHÔNE I prefer these Syrahs fairly young: 1978, 1982, 1983, 1985, 1988, 1989, 1990, 1991, 1995, 1996.

SOUTHERN RHÔNE Likewise with these blends: 1978, 1979, 1981, 1983, 1985, 1988, 1989, 1990, 1995, 1996, 1998.

ITALY

PIEDMONT Nebbiolo's power carries these wines far: 1970, 1971, 1974, 1978, 1979, 1980, 1982, 1985, 1988, 1989, 1990, 1995, 1996, 1997, 1998.

VENETO (AMARONE) The power in Amarone makes these wines long-lived: 1970, 1971, 1974, 1976, 1979, 1983, 1985, 1988, 1990, 1993, 1995, 1997.

ITALY (CONT)

TUSCANY Like the Rhônes, I prefer to attack early: 1975, 1978, 1979, 1982, 1983, 1985, 1988, 1989, 1990, 1994, 1995, 1996, 1997.

GERMANY
Riesling loves the long haul: 1971, 1975, 1976, 1983, 1985, 1988, 1989, 1990, 1992, 1993, 1994, 1995, 1996, 1997.

PORT
No surprise, port is the keeper of them all: 1927, 1931, 1945, 1948, 1955, 1963, 1970, 1977, 1983, 1985, 1991, 1992, 1994, 1997.

SPAIN
I like to drink Riojas when they still have a lot of fruit: 1981, 1982, 1985, 1987, 1989, 1990, 1991, 1994, 1995, 1996, 1997.

SOUTH AFRICA
Rare to find older examples and not much variation from the best producers due to largely uniform weather conditions: 1986, 1987, 1989, 1991, 1992, 1995, 1997.

USA

CALIFORNIA Not the longevity that you might expect, as they mature early on the whole: 1984, 1985, 1987, 1990, 1991, 1992, 1993, 1994, 1995, 1996, 1997.

OREGON AND WASHINGTON Ditto California, impossible to find old bottles: 1988, 1989, 1990, 1991, 1992, 1995, 1996, 1997.

CHILE AND ARGENTINA
Very little vintage variation due to uniform weather conditions.

AUSTRALIA
I like these wines young: ten years old is probably the peak, save for only one or two labels: 1984, 1985, 1986, 1987, 1988, 1990, 1991, 1994, 1995, 1996, 1997, 1998.

NEW ZEALAND
Almost always drunk young, few reds would last more than ten years: 1989, 1991, 1994, 1995, 1996, 1997.

digestif

GLOSSARY

VITICULTURAL TERMS

**Botrytis cinerea/
noble rot**
Usually shortened to *botrytis*, it is a welcomed fungus that attacks bunches of white grapes. Living off the water in the bunch, it concentrates the sugar content of the grapes enabling a wine made from these affected grapes to have high potential alcohol. These grapes are ideal for sweet wines. If botrytis attacks red grapes, the resulting flavours are 'off', rotten and the wines lack colour. The French term is *pourriture noble*.

black rot
A fungal disease that occurs in wet weather. The crop can lose up to eighty per cent of its yield.

Bordeaux mixture
A mixture of copper sulphate, lime and water, very effective in controlling fungal and bacterial diseases on vines. Permitted in organic viticulture.

budbreak/budburst
The moment when the first shoots emerge from the buds in spring – dangers of frost abound. Eight months to go until harvest.

budding
The process of grafting a single bud to a rootstock.

canopy management
Vine-training techniques that expose the leaves and bunches of grapes to the sun in order to maximise the yield and quality of the fruit.

cépage
French term for grape variety or varieties, if a blend.

chlorosis
A vine disorder due to iron deficiencies in the soil which leads to a lack of chlorophyll, resulting in the leaves turning yellow.

clone
A superior selection within a specific variety of vine, often taken from a cutting or a bud from a single, successful mother-vine.

coulure
Flowers or small berries fall off the vine resulting in a diminished crop due to climatic conditions – cold and wet weather reducing photosynthesis; disease; or lack of minerals in the vine tissue causing the stems to shrivel.

downy mildew
Also known as *Peronospera*, a fungus affecting vines, particularly in humid summers. Use Bordeaux mixture to treat.

drip irrigation   A watering system that allows drips of water to fall on to the vine from a system of pipes.

eutypiose   A fungal disease that rots the wood section of a vine. Often caused by pruning wounds.

flowering   The process prior to fertilisation that leads to fruit set. This usually takes place two to three months after budbreak. Time to pray for good weather.

Geneva double curtain   Often shortened to GDC, a training technique that divides the canopy into two hanging curtains, maximising the sun's effect. Useful on wide-row spaced vineyards with vigorous soil, resulting in higher-quality larger yields.

gobelet   A training system that makes the vine look like a goblet. The vines are free standing, without a trellis and with short trunks. The growth on short arms resembles a little tree (also called 'bush vine' training in the New World). Used in low-vigour, hot-climate vineyards.

grafting   The process of connecting two pieces of plant together to make one vine; usually a vine variety on top and a resistant rootstock below. Essential to avoid the *Phylloxera* louse living in the soil.

grey rot   An infection of the vine, also known as *pourriture grise*. This is the bad version of botrytis that breaks down the skin of the grape and results in rotten fruit unsuitable for wine.

Guyot   After Jules Guyot whose name lives on as the training system; either single Guyot or double Guyot, referring to the number of laterally trained canes from which the buds burst.

hectare (ha)   Vineyard area measurement equivalent to 10,000 square metres or 2.47 acres.

hectolitre (hl)   100 litres.

irrigation   The application of water to vines where there is insufficient rainfall. Not allowed in certain countries, such as France.

late harvest   Vines that are picked later than normal in the quest for extra ripe grapes with which to make sweet wines.

microclimate   The precise climate of a vineyard, or group of vineyards.

millerendage   Uneven berry sizes on the same bunch, also known as 'hen and chicken'. This is brought about by inclement weather during flowering and can cause a loss in crop volumes, but can concentrate the flavours within the harvest.

monopole
A French term for a Burgundian vineyard in single ownership.

oidium
Another fungus, this time known as 'Powdery Mildew'. Unlike other fungal diseases this one doesn't need humidity to thrive. It likes shaded canopies and does not like direct sunlight. Spray sulphur, lime and water to control it, or open up your canopy!

Phylloxera vastatrix
A parasitic louse that feeds on the rootstocks of *vitis vinifera* vines and caused devastating damage to vineyards in the late nineteenth century. The grafting of *vinifera vines* on to resistant American *vitis lambrusca* rootstocks has prevented further damage.

pruning
A combination of shaping the vine, controlling its vegetative growth and concentrating its fruit quality by means of careful cutting by hand-held secateurs or various mechanical equipment.

rootstock
The plant forming the below-ground root system of a vine on to which the fruiting variety (scion) is grafted.

scion
The piece of fruiting vine that is grafted on to the rootstock (see above).

terroir
A French word that rolls an entire vineyard's attributes such as microclimate, soil, drainage, altitude, aspect, exposure and slope, into one.

training
The structure along which a vine is encouraged to grow, in order to maximise its quality and quantity of output. Geneva Double Curtain, Lenz Moser, Gobelet, Cordon de Royat, Espalier, Guyot, Lyre, Pergola, Scott Henry and Tendone are but a few.

tri
Usually employed when harvesting botrytised grapes, a tri is one of a series of trips through the vineyard selecting only the bunches that are ready to be picked and leaving the others until they are at their optimum ripeness.

triage
A sorting procedure of the harvested grapes to spot any unripe or out-of-condition bunches and throw them away.

veraison
The moment on the vine when the small, hard, green berries change into their bigger, softer, yellow or red coloured grapes. This is the start of the ripening period.

Vitis lambrusca
North American vine species, whose rootstocks are Phylloxera resistant. It produces table grapes and grape juice.

Vitis vinifera	The vine species from which most of the world's wine is made.
yeast	The dusty bloom on grapes is wild yeast that can kick start fermentation when the grapes are crushed. Some wine-makers prefer this, others prefer to use cultured yeast.
yield	A word that refers to the amount of grapes or wine that a vineyard produces. A high yield = a big crop. A low yield = a small, but probably concentrated crop. E.g. '50 hectolitres per hectare' is a useful wine-maker's calculation of the amount of wine resulting from a standard vineyard area. Yield can be measured in tons per acre in which case this is a measurement of the harvested grapes, not the resulting wine. (On average one ton/acre = 17.5 hl/ha.)

VINIFICATION TERMS

acid	Chemical compounds that give wines freshness and a sharp, clean taste on the palate. Tartaric and malic are the two most important acids in wine production. Malic acid transforms into lactic acid during malolactic fermentation. Tartaric acid can be added during wine-making if a wine lacks natural acidity. Acids keep wines stable as they ward off bacteria.
alcohol	The common name for ethanol, measured as a percentage of the volume of the wine. Alcohol is the result of fermentation, when sugar is combined with yeast.
autolysis	A process occurring during bottle-fermented sparkling wine production. The flavour of the wine is enhanced, due to the fact that the wine is aged on its lees (dead yeast cells) for an extended period.
barrel-fermented	A white wine that has been fermented in oak barrels giving rise to a stronger flavour than those wines merely aged in oak barrels.
barrique	A traditional 225 litre Bordeaux oak barrel or international term covering just about any 'small' oak barrel.
bâtonnage	French term for 'lees stirring'.
baumé	A scale of measurement of the sugar in grape must.
bentonite	A type of clay used for fining.

blending	Mixing together several different batches of wine to create a final wine that is hopefully greater than the sum of its parts. This usually occurs after vinification, just before bottling. The French term is *assemblage*.
Bordeaux blend	A wine consisting of Cabernet Sauvignon, Cabernet Franc and Merlot. Occasionally Petit Verdot can sneak into this equation.
cap	The mass of grape solids that floats on top of red wine during fermentation. The French term is *chapeau*.
carbon dioxide (CO_2)	A gaseous by-product of fermentation, which can be trapped on purpose and dissolved into wine, later to be released as bubbles. Also used as a blanket to protect grapes against oxidation.
carbonic maceration	Fermentation of uncrushed grapes in a sealed tank in the absence of air, resulting in vibrant, fruity, forward red wines. The French term is *macération carbonique*.
centrifugation	A clarification process used to spin out unwanted heavy elements (yeast cells) from a wine.
chaptalisation	The addition of sugar or concentrated grape juice to raise the final alcoholic strength of a wine.
clarification	The removal of suspended solids or lees from grape juice or wine.
cold stabilisation	The extended chilling of a wine to encourage the precipitation of tartrate crystals which are then removed, preventing any crystals forming in the bottled wine.
cru	A confusing French term for a specific vineyard's quality status, as in Burgundy's 1er Cru and Grand Crus, and Alsace's Grand Crus. In these cases the individual name of the vineyard would be attached to the 1er or Grand Cru prefix, e.g. Meursault 1er Cru Perrières, where the vineyard of Perrières is the 1er Cru rated vineyard from the village of Meursault. (Unless the wine was a blend of several 1er Crus, in which case it would not list each vineyard involved, just state 1er Cru.) The other meaning is growth, as in 1er Cru, 2ème Cru, down to 5ème Cru, translating as 1st growth, 2nd growth, etc. This is the classification of Bordeaux top-ranking Left Bank Châteaux such as Château Lafite-Rothschild 1er Cru Pauillac, a very serious drink indeed!
cryoextraction	Freezing grapes to extract as much sugary juice as possible leaving the water content behind in the press. Used for sweet wine production, particularly in wet years. A cheat version of Eiswein.

cuvaison	The total time that a red wine spends in contact with its skins.
cuve	French term for a vat or tank in which fermentation takes place.
cuvée	An individual barrel, a blend or a style of wine.
débourbage	French term for settling out the less desirable solids from must or wine.
egrappoir	French name for the machine that removes the stems from bunches of grapes.
elevage	No real translation in English, this word means the 'bringing-up' of a wine in the maturing sense, or the time spent from vinification to bottling. 'Elevé en Fût de Chêne' means brought up or aged in an oak barrel.
fermentation	The conversion of sugar to ethanol (alcohol) and carbon dioxide (CO_2) by the addition of yeast.
filtration	The straining of solid particles from a wine.
fining	The clarification and stabilisation of must or wine by the addition of a fining agent, such as bentonite, isinglass (fish bladders) or egg whites, which coagulate or absorb solids and fall to the bottom or the tank or barrel. The clear wine is then decanted off this sediment.
fortification	The addition of alcohol (usually grape spirit) to a fermenting wine (or after in the case of sherry) to prevent further fermentation resulting in a fortified wine.
free-run juice	The finest quality grape juice that runs out of the grapes even before the press has been started as a result of the crushing process.
lees	The dregs or sediment that settles at the bottom of a barrel or fermentation tank made up of dead yeast cells, grape-skin fragments, grape seeds and tartrates.
maceration	A period of contact between red grape skins and must or wine.
malolactic fermentation	The chemical conversion of harsh malic acid to softer lactic acid, often shortened to malo.
maturation	The ageing of a wine. 'Oak-aged' is the same as 'oak-matured'.

méthode traditionnelle	Along with méthode classique, the accepted terms for the finest process of sparkling wine production where the second fermentation occurs in the bottle in which the wine is sold. The old term was méthode Champenoise.
must	Unfermented grape juice.
oak	The wood used to make barrels in which to mature wine.
oak programme	A wine-maker's oak barrel 'formula' designed to result in the best wine possible. Various combinations of barrel age (new, 1-year-old, 2-year-old, etc.); barrel type (barrique, cuve, piece, hogshead, Italian botti, etc.); origin of oak (American, Slovakian, French, etc.); cooper (various companies); degree of toasting (low, medium and high); length of time spent in barrel (from a few months to several years).
oenology	The study of wine, i.e. wine-making. Practised by an oenologist (wine-maker).
oxidation	The chemical reaction of air with crushed grapes, must or wine. More of a danger to whites than reds. Excessive oxidation results in the colour browning and eventually to spoilage. Some wines are deliberately oxidised such as Madeira, Tawny port and sherry.
pasteurisation	Heating wines to high temperatures to kill bacteria and yeasts.
pH	The level of acidity or alkalinity of a wine expressed as a number. Low pH is high acidity, 7 is neutral, wine is generally between 3 and 4.
pomace	The 'cake' of grape skins and pips left over after the wine has been drained off (after fermentation). This is often distilled into brandy. The French term for the pomace itself and the resulting brandy is *Marc*.
pre-fermentation maceration	The period of time before fermentation when the juice of the grapes is left in contact with the skins, thus enhancing the varietal character of the wine.
press	The grape-squeezing apparatus.
press wine	The strongly coloured and flavoured wine resulting from pressing the pomace of grape skins after fermentation. Used for careful blending.

pumping over The process of circulating the fermenting red must over the floating cap in order to release more colour and flavour. The French term is *remontage*.

punching down French term is *pigéage* which means pushing the 'cap' down, manually or mechanically, into the fermenting red must to extract more colour and flavour.

racking Removing clear wine from the sediment in a tank or barrel, by pouring using gravity.

residual sugar The amount of unfermented sugar left in a finished wine, measured in grams per litre.

skin contact The process of extracting more flavour compounds from the skin of a grape into the juice. The same idea as maceration, but this term is used for white wines. The French term is *macération pelliculaire*.

stuck fermentation This is an unwanted condition when fermentation stops before it is completed, often because the temperature has reached a level at which the yeasts present are killed.

sugar Sugars in a grape produce sweetness and ferment to form alcohol. The total sugar content of a grape ('must weight') is a measurement of a grape's ripeness, which in turn can act as a pointer to a harvest date. Sugars are measured in degrees Baumé which conveniently translate to potential degrees of alcohol if the wine was fermented out dry (e.g. 12 Baumé would give a 12% vol. wine. The other methods of measurement – Brix used in America, Oechsle in Germany and KMW in Austria – require a calculator and tables to figure out.

sulphur dioxide (SO_2) Used as a preservative in finished wine, with care, otherwise it can give rise to an unattractive, pungent odour; an all-purpose disinfectant that kills yeast and bacteria; an antioxidant that prevents oxidation of grapes and wine thus avoiding colour loss and off flavours.

tannin The bitter, astringent flavour that is found in grape skins, seed and stalks as well as oak barrels, that softens as red wines age. Often referred to as a wine's natural preservative, they are prominent in young red wines. Tannins are undetectable on the nose, but give rise to drying in the mouth and a harsh feel on the inside of the cheeks.

tartrates The harmless crystals that are deposited during wine-making and occasionally form in bottles of wines that have not been 'cold stabilised'.

vin de liqueur	An unusual fortified wine made by the addition of alcohol to grape must before fermentation, resulting in a 17-18% sweet aperitif style of wine. Pineau des Charentes and Floc de Gascogne are two examples, made in Cognac and Armagnac respectively.
Vin Doux Naturel (VDN)	A fortified wine made by the addition of alcohol to grape must during fermentation. Usually sweet wines and after-dinner drinks, Muscat de Rivesaltes and Muscat de Beaumes-de-Venise are two of the most famous white styles whilst Banyuls and Maury are two lesser-known reds.
vintage	The year in which a wine was produced.
yeast	The agent that transforms the sugar in grape juice into alcohol and CO_2 via fermentation. Yeast is naturally found on grape skins or can be added by the wine-maker in a process called *inoculation*.

TASTING TERMS

acid	Crucial natural balance element that gives a wine freshness, vitality and life.
aggressive	A sensation resulting from an excess of tannin, acidity or both.
alcoholic	A 'hot' feeling on the palate, from high levels of alcohol.
angular	A wine lacking in fruit and depth, without a 'smooth' taste.
apple	A common nose and taste in young white wines, connected to acidity (malic acid).
apricot	A sure-fire sign of Viognier in a dry wine or botrytis in a sweet wine.
aromatic	Strongly scented wines like Gewürztraminer, Muscat or Tokay-Pinot-Gris.
asparagus	A common tasting note for the nose on a Sauvignon Blanc.
astringent	A drying or souring sensation on the palate usually from high tannin or acidity levels. Generally an indication of youth.
attack	The initial burst of flavour in a wine.

austere	Quirky, or maybe a little too young. Wines that seem difficult to appreciate, perhaps 'closed', atypical or 'funky'.
backward	A wine that still tastes young despite its age leading you to believe that it should be drinking.
baked	A 'hot' smell or taste usually from hot-climate wines that give the impression that they were lacking in water in the vineyard – raisiny.
balance	A wine that is in harmony, with all of its elements complementing each other.
banana	A red wine's aroma resulting from carbonic maceration.
big	A wine full of flavour.
biscuity	A quality usually associated with the nose and palate of champagne. Connected to yeast autolysis.
bite	The fresh flavour that acidity brings to a wine.
bitterness	The acid and tannin taste resulting from over-pressing grape-skins, pips or stalks.
blackcurrant	The classic Cabernet Sauvignon aroma and taste.
black fruit	A mix of all black-coloured fruit. A useful term for nose and palate if one individual flavour does not stand out.
blind-tasting	A tasting where the identity of the wine is unknown.
blowsy	A low acidity wine that appears too fruity.
body	The weight of a wine on the palate (light, medium and full).
bottle stink	A initial unpleasant pong when opening a bottle of wine that disappears with a little contact with air.
bottle shock	A recently shipped wine that appears to be jet-lagged and needs to settle down.
bouquet	The smell, aroma or nose of a wine.
Brettanomyces (brett)	A yeast that gives rise to a peculiar 'mousey' smell on a wine. Not unpleasant, just unusual. Not a true wine fault, just an idiosyncrasy.

briary   A term used to indicate a mixed berry fruit flavour, coupled with spicy notes. Often very attractive.

bright   The appearance of a clean, clear wine.

brilliant   Apart from the obvious explanation, this word is also used to describe the clear colour of a wine.

buttery   A classic Chardonnay tasting note on the nose and palate.

caramel   A burnt toffee flavour found on old sherries and Madeira.

cassis   French for blackcurrant – a Cabernet Sauvignon tasting note.

cat's pee   Not being a 'cat-man' I cannot vouch for this term, but it is a popular description for the nose on a Sauvignon Blanc.

cedarwood   The nose on an oak-aged Cabernet Sauvignon or Merlot, particularly found in fine clarets.

chaptalised   Often a slightly disjointed character occurring from the addition of sugar to fermenting must in order to raise the alcoholic strength of a wine.

cheesy   Not uncommon nose of very expensive Chablis; however, cheesiness is usually a sign of poor hygiene in a winery!

cherry   Black or red, a useful aroma to spot on Burgundies, Beaujolais, Nebbiolos, Zinfandels, Riojas and many other red wines. The ultimate tasting note is the chocolate and cherry combination of Blackforest Gâteau, found on some Californian Zinfandels.

chewy   This refers to the palate of a richly textured, often high-alcohol wine. The taste is so dense you can almost chew it.

chocolate   Dark chocolate can be found on many big red wines, perhaps in the combination of aroma and texture.

cigar-box   Another classic red Bordeaux term for the aroma of oak and fruit combined.

classic   Overused in my tasting notes, denoting a wine that tastes exactly as it should from previous experience.

classy   A distinguished taste. Usually referring to a complex, balanced flavour – more often than not from an expensive bottle.

clean	A pure, unencumbered smell or taste, usually referring to white wines.
closed	A wine that is somewhat subdued, not giving away much in the way of aroma or flavour. Often needing more time to age.
cloudy	A bad sign. A wine that has not been stabilised, exhibiting suspended yeast, bacteria or micro-organisms; or a result of sediment in a red wine being shaken up unwittingly.
cloying	Mouth-coatingly sweet, often lacking in balancing acidity.
clumsy	A simple, if slightly out-of-balance wine, lacking in elegance.
coffee	A self-explanatory red wine descriptive term often found on New World Cabernet Sauvignons and Pinot Noirs.
commercial	Not a derogatory expression but an indication of a crowd-pleaser that is usually of the inexpensive, glugger style.
complex	The sign of a fine wine, having a multi-layered flavour. A wine that reveals different aromas and flavours every time you taste it.
confected	Seemingly a 'chemistry-set wine' made in the winery rather than grown in the vineyard. A wine reminiscent of confectionery.
cooked	The feeling that the fermentation was too hot and the wine became 'stewed', leading to high alcohol and lacking in balance.
corked/corky	A faulty wine spoiled by a mouldy cork.
crisp	A white wine with refreshing levels of acidity.
depth	The concentration or richness of flavour.
developed	A term to indicate maturity.
dirty	Unpleasant, unclean wine-making.
dried-out	A wine lacking in fruit flavours.
drinking	Ready to drink or at its peak.
dull	Uninspiring wine that lacks character or interest.
dumb	A wine with no nose at all.
dusty	A palate sensation usually associated with tannin levels, almost as if there was a dusty coating to the wine.

earthy	Another dimension to the aroma and palate, coming from the soil. A good element in the complexity of a wine.
eggy	Phew, a bad sign of over-sulphuring a wine. (Or perhaps just a Dolcetto in disguise!)
elegant	An even, lingering flavour, that is pleasing, refined and not too overblown.
eucalyptus	Found on the nose, this distinctive smell often pops up on New World Cabernet Sauvignons.
explosive	A massive, unexpected nose or flavour.
extract	The 'guts' of a wine, making up its body.
farmyardy	An accurate, if surprising, aroma on red Burgundy.
fat	A big, rich wine lacking in definition, full-bodied and a little too heavy.
fine	There are two meanings to this. 'Fine Wine' is a term for expensive and possibly rare wine. 'Fine' on its own implies a degree of class and complexity.
finesse	Often used in the same breath as elegance, this is another word used for a complex if slightly lighter-bodied wine. Nearly always mentioned in the context of expensive champagne.
finish	The end flavour left on the palate, measured in terms of length.
flabby	A wine lacking in balancing acidity, one stage worse than blowsy.
flat	A muted nose and palate on a wine. Not quite as dull as 'dull'.
flinty	A gunflint or smoky scent picked up on Loire Sauvignon Blancs, coming from the French word *fumer* – to smoke (as in Pouilly-Fumé).
flowery	Bunch of flowers aroma, evoking a fragrant summer meadow.
forward	A wine that can be drunk earlier (in its lifetime) than expected.
fresh	A wine with perky acidity and a lively flavour.
fruity	A reassuring ripe-grape nose and palate.

funky

Not always complimentary, this term can mean that a wine is a touch faulty but not enough to detract from the overall impression of the wine. If we were talking about art, the term might be 'distressed'.

gamey

As the word implies, a scent or taste of game that is meaty, fairly strong and a little rotten, in the nicest sense of the word. Only found on red wine (usually older bottles). Another Burgundy trait, although often associated with any of the Rhône grape varieties.

generous

As in any polite word meaning 'in abundance'. Top-heavy, ample, copious amounts, voluptuous, overflowing, etc. Perhaps I am getting a little side-tracked.

glugger

A jokey word for a simple, undemanding, easy-to-drink wine that would please everybody's palate. Perfect for a party.

glycerine

The oily feel in a wine that makes it taste more textured on the palate.

gooseberry

The benchmark Sauvignon Blanc nose.

grapey

The actual smell and taste of grapes, only really applicable to wines made from the Muscat variety.

grassy

The green smell, often reminiscent of cut grass (cricket pitches), found on Sauvignon Blanc and Cabernet Franc.

green

An unripe smell and taste often found on thin Merlots and Cabernet Francs, associated with an unripe crop resulting from over-production or a bad vintage. Green wines have raw acidity on the finish.

grip

The firm feeling on the back-palate brought about by dominant acidity or tannin. Essential in very ripe wines.

hard

Almost always followed by 'tannins'; i.e. too young to drink.

harsh

Another acidity and tannin adjective, suggesting a high degree of one or the other, or both.

heady

A dizzy-making feel to a wine. Not for quantity reasons, just alcohol levels.

heavy

Used to explain the weight of a wine on the palate.

herbaceous

Not to be confused with green, this word conveys the scent of greenhouses or garden centres. A pleasant extra dimension to a wine.

herbal	As the word suggests, any scent or flavour reminiscent of fresh or dried herbs.
hollow	A wine that has attack and a finish, but a gap between. A disappointing dip in concentration on the palate.
honeyed	A regular tasting note for sweet wines, particularly Sauternes and Loire sweeties. Sometimes used for dry whites to imply a degree of texture and richness.
horizontal tasting	A wine tasting consisting of a number of different wines from the same year (vintage).
horsey	A bit like farmyardy and leathery, although more specific. Not a bad term, particularly when connected to red Burgundies.
hot	Wines with high alcohol.
insipid	Watery wines lacking in structure and character.
jammy	Self-explanatory: smells akin to the fruit preserve, often as a result of hot climates.
lanolin	An oiliness found in some heavy white wines.
leafy	See 'herbaceous'.
leathery	Another superb descriptive word that conjures up the smell of new shoes, motorcycle gear, tack rooms and all manner of leather goods. Leather is found on Syrah, Grenache and many of the Bordeaux reds. Similar to the cigar-box and tobacco feel.
legs	The patterns made by wine sliding down the inside of a wine glass, as a result of its viscosity. Also known as tears.
lemon	Usually found on youthful white wines with a citrusy freshness.
length	The time that the wine's flavour lingers on the palate – the finish.
light	Used to explain the weight of a wine on the palate.
liquorice	Can be picked up on many red and white wines, offering an unexpected, enjoyable flavour.
lively	A reference to the acidity in a young wine.
long	The most desirable degree of length.

luscious	A ripeness and smoothness found in equal measure.
lychees	Found on the distinctive nose of a Gewürztraminer.
Madeirised	The sweet pungent aroma of over-mature or oxidised wines, often accompanied by a browning in the colour. At its most typical in the wines of Madeira.
malic acid	The aroma of unripe green apples, suggesting that a wine has not completed its malolactic fermentation.
meaty	Always with reference to a huge red wine – you may need a knife and fork!
mellow	A character trait bought on by age, this usually means soft and smooth with a harmonious palate.
metallic	Sometimes found on the palate of inexpensive wine, arising from sloppy wine-making. Not very pleasant.
minty	A New World Cabernet Sauvignon hallmark.
mocha	Somewhere near a coffee aroma, usually found on New World Shiraz or Bordeaux Blends.
mouth feel	A superb self-explanatory term referring to the sensation of a wine on the palate.
mulberry	Another berry flavour often associated with Sangiovese and Merlot.
musty	A hygiene problem somewhere along the line leading to a stale aroma or taste. Usually disappears with aeration.
nose	The aroma, bouquet or smell of a wine.
nutty	Usually a nose-detected quality resulting from oak-ageing, somewhat akin to dry-roasted nuts/charred or toasted barrels. Chardonnay often has this aroma.
oaky	The smell and taste of oak barrels. Should not be too intrusive.
organoleptic	A fancy word for 'testing by using one's senses' or sensory assessment with regard to wine (and food).
out of balance	As the expression suggests (see *balance*). Can be shortened to O.O.B. in tasting notes.

out of condition	Faulty. Can be shortened to O.O.C. in tasting notes.
oxidised	A wine spoiled by oxidation. Browning in colour and stale on the nose and palate.
palate	The flavour of a wine and also a word for your mouth.
peaches	A Viognier pointer. Found on many aromatic white wines.
perfumed	Highly scented or fragrant nose.
pepper	Absolutely guaranteed on the Syrah noses of northern Rhône reds. Also found on any Syrah blends from the southern Rhône and Provence. Evident on Syrahs outside France, like the Shiraz from California, Australia and further afield. Can often be detected on top quality Cru Beaujolais.
petrol	Older Rieslings have this unusual, pungent scent.
plummy	A rich, ripe red wine, particularly Merlot or Pinot Noir, can have a nose and flavour reminiscent of plums.
poor	Not nice.
price point game	A guessing game played when tasters are trying to assess whether a wine is good value or not. Quite simply, have a guess at the price. If you guess too low then you would obviously not want to pay more for the wine, so, in your opinion, the bottle was not worth the money. If you guess too high, you must think that the wine is good value and you may want to buy a bottle for yourself. This thought-process is used whenever a wine buyer selects a wine.
pungent	Strongly scented.
quaffing	Drinking with purpose (see *glugger*). This is what you would do with a case of gluggers!
raspberry	A lighter red wine aroma associated with Pinot Noir and Gamay.
red fruit	A collection of red-skinned fruit like strawberries, raspberries, cranberries, redcurrants etc. A red wine tasting note, when no specific red fruit is precise enough.
reductive	A word associated with a skunky smell on a wine. This smell is of sulphur compounds such as hydrogen sulphide that will subside with aeration. Decant the wine and wave it around!
residual sugar	The remaining sugar in a wine that accounts for its degree of sweetness.

rich	A word used to describe texture and smoothness of a medium- to full-bodied wine.
ripe	The taste of a wine that has reached its physical peak of development at harvest.
robust	A firmly structured wine. Always used for red wines, never whites.
rose	Either rose-petal or rose-water can be found on the nose of some aromatic varieties like Gewürztraminer. Occasionally red wines can have a rose nose.
round	This refers to a wine's body, meaning that a wine is balanced and complete.
rubber	A sulphurous nose if too strong, but can actually be an attribute of some New World reds, or Italian Dolcettos.
salty	Most often found on sherry, particularly Manzanilla. Also can be picked up on some top flight Muscadets.
sediment	The solids found at the bottom of some old red wines.
sharp	A term used for acidity beyond that of a balanced nature.
short	A disappointing length.
shows	As in 'exhibits'. 'This wine shows mint on the nose' = 'you can smell mint on this wine'.
sinewy	A lack of juicy fruit character, exposing the acidity and tannin elements of a red.
silky	Very smooth on the palate.
smoky	In reds, smoky can be found on a range of wines particularly, Syrah, Nebbiolo, Mourvèdre and Grenache. In whites it is only really used for Pouilly-Fumé (see 'Flinty' above. Flinty is much better, anyway).
spicy	Regularly making it into my tasting notes, spicy means just that. Often countering a fruity flavour, a herbal spiciness on whites and a dried-spice character on reds is commonplace.
spittoon	The correct term for the bucket that you spit into (or not, as the case may be!).
spritz	A gentle prickle of fizz on the palate. Found on young white wines.

stalky	One stage beyond that of green, this word is used for a particular type of harsh tannin resulting from the inclusion of too many grape stems into the fermentation.
steely	A lean, acidic crispness in a white wine that can be refreshing if balanced with sufficient fruit flavours.
strawberry	The benchmark Burgundy fruit nose and flavour that is also unmissable on Rioja.
structure	The physical framework on which a wine's flavours are hung.
subtle	Subdued flavours that are in balance but require some concentration to track down.
sulphur	Similar to the smell of a struck match, sulphur is detectable on the nose but should disappear when the wine comes into contact with air.
supple	A lush, round style of wine with no obvious acidity or tannin.
tannic	The natural preservative for red wines found in grape skins that lends a peculiar dry, harsh flavour to a wine in its youth, but thankfully softens with age. There are many expressions for tannic wines including cheek-sucking, teeth-furring and mouth-puckering.
tangy	A pleasant feeling of acidity on the palate of white wines.
tart	A raw feeling of acidity on the palate of white wines.
toasty	The nose associated with oak-aged wines, on account of the insides of the barrels being charred or toasted, reminiscent of burnt toast.
tobacco	See 'Cigar-box'.
truffles	A really beautiful mushroomy aroma found on some red wines, usually red Rhônes and Nebbiolos from Piemonte – both, curiously, where actual truffles are found.
unctuous	Intense, oily character usually associated with sweet wines.
upfront	The immediately appealing characteristics on a wine. An up-front nose or palate means that they are instantly recognisable.
vanilla	An aroma resulting from oak-ageing, particularly in American oak.

varietal	A wine that displays textbook grape variety characteristics e.g. 'gooseberries and asparagus on the nose with keen acidity and fresh citrusy fruit on the palate' depicts a 'varietal', as in typical Sauvignon Blanc.
vegetal	A word that groups together various vegetable smells and tastes, mostly with reference to red wines. Not always a derogatory term.
velvety	The smoothest and most luxurious of textures on the palate. Merlot and other sensuous red varieties can attain this character if they are of the finest quality.
violets	Purely a nose note, violets can be found on a number of red grapes like Sangiovese, Pinot Noir and Cabernet Franc.
vertical tasting	A wine tasting consisting of a number of different vintages of the same wine.
volatile acidity (VA)	Acetic acid, that in certain concentrations (above 1.5g/l) gives an off-putting vinegary smell. This is usually brought about as a result of shoddy wine-making.
woody	Over-oaked, when the nose or palate stops tasting like well-integrated oak and starts tasting like tree!
yeasty	The fresh-baked bread nose found on champagne and other white wines mainly using Chardonnay.
zesty	A citrus taste associated with acidity and also with some white grape varieties like Sauvignon Blanc and Sémillon.
zippy	A term used to describe refreshing levels of acidity.
zingy	See above.

N.B. I have not included *cheeky, train-brakes, impudent, wet park benches, bashful* or *precocious*, as such terms reveal more about the taster than the wine.

FRENCH TASTING TERMS

agressif	High acidity, harsh.
arôme	Aroma or nose.
bouchonné	Corked.

brut	Dry.
charpente	Literally 'carpentry', this refers to wines with good structure.
clairet	Light red colour, deeper than rosé.
crémant	Literally 'creaming', slightly sparkling or frothing.
dégustation	Tasting, as in wine tasting.
demi-sec	Literally 'half-dry', therefore medium-dry.
doux	Sweet.
equilibré	Balanced.
fruité	Fruity.
goût de terroir	A French term meaning the distinct taste of the soil, found in wines typical of specific regions or villages.
moelleux	Sweet, with reference to pudding wines, although sometimes this means rich, smooth and ripe but not overly sweet.
mousse	The fizz on the surface of a glass of sparkling wine or champagne.
pétillant	Gently sparkling.
piquant	A refreshing level of acidity.
robe	The colour of a wine.
sec	Dry.
souple	Supple, balanced, harmonious.
vif	A lively, youthful flavour.
vin de garde	A French term for a wine that is worth laying down, as opposed to drinking young.

GENERAL WINE TERMS

abboccato	Italian for medium-sweet.
abocado	Spanish for medium-sweet.
amabile	Italian for sweet.
amarone	Italian for wines made from dried grapes, such as Amarone della Valpolicella.
ampelography	The study of vine species and varieties.
Anbaugebiet	A German term for a wine region, of which there are thirteen in Germany.
AOC	An abbreviation for the French term Appellation d'Origine Contrôlée – a control system that protects and polices regionally specific wines. Often shortened to AC.
AVA	American Viticultural Area: a somewhat confused attempt at a meaningful AC system (see above).
aperitif	A drink used to gets the taste buds humming, before a meal. See 'kir'.
Auslese	A German style of wine meaning 'selected harvest'. The grapes will be harvested later and riper than normal, often giving rise to sweet wines.
Azienda Agricola	The Italian equivalent of _Domaine_, where the grapes are grown and made into wine on the estate.
Bacchus	The Roman God of Wine – what a job.
Bereich	A German term for a wine district containing 'Grosslagen' areas.
Beerenauslese	German for a sweet style of wine made from individually selected overripe berries, one notch up from 'Auslese'.
blanc de blancs	French for a white wine made using white grapes only. On a bottle of champagne it would signify a wine made solely from Chardonnay.
blanc de noirs	French for a white wine made using red grapes only, removing the skins from the must before any colour leaches out.

bianco	Italian word for white, usually followed by 'di' then a place name.
blanco	Spanish word for white.
bodega	Spanish word for a winery.
butt	A barrel used for the production of sherry usually made from American oak and with a capacity of approximately 600 litres.
capsule	The covering protecting the cork in a bottle of wine. Nowadays made from all manner of weird and wonderful materials. They used to be made from lead.
casa vinicola	Italian equivalent of a French *négociant*.
case	The traditional trading unit of a dozen bottles of wine. (Not crates!)
claret	English term for any red wine from Bordeaux.
climat	Burgundian term for an individually named vineyard site. See *lieu-dit*.
clos	French term for a walled vineyard.
co-operative	A winery owned by a number of different members who pool their resources, combine their harvests, and save considerable money on buying wine-making equipment, as they all share the one site.
coteaux	French term for a collection of hills.
côte	French term for a slope or hillside.
crianza	Spanish term for a wine that has been aged for two years before release, of which a minimum of one year is spent in a barrel.
cru bourgeois	A Médoc classification for wines one step below that of Cru Classé.
cru classé	Literally a 'classed growth', this French term refers to a classification system covering all of the finest Left Bank Bordeaux Châteaux.
decanting	The process of pouring a wine out of its bottle into a decanter or jug to remove its sediment or let it breathe.
digestif	A smart word for an after-dinner drink. Whether it be Cognac, Armagnac, Calvados, Eau de Vie, Whisky or any of the other huge range styles of nose and swirl drinks, I think they are a fine curtain-call to finish off a good dinner.

Dionysus	The Greek God of Wine – the other enviable position; though on current form, I would prefer to be in Rome, than Athens for cellar-selection.
DO	*Denominación de Origen*, the Spanish version of AC.
DOC	*Denominazione di Origine Controllata*, *Denominación de Origen Calificada* and *Denominação de Origem Controlada*: respectively, the Italian version of AC, the Spanish equivalent of Italy's DOCG and the Portuguese version of AC.
DOCG	Add '*e Garantita*' to the Italian DOC term and this is the classification for the supposedly finest Italian wines.
domaine	French word for a winery that owns its own vineyards and makes its own wine.
double-decanting	Pouring a wine into a decanter, then back into its original bottle after having washed out any sediment. This means that you can enjoy the wine without the worry of the sediment ruining the last few glasses, and also see what wine it is you are drinking.
eau de vie	A spirit made from distilled fruit. Some people keep their bottles in the freezer like vodka, so that when it is poured it is as cold as possible. This is not the best way to appreciate these digestifs. Bottles should be kept in a normal fridge and the glasses kept in the freezer. They will take up less space in the freezer than the bottles and when poured will look fantastic. The aroma will explode on the nose when the cold Poire hits the freezing glass and tastes superb.
Einzellage	German for a named single vineyard site, like a *lieu-dit* in French.
Eiswein	German name for wine made only in vintages where the grapes freeze on the vine. They tend to be affected with noble rot, and when frozen the water content is captured such that the juice emerging from the wine-press is so concentrated in sugar that they result in tooth-achingly sweet wines that cost a bomb. This style of wine is made in Austria and Canada. See 'Cryoextraction'.
en-primeur	Any wines that are offered for sale before they have been bottled, similar to buying a 'future'. In theory, the buyer gets the opportunity to reserve a wine at a low opening price with a view to speculating on the quality of the wine and its eventual worth. This is one way to invest in wine, attempting to realise a profit as the wine matures and nears its period of drinking. Duty, shipping costs and taxes are due when the wine is released from the winery.
fût de chêne	French term meaning oak barrels.

generoso	Spanish or Portuguese term for a wine that is fortified.
gran reserva	Spanish for a wine that has been aged for five years before release, of which a minimum of two years is spent in a barrel.
Grosslage	German for a collection of vineyard sites.
Halbtrocken	German term meaning 'half-dry', so one up from *Trocken*, with a little more residual sugar.
hectolitre	100 litres.
ice wine	See 'Eiswein'.
IGT	Italian term *Indicazione Geografica Tipica*, meaning the equivalent of French Vin de Pays, except it can be used for some 'Super' style Italian wines instead of Vino da Tavola.
jeunes vignes	French term for young vines.
Kabinett	German term for the first grade of QmP wines, usually light and dry.
kir	A refreshing aperitif made by adding dry white wine to a few drops of Crème de Cassis in the bottom of a wineglass. (Crème de Cassis, a blackcurrant liqueur, is very potent and only a dribble is needed to give the wine flavour and colour.) Use the best you can afford, as this is the predominant flavour. Use a very neutral white wine, nothing oaked and nothing off-dry. Usually a French table wine is best for the job, traditionally Aligoté.
Landwein	German equivalent of French Vin de Pays.
lieu-dit	French term for a specific named vineyard site. This name might appear on the wine's label, thus raising it to a higher quality level than a straight 'village' wine.
millésime	French term for vintage.
mousseaux	French term for sparkling.
négociant	A French producer who buys in grapes or wine for vinification, bottling, labelling and selling. (The opposite of a domaine.)
organic	A wine made from grapes grown without the use of chemical herbicides, pesticides or fertiliser.
O.W.C.	Original wooden case.

passito	Italian term for a wine made from dried grapes.
puttonyos	The level of sweetness of Hungarian Tokaji (1-6).
QbA	A German term – *Qualitätswein bestimmter Anbaugebiete* – meaning 'quality wine'. Don't believe it, this term is on bottles of Liebfraumilch! These wines are usually boosted with added sugar.
QmP	A German term – *Qualitätswein mit Prädikat* – meaning 'better quality wine'. This is the one to look for, as no sugar is added. This term covers all levels of ripeness from Kabinett to Trockenbeerenauslese.
recioto	Italian term for a strong sweet wine made from dried grapes.
récolte	French term for harvest.
reserva	Spanish term for a wine that has been aged for three years before release, of which a minimum of one year is spent in a barrel.
rosso	Italian word for red, usually followed by 'di' then a place name.
sélection des grains nobles	The ultimate in sweet wines from Alsace or the Loire. Literally meaning 'a careful selection of noble-rot affected grapes'.
single varietal	Wine made from one single grape variety.
Spätlese	German style of wine that is late-harvested but not always sweet. Usually less sweet than 'Auslese', these wines can be fermented out dry to result in a higher-alcohol, more 'foody' wine. See 'Trocken'.
sur lie	French for 'on its lees', with reference to higher quality Muscadet and other white wines that are made in contact with their lees.
TCA	The full name is '2,4,6-trichloroanisole', the unpleasant, musty-smelling compound that gives rise to the corkiness in tainted wine.
tenuta	Italian for an estate, or collection of vineyards including a winery.
tinto	Spanish and Portuguese for red.
throw	As in 'to throw a sediment', a quaint expression for a wine that has developed sediment.
Trocken	German for dry.

Trockenbeerenauslese	A German mouthful in all senses of the word. Mega-sweet, mega expensive style of wine, made from noble-rot affected grapes in tiny quantities. Even the wine-press is miniature. Usually shortened to TBA to save five minutes' effort.
unfiltered	Just that: a wine that is not filtered. More likely to throw a sediment and may, in time, require decanting. French term is *non filtré*.
ullage	The space between the top of the wine and the bottom of the cork in a bottle of wine.
vendange	French for harvest.
vendange tardive	French for late-picked or late-harvested. Used for sweet wines.
vendemmia	Italian term for vintage.
VDQS	French for Vin Délimité de Qualité Supérieure, the breeding ground for wannabe AC regions, higher than Vin de Pays.
vieilles vignes	French for 'old vines'. This should signify a superior wine, with a more concentrated flavour.
vigna	Italian word for vineyard.
vigneron	French vineyard worker.
viña	Spanish word for vineyard.
vin de pays	French classification for 'country wine', an intermediate category for French wines between Vin de Table and AC. The term Vin de Pays is always followed by 'de . . .' indicating where the region is, e.g. Vin de Pays de l'Ardèche.
vin de table	French classification for table wine, the basic level of French wine. In Germany the term is *Tafelwein*, in Italy *Vino da Tavola*, in Spain *Vino de Mesa* and in Portugal, *Vinho de mesa*.
vino de mesa	A blended Spanish table wine from unclassified vineyards.
vino comarcal	A regional Spanish table wine.
vino de la tierra	The Spanish equivalent to French Vin de Pays.

BORDEAUX

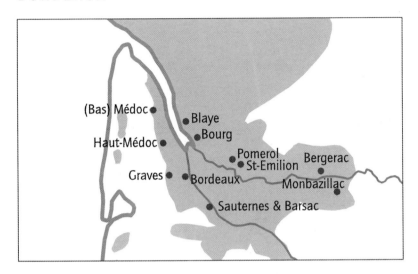

BURGUNDY

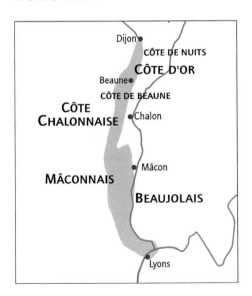

 vine growing areas